A Handbook of Classroom Assessment

ASHTON D. TRICE
JAMES MADISON UNIVERSITY

 LONGMAN

An imprint of Addison Wesley Longman, Inc.

New York • Reading, Massachusetts • Menlo Park, California • Harlow, England
Don Mills, Ontario • Sydney • Mexico City • Madrid • Amsterdam

Editor-in-Chief: Priscilla McGeehon
Acquisitions Editor: Amy Cronin
Marketing Manager: Marilyn Borysek
Full Service Production Manager: Patti Brecht
Project Coordination, Text Design, and
    Electronic Page Makeup: Pre-Press Company, Inc.
Cover Designer/Manager: Nancy Danahy
Senior Print Buyer: Hugh Crawford
Printer and Binder: The Maple-Vail Book Manufacturing Group
Cover Printer: Coral Graphic Services, Inc.

Library of Congress Cataloging-in-Publication Data
Trice, Ashton D.
    A Handbook of Classroom Assessment/Ashton D. Trice
       p.   cm.
    Includes bibliographical references (p.   ) and index.
    ISBN 0-321-05397-4 (alk. paper)
    1. Educational tests and measurements.   I. Title.
LB3051.T6734   2000
371.27—dc21   99-16437
                                                   CIP

Please visit our website at http://www.awlonline.com

ISBN 0-321-05397-4

123456768910—MA—02010099

CONTENTS

■

PREFACE

■

This book is a first textbook in testing for classroom teachers. It grew out of my frustration in searching for a text for a course in assessment for prospective teachers that would help them understand the basic issues of assessment and combine the best of traditional testing theory and practices with the ideas and practices growing out of the authentic assessment movement and the requirements of assessing special students. The text begins with the idea that assessment is not an ancillary activity to instruction but an integral part of the seamless process of teaching that involves the traditionally distinct areas of curriculum, instruction, and assessment. It assumes that teachers will have to construct traditional paper-and-pencil tests, give grades, use standardized tests, and interpret them to parents. It also assumes that such traditional testing approaches cannot be the end point of student assessment, and so it examines performance-based assessments using portfolios, journals, group work, and other nontraditional approaches. This assumes that teachers will be part of the identification process of special needs students and therefore need to understand the meaning and limitations of intelligence tests scores. It assumes that teachers will work daily with special needs students and need to know how to accommodate their assessment practices to meet those students' special requirements.

What disturbed me about many of the texts available was that they were more polemical than helpful. Most texts were squarely either in the "authentic" camp or the "traditional" camp, without recognizing that all forms of assessment have limitations and all forms of assessment have their uses. As college professors often removed from the demands of teaching elementary and secondary students, text writers develop a heightened sense of "critical thinking" that at times can be so critical it leaves nothing for the students except doubts about every possible procedure. Even the often maligned multiple-choice item has its legitimate uses, and even the often-touted portfolio has its hazards. In this book, I have tried to constrain my negative critical sense and help teachers understand the benefits and limitations of each kind of assessment procedure.

This book takes a practical approach and focuses on what teachers need to be able to do. Each topic begins by developing specific examples and the reasons behind the various choices teachers have. I have tried to use real problems that I have encountered in more than 25 years of involvement in public schools. Only the names have been changed to protect the innocent, as well as the guilty. Often the guilty party has been myself. I hope that students will learn something by my being forthcoming about some of the blunders I have made along my professional way.

This book is structured as a handbook with 30 short chapters. Each is centered around a major issue or procedure in assessment. The chapters are subsumed under four major parts: Characteristics of Assessments, Traditional Teacher-Made Tests, Performance-Based Assessments, and Standardized Tests. By using short chapters, I hoped that after the students become teachers, they would be able to refer back to issues and, with a relatively small amount of effort, renew their acquaintance with a brief, but thorough, development of those issues. Extensive cross-referencing allows the book to be used as a reference book. The chapters are designed, however, to be read in order as a comprehensive introduction to testing.

The text is deliberately short. Whole semester-long courses in assessment at the initial certification level are relatively rare. One possible use for this book is as one of several texts in a course in which assessment is only one emphasis. Even in my semester-long, three-semester-hour graduate course in assessment, I wanted a short but comprehensive book, because I wanted students to do much more than read a text and take tests on it. I wanted students to learn about specific standardized tests, develop teaching and assessment units, and write critical papers based on research. In short, I wanted them to engage in application, analysis, synthesis, and evaluation activities, not just knowledge and comprehension ones. A lengthy text that needed to be studied from cover to cover would preclude such activities.

The text is also short because some topics, which seem unnecessary for a first introduction to assessment for teachers, are not covered. I have not, for example, discussed stanine, quartile, and CEEB standardized scores. When such information is available, percentiles are also invariably there, as well. I have not delved into readability scores, partial correlations, or many of the issues in evaluating athletic performance. I have made the assumption that what is needed in this text is a generalist's knowledge of assessment. My intention was to provide a foundation so that more content-specific techniques could be learned easily later.

In addition to my belief that each of the four major assessment perspectives—norm-referenced psychometrics, traditional criterion-referenced testing, authentic assessment, and special education—have their role in the assessment of student progress, this book has several emphases that I found lacking in many other books:

- A focus of the text is assisting teachers in explaining assessment procedures and the information such activities generate to parents. Beginning teachers often express that dealing with parents is one of the most stressful parts of their jobs.
- The process by which assessment results are transformed into grades and other forms of evaluations is emphasized throughout. Prospective teachers not only need to think about ideal grading procedures, but also about how they might adapt to the demands of their school districts.
- Statistics are developed through examples and arithmetic rather than deductively through higher-level mathematics. For faculty who do not want to go into statistical details, all of the statistics are contained in three chapters, which could be omitted. By concentrating the statistical information into three chapters, the book may serve teachers well as a handy reference as they implement the new emphasis on statistics in the early grades, brought about by the new National Council of Teachers of Mathematics standards.
- I have included the topic of teacher evaluation. Beginning teachers need to think about how they will be evaluated and how they may contribute proactively to that process.
- The book is based on more than 100 interviews with preschool, elementary, middle school, high school, and K-12 special education teachers about their current practices and their perceived needs for information about assessment. I conducted about half of these interviews, while the remaining were conducted by students in the earlier versions of my assessment course. What these teachers had to tell me generally confirmed my suspicions: They wanted a more comprehensive and more practical approach to assessment than they had gotten as teachers-in-training. Many indicated that they thought group work, journals, and other project-focused activities were important for students, but they were at a loss as to how to include them in their overall assessment and grading practices.

Cases and teaching suggestions are integrated into the text. The book also has a glossary of technical terms. I have not included multiple references to back up every assertion made in the text. Rather, I have developed an annotated bibliography of technical and nontechnical references for teachers that can assist them in pursuing the ideas and techniques encountered.

Four people need to be thanked for their contributions to the development of my ideas regarding assessment. The first is my first measurement teacher, the late Donald Thompson of Mary Baldwin College. Don made statistics comprehensible to me and helped me understand that there was always more than one way to do a particular job. Second is my graduate professor at Johns Hopkins, Julian Stanley. Professor Stanley shared with me a long and lively involvement in educational assessment, and it was he who got me excited about the area of assessment. Third, I must thank

Dr. Mary Gendernalik-Cooper, now of Augusta State University, who pro-voked me to teach the assessment course in the Mary Baldwin M.A.T. Program and who supported my decision to find a middle ground, when strong voices suggested a one-sided approach. Finally, I must acknowledge a life-long debt to my father, Professor Emeritus O. Ashton Trice, who was trained as a chemist and an experimental psychologist, who taught himself to be a school psychologist and clinician, and who developed a broad view of assessment through his experiences. During the writing of this book, I had almost daily conversations with him. He offered practical advice and encouragement. Without both that advice and encouragement, this book would not exist.

Thanks are also due to the following reviewers: Craig Mertler, Bowling Green State University; David Tanner, California State University at Fresno; Peggy Perkins, UNLV; James Divine, University of Southern Indiana; Cordelia Douzenis, Georgia Southern University; John Tenny, Willamette University; Judith Kennison, Ithaca College; Mary Bicouvaris, Christopher Newport University; and Dan Fennerty, Central Washington University.

The usual caveat pertains: What is good about this book can be ascribed to my good mentors, and the errors belong entirely to myself. This book is not perfect, but I hope it represents a step forward in making assessment more reasoned, balanced, and student-relevant.

Ashton D. Trice

PART I

■

Characteristics
of Assessments

$\mathcal{I}$n this section we examine qualities of all tests and assessments. We begin in Chapter 1 with the traditional definition of tests as samples of behavior taken under standard conditions, then examine specific tests. In Chapter 2 we see how our current ideas and practices of assessment have developed over hundreds of years, usually in response to major changes in education. We then examine how our goals and objectives determine what we will teach, how we will teach, and how we will assess student progress. We discuss seamless teaching, which considers curriculum, instruction, and assessment not as separate acts, but as integrated processes in the act of teaching.

We then turn our attention to the issues of reliability (Chapter 4) and validity (Chapter 5). *Reliability* refers to how accurate a test is. Tests can be inaccurate for a number of reasons, including student guessing on objective tests and poorly defined scoring criteria when the tests are "subjective," such as essay tests, oral reports, or projects. *Validity* refers to whether a test is useful in measuring specific objectives. Tests can be valid for one purpose but not for another. A computational mathematics test, for example, can be valid if our objectives are for students to master math facts, but it is not valid if our intention is to see whether students can use math facts to solve word problems. A journal can help students reflect on their learning, but it may not always be useful in determining whether students have mastered content. Several kinds of reliability and validity will be developed.

In the last last two chapters of this section we develop basic statistical procedures. In Chapter 6 we discuss measures of central tendency and dispersion, and see how these measures tell us different things about student performance. In Chapter 7 we develop the idea of correlation. Correlation is useful in describing the reliability and validity of tests. Although classroom teachers will only need to use and interpret correlations occasionally, there are important occasions when an understanding of correlations is essential, as when teachers explain their grading or the findings from standardized tests to parents, when they select standardized tests for classroom use, and when they serve on child study teams.

1

Basic Definitions

A kindergarten boy is sitting on the floor with his teacher, having what appears to be a friendly conversation. In the space between them is a piece of paper with geometric shapes on it. The teacher asks him to point to the triangle. When he does so, she asks him how he knows it is a triangle. He says, "Because it has three points." She asks him to name something that has that shape. He thinks a minute and says, "A Christmas tree." She puts three checks beside *triangle* on another piece of paper, under the headings of recognition, definition, and example. She talks to him for a minute about Christmas trees and then goes on to the the topic of *square.*

Across the building five second-grade students are drawing a mural on butcher paper of their ideas of everyday life in ancient China. They consult a pile of books from the library and decide to paint the houses red because they notice many of the buildings in the books are painted red. One student draws a banner and attempts to copy some Chinese calligraphy on it. Another student does her best to show three farmers in a rice field.

In a sixth-grade classroom, half of the students are writing essays about the First Constitutional Convention, while the other half of the class is completing a worksheet relating to a video tape about caterpillars.

In a ninth-grade classroom across town, teams of students are recording the numbers of different kinds of insects they have found in a square foot of dirt they dug up that morning. At the end of the exercise, they enter the numbers in a computer, which then produces a bar graph.

In another ninth-grade classroom six students are rehearsing a play they wrote about the winter at Valley Forge. Their classmates have chosen other ways of showing what they learned about this event. Some are producing and illustrating books. Two boys with a strong interest in computers are scanning pictures from a history textbook for a hyperstack presentation.

In another second-grade classroom the teacher stands in front of the class and tells the class to close their books and take out a piece of paper. She calls out ten spelling words, and the students write them down as best they can. They put their names at the top of the paper and pass the papers forward.

Each of these varied activities is an assessment. They vary a great deal in the way they look; each one is designed to show whether the students have learned the material. Assessment comes in a wide variety of forms, depending on the objectives the teacher set for the instruction, the age and ability of the students, and the philosophy of the teacher.

▨ DEFINITIONS

For the last 80 years most textbooks on psychological and educational assessment have opened with the definition of a **test** or an **assessment**[1] as *a sample of behavior taken under standard conditions.* This definition is still a workable place to start, although at first glance it may seem overly formal or not what we usually mean by a test. It contains, however, the three essential properties of tests: They are samples; they consist of behavior; and they are given and taken under standard conditions. We will first examine each of these components before looking at an important way in which this definition is incomplete.

A Test Is a Sample
We do not assess every fact or skill. Instead, we select important representative items and we include these in the assessment process. That is why tests are samples. A **sample** *is a subset* of all the facts and skills we expect students to have learned. There are many ways of creating that sample. One kind of sample is a **random sample.** Many textbooks now come with test item banks prepared by the textbook publishers. Many of these test banks come on CD-ROMs; teachers can tell their computers to select a specific number of items randomly, and the computer will print out a test. A random sample is *unbiased* because *every fact or skill is equally likely to be included on the test.* A random sample has the advantage of covering everything equally. Sometime during our education we have taken tests that concentrated on only part of what we had studied, and we either felt lucky that we studied the right material or felt that the test was unfair because we studied the wrong material.

---

[1]Many teachers are surprised there are no differences in definition between *test* and *assessment*. We are in the habit of calling paper-and-pencil assessments *tests* and other kinds of assessments, *assessments*. In this book we will use the words *test* and *assessment* interchangeably. When we are talking about an *item* on a test, we are talking about more than a multiple choice item on a paper-and-pencil test. We might be talking about an essay, an item on a checklist for evaluating an oral report (e.g., "The student had a clearly stated thesis statement"), an oral question asked to a kindergarten student about counting, a grading rubric for evaluating a student's social studies portfolio, or a drawing to see if the student has understood the Pocahontas story.

We can also develop an assessment through a **rational sample:** The teacher has a deliberate plan on what to include and what not to include. For example, you may decide to exclude some content on a test because you do not feel you covered it sufficiently well. You may include other material you want students to know before moving on to the next unit, and you may ask extra questions to be sure students understand all of the material. One form of rational sample is a table of specifications (discussed in Chapter 9) in which instructional objectives are used in a very deliberate way to select items for an assessment. Unfortunately, teachers often use less systematic ways of developing a test.

A rational sample is biased, but that does not mean it is unfair. In a rational sample you bias your selection of items toward important content or the content you emphasized and away from content that you feel was not adequately covered. You may decide not to include items you are confident all students have mastered or the majority has not yet mastered. *Biased* is a technical term used to describe nonrandom samples and should not be equated with the term *unfair.* An unfair test might include items that the teacher did not teach or which favor one group of students over another.

Tests Are Behavior

As much as we would like to assess what a student really knows or really feels, we end up assessing what the student produces. The student produces **behavior,** *observable activity:* a physical movement, a written response, a spoken sentence, a sung tune, the act of drawing or painting. It may be writing an essay, giving an oral report, making a drawing, writing the answers on a true-false test, or making the final product of a four-week project.

There are many reasons a student's behavior may not represent what he or she really knows. The child might be tired. The child might not understand the question posed to him because of the wording or because he does not understand a vocabulary word in the directions. Sometimes children might try too hard or not try hard enough. But behavior is what we get on assessments, and we need to understand it for what it is, and for what it is not.

The importance of assessments being about student behavior is underscored when we attempt to assess products of which we have little knowledge, including the behavior that produced them. An example is the dilemma of what to do about out-of-class projects where we suspect parents did most of the work. The distinction between behavior and the products of behavior is an important one, which will be dealt with throughout this book.

Tests Are Given Under Standard Conditions

When someone uses the phrase *standard conditions,* we may automatically think of the conditions under which many standardized tests are given: machine scored, timed to the second, heavy security around the content of the tests, etc. In fact, *standard conditions* and *standardized test* refer to two very different standards. A standardized test is scored to a standard. Scores on the Praxis Examination will not be reported by the percent correct, but by comparison to other students taking the test. The score will be compared to a standard of performance.

Standard conditions mean that everyone took the test under the same rules. If the test was timed then it was timed for everyone. If some people were allowed to take the test without time constraints, there was a standard reason for the exception; for example, we allow students with documented learning disabilities to take many tests untimed. Everyone was given the same directions for their projects, and they were all assessed by the same standards (or students within different ability groups were assessed by the same standards). On a paper-and-pencil test, usually everyone has the same items, and the correct answer is the same for everyone.

Some recent ideas in assessment theory seem to challenge the standard condition requirement of assessment. The theorists responsible for these criticisms have suggested that assessment should be individualized for each student. As we will see in Chapter 14, there are still standard conditions here, although fewer than in more traditional assessment. For example, in a second grade unit on the water cycle, students may be allowed to choose whether to demonstrate their knowledge by publishing a book, drawing a picture, performing a skit, producing a CD-ROM hyperstack, or taking a written or oral test. As the teacher assesses these products, he will use the same criteria: Does the student include all the steps in the water cycle? Does she show how and when water changes physical state? Does she know the word evaporation? etc. Classroom assessments can take many forms, and the extent of standardized conditions may vary from situation to situation and according to the testing philosophy of individual school districts and individual teachers. Standards may be different for different ability or interest groups, but there are, inevitably, standards when we are assessing students' products.

Sometimes you will encounter the term **informal assessment** as you read the instructional literature, particularly in the area of reading assessment. To an assessment specialist, this term has little meaning. In some way an assessment must always be formal. If a third-grade teacher asks each student in her class individually to define five key terms in a unit on maps, this may seem less formal than a paper-and-pencil test; however, it is still a formal assessment, because the teacher asks everyone the same questions, even though she may try to break the tension of a timed test. If another teacher asks each student a few spontaneous questions, this is not assessment. Assessment must have some sort of standard/formal procedures for it to be considered assessment. This is not to say that such informal questioning of students is not useful to the teacher; it is only to suggest that such questioning does not constitute an assessment of student learning.

▣ THE PURPOSES OF ASSESSMENT

Our basic definition leaves out the purpose of assessment, probably because tests have many different purposes. Often we assess students' knowledge and skills before instruction to determine what they already know. We will then spend less time on those things that students seem already comfortable with and more time on those things they have not yet mastered. We may even have to go back and rework our instructional plan if this assessment indicates students have not yet mastered skills we thought they should have already learned. This kind of assessment is called **diagnostic testing** or **diagnostic assessment.**

After teaching part of a unit, a teacher may administer an assessment to see how students are getting along. For example, we may give students a worksheet on carrying after we have spent three days on the addition of two-digit numbers. If all students have mastered the material, we may go on to the next step. If some students have mastered the ideas while others have not, we may divide the group into those who can move on to the next step and those who are given more practice with the carrying material. If the majority of students are unsure of carrying skills, we may decide to reteach the material to the whole group using another technique. This kind of assessment is called **formative assessment.** Formative assessment is largely an evaluation of our own teaching and shares with diagnostic assessment an emphasis on our own accountability in developing appropriate instruction, and less emphasis on evaluating individual students.

After carefully crafting our instruction based on diagnostic assessment and formative assessment, we will eventually come to the end of a unit of study. At this point we will want to assess students in terms of our instructional objectives. Here the emphasis has changed from the evaluation of instruction to the assessment of individual student progress. This process is called **summative assessment.** In diagnostic and formative evaluation, the teacher accepts responsibility for student learning. She modifies her instruction based on the feedback provided by the assessments. In summative assessment the teacher shares responsibility with the student.

Summative assessment is an important component of **grading,** although there are important differences between the two processes. Grading is an administrative process and it may include information other than summative assessment. Teachers commonly give students who try hard higher grades than those who do not, even though their summative assessments may indicate the same level of mastery of the material. Some teachers are tougher graders than others. Some teachers use formative assessment information in constructing grades, while others do not. Diagnostic assessment is rarely part of the grading process. Grades are influenced by administrative and instructional standards. For example, some school districts use letter grades, some use number grades, others use narratives.

Grading is one form of **evaluation**. Evaluation either provides labels for children's behavior (such as awarding letter grades) or guidelines for administrative actions based on the assessment (retaining or promoting students, placing students in gifted or special education classes, etc.).

We may sometimes ask students how they feel about what they are learning—if they liked or understood a book, for example. We may ask students what was hard about a project and what was fun. This is called **satisfaction assessment**. Satisfaction assessment can sometimes be useful to a teacher, but the teacher should always be conscious that students' feelings about learning do not always reflect the learning itself. Students may be having a great time but learning very little, or struggling and learning a great deal.

Some assessments in education are not focused on individual student learning. School districts routinely use standardized tests to assess how well their students stack up against other students in the same state or in the same neighborhood type (urban, rural, suburban), or compared to all students nationally. Sometimes student test results are used to evaluate the performance of teachers, although this practice is controversial.

THE QUALITIES OF ASSESSMENT

Although tests are discussed in more detail in later chapters, it is important to distinguish four types of tests. Most of the tests we are familiar with are **quantitative assessments** where a number is assigned to the level of a student's performance. A 91 percent on a paper-and-pencil examination is an example of quantitative assessment. More recently, much assessment in elementary and secondary schools is **qualitative.** Rather than applying a numerical label, those who advocate qualitative assessment will apply labels such as *Good* or *Excellent,* or write descriptive comments to students or parents. Teachers often use both qualitative and quantitative assessment, particularly in the areas of writing and oral reports.

Some tests are **norm-referenced tests**, *assessments that show where a student's performance is compared to others.* As mentioned above, scores on the Praxis Examination are norm-referenced. Sometimes teachers use curving: the top 20 percent of students make A's, the next 30 percent get B's, the next 30 percent get C's, and the bottom 20 percent get D's, regardless of what their percentage scores are. Most classroom assessments, however, are **criterion-referenced tests**. In this case *a student's performance is compared to a standard of performance called the criterion*: 90 percent correct merits an A in many college classrooms, and anywhere from 0 percent of the students to 100 percent could earn A's. Teachers will often employ a criterion before moving students on in the instructional sequence. A teacher may feel that before students can move on to adding three three-digit numbers, they should be able to add two two-digit numbers with 90 percent accuracy. That level of accuracy is the criterion used in deciding who moves on and who gets additional instruction. Most often, norm-referenced tests are quantitative; criterion-referenced tests can be quantitative or qualitative.

Questions for Reflection

1. Find five syllabi for courses at your college, either courses you are taking, your friends are taking, or courses on the Web. List the activities that are used to assess student performance. See if you can determine whether these are quantitative or qualitative assessments. Compare your findings to those of another student in this class.

2. Think back on your days in middle school or high school and recall a time you thought an assessment was unfair. Describe the situation. Using the vocabulary in this chapter, express why you think the assessment was unfair. Now that you are beginning to think about assessment professionally, how would you remedy this situation?

3. You have just given a test to a class of students. You think you taught the material well, but the class grades were well below your expectations. Your school district defines passing as 70 percent, but no student got any higher than 68 percent. Make a list of possible actions you could take. Compare your suggestions to those of another student in this class.

2

History of Testing

$\mathcal{J}$t is surprising to many teachers that the tests we have been exposed to since we entered kindergarten have not been around very long. It also comes as something of a shock to discover that the tests we are used to are not commonly used in other countries. Written teacher-made tests, for example, are fairly uncommon in most Western European schools. In Italy most tests are oral, and public, until children begin to prepare for university entrance examinations. In most Eastern European schools annual written examinations come from and are graded by the national departments of education. Teachers may give practice tests to their students to prepare them for the national examinations, but they do not grade them, and the students' grades are completely dependent on the state tests. Because children are automatically promoted every year during the elementary school years in Japan, few tests or grades are given until junior high school. Teachers are very free with their opinions about who is doing well and who is not.

▓ UNIVERSITY TESTS

Tests, however, have been around a long time. The Chinese used tests as early as 1200 B.C. to determine who would become a member of their civil service. These tests were administered locally, regionally, and nationally: One had to pass the local tests before going on to the regional tests, and the regional tests before the national ones. The tests were offered only every five to seven years; it took up to 20 years to pass them all. When Britain and the United States began civil service tests in the mid-1800s, they sent delegations to China to study their system (Linden & Linden, 1968).

As early as the 13th century, oral examinations were administered by the faculties of European universities for those students who were sitting for the Ph.D. degree. All teachers at the university could examine the candidate on any subject. These oral examinations often lasted all day for ten days to two weeks and were the origins of our five-part grading system. A candidate was awarded grades of excellent, high pass, pass, charity pass (usually reserved for the nobility, the origins of the "gentleman's C"), and fail. Around the year 1500, at Cambridge University, a similar examination limited to the student's subject specialization began to be given for undergraduates. Students who passed the examination were given a master's degree; those who avoided the examination or failed it were given a bachelor's degree. These same kinds of tests are still administered in most older European universities. There are no course grades; rather, the student's entire undergraduate or graduate experience is determined by his or her performance on the final, exit examination.

Until about 150 years ago, these were the only tests of consequence given to students. In the 1870s the American educational reformer Horace Mann suggested exit examinations, based on the university model, be administered to all high school graduates to ensure a high school diploma had some meaning other than that the student had put in the requisite eight or nine years in the classroom. Usually, such examinations were administered orally by a group of teachers. Today, we might wonder whether these practices should truly be called tests because there were few real standards. Students were asked different questions, depending on the teachers who examined them. The only standard condition was probably stress.

▦ RICE AND EDUCATIONAL EVALUATION

Historically there were few assessments in school because assessing students was very labor intensive. Today, one teacher can give a test to dozens or even hundreds of students at the same time. Until the 1890s it took several teachers to administer a test to a single student because tests were administered orally. Usually we think of technological breakthroughs in education as involving machines, such as televisions and computers, but in the 1880s two technological breakthroughs occurred to revolutionize testing: the development of the pencil and the development of cheap, pulp paper. Until this time paper and ink were too precious to be used for assessment. After these innovations written tests became commonplace.

One of the leading exponents of the use of written tests, J. M. Rice, became very concerned about educational inequality. He began his career as a critic of educational practices by administering spelling tests to students in 20 different school districts throughout the United States. He published a number of papers based on this research, showing how students in some school districts seemed to be shortchanged in their educational preparation. He later went on to develop tests in many other subject areas (DuBoise, 1970).

Educators are often wary of the use of standardized tests to make comparisons among schools, but it is instructive to note the degree of difference

Rice found. The curriculum at this time was seldom standard: There were few textbooks and no teacher certification. Rice found that the typical student in some school districts knew less than half of what students from other school districts knew. Rice's findings were a major impetus to developing standards of instruction and teacher preparation.

About the same time, a Scottish clergyman named MacKenzie developed our abecedarian (A–F) form of grading. He believed such rankings were useful not only in making comparisons among students, but they could also be used to determine individual students' strengths. Particularly, he believed that if teachers graded students year after year and kept a record of these grades, when the child was ready to leave school, there would be a wealth of information to help make decisions about careers and further education.

However skeptical one may be about some current practices regarding standardized tests or grading, historically they were major steps forward toward educational equality and helped provide the basis for the American educational system. Assessments used to compare school districts forced local politicians to be less stingy with funds for education. Annual grades were an impetus for some students to try harder. Records of annual accomplishments gave a much better picture for college admission or employment of a student's overall performance than the opinions of the students' senior year teachers alone.

▦ THE PROGRESSIVE MOVEMENT

Almost as soon as the reforms brought about by Mann and Rice were in place, they began to have their critics. One group of critics were the Progressives, whose main spokesperson was the psychologist John Dewey. Dewey wanted to build on the reforms of Mann and Rice: He felt that they had not gone far enough. Most education at this time was based on rote learning and recitation. Children often sat quietly all together as a class and repeated factual information such as lists of state capitals, poems, and multiplication tables. Often the content of schooling had little relation to what children would eventually be doing with their lives. Dewey wanted children to be more actively involved in their learning, and he wanted there to be clear relationships between schooling and work. The slogan that we associate strongly with Dewey is "Learning by Doing." Dewey pushed for the inclusion of science in the curriculum and the use of the scientific method in solving problems. He also helped develop vocational education.

Some Progressives were critical of the kinds of assessments that Rice and MacKenzie had developed because they saw them closely associated with rote learning. The Progressives emphasized science experiments as the model of learning, but other than this, they failed to propose any real assessment alternatives to the factual tests of Rice.

▓ ASSESSING EXCEPTIONALITY: BINET AND TERMAN

In 1797 a young boy, who had apparently been abandoned by his parents at an early age, was found in the woods in Southern France. Victor, as he was called, was taken into the household of a physician named Itard, who attempted to teach him basic skills. Itard's accounts of his efforts were widely read. (In fact, Victor was something of a tabloid celebrity at the time.) Victor learned many social behaviors: wearing clothes, eating politely, and taking care of himself. While he learned to follow complex instructions, both spoken and written, he did not learn to talk.

Itard and his student Seguin interpreted his failures in terms of the concept of critical period. Language, they believed, could only be learned during the period of early childhood. After the critical period had passed, language learning was impossible. They reasoned that had Itard gotten to Victor earlier, the results may have been more profound. The work of Itard and Seguin led to the establishment of many special schools for children in France. When Seguin ran into political trouble during the Napoleonic Wars, he came to the United States and set up schools in Massachusetts and New Jersey (Lane, 1976).

More than a hundred years later, a committee of concerned French educators approached the leading psychologist of his day, Alfred Binet, to develop a way of identifying students who would not learn from the usual curriculum. At that time children entered school at the age of seven, and many children had limited reading and writing skills by the end of the second grade. Some of these children went on to be successful in school, but many did not. Remembering the idea of a critical period from Itard and Seguin, the committee reasoned that if the children who would have difficulty in school could be identified early and given compensatory educational experiences, they would have better outcomes.

In 1905 Binet published the Binet-Simon Scale, often identified as the first IQ test. Binet specifically said the test did not measure all aspects of intelligence; he was trying to identify early what we would now call educable mental retardation (Binet & Simon, 1905). He was specifically trying to predict which children would not profit from normal school practices. Binet used complex verbal questions, such as asking for the definitions of words, asking children to repeat complex sentences, and asking children to identify the thumb by name to asking them to tell a difference between Catholicism and Protestantism. The Binet-Simon Scale was very successful in identifying children with severe learning problems, and the test became the pattern followed by most other IQ tests.

In 1913 the American psychologist Lewis Terman began developing an American version of the Binet test, the Stanford-Binet, named after his institution, Stanford University. Terman grew up poor in a rural county in Indiana that did not have a secondary school, and his high school and university education came through a series of lucky and unlucky breaks. He decided to become a teacher after he developed tuberculosis. He felt that many gifted and talented students like himself were being undereducated because of the luck of their birth place. While Binet had developed his test to select those students who would not profit from traditional instruction, Terman envisioned a national testing program that would identify and assist bright children in getting at least a high school education. Binet wanted to test children as early as possible. Terman developed his test for somewhat older children so they would have time to excel at school work.

Current IQ tests are directly built on the work of Binet and Terman. They are an important component of identifying gifted, talented, mentally retarded, and learning disabled children, as we will see in Chapter 27. These are the purposes for which these tests were designed, and they are useful in this process. These tests have also been used for other, more controversial purposes, as will be discussed throughout Part IV of this book.

▨ THE RISE OF STANDARDIZED TESTING

Building on the work of Binet and Terman, educators and psychologists in the 1920s through the 1950s began developing new ways of assessing students. Two kinds of tests emerged, **achievement tests,** *which determine what a student knows,* and **aptitude tests,** *which try to predict future achievement.* The tests you took throughout elementary and secondary school every few years, such as the Iowa Tests of Basic Skills (ITBS) or the Stanford-9, are examples of achievement tests because they try to assess how much students know of the standard curriculum. The Scholastic Aptitude Tests (SATs) are considered aptitude tests because they try to predict how successful one will be in college.

Like IQ tests, achievement and aptitude tests have legitimate and controversial uses. An entire section (Part IV) of this text addresses these tests because teachers need to be aware of the legitimate uses of these tests and to be informed critics of improper uses.

▨ FEMINISM AND TESTING

Since the late 1960s feminism has become an important force in American education. In the area of assessment, feminist educators have criticized the competitive nature of testing in American education, which they believe is the result of male dominance in education. Contemporary feminists are more influenced by structural sociological theory than by individual psychology, and they tend to see tests as barriers to self-actualization rather than assessments of individual strengths and weaknesses that individuals can use to develop their potential.

For example, feminists have been concerned about the sociological concept of **labeling,** or *the effects on children of being given a specific classifi-*

cation, such as gifted or retarded. Concerns about labeling come from the concept of roles. Individuals tend to conform to the roles in which they have been assigned, and therefore one must be concerned that identifying a student as learning disabled or gifted or behavior disordered will influence the student to act in a manner typical for that group. Sociologists tend to view the behavior of children in a gifted class as caused less by their abilities than by the label applied to them. Psychologists, on the other hand, tend to think the behavior of gifted children is primarily caused by their special intellectual ability rather than their identification as gifted. Psychologists do believe there are advantages in labeling students gifted: If they are surrounded by other gifted students, they will learn from them and be challenged by them. Psychologists are concerned about the possibility of the dangerous effects of a mislabel. Both psychologists and sociologists also recognize the problem of informal labeling. A child in a class who is not doing well may be labeled lazy or stupid by his parents, his teacher, and other children, and this kind of labeling is as damaging as a formal mislabel.

Another concern related to the issue of labeling is **tracking,** *the practice of placing students in ability groups for instruction.* Two forms of tracking have been common in American education. **General ability tracking** is *the placement of students for all subjects in a group based on a measure of their general ability.* For example, many high schools have college-bound and vocational tracks. Students in the vocational tract may not be allowed to take algebra, even though they are good at mathematics, because their general ability is relatively low. **Subject ability grouping,** on the other hand, *groups students on the basis of their current skill level on a subject-by-subject basis:* A student may be in a high group for mathematics, an average group for social studies and science, and a remedial group for reading.

Educators are now in agreement that general ability tracking is bad for students because it limits many students' opportunities: It excludes lower-track students from higher-level subjects in which they could succeed, making school dull and boring in some areas. Higher-level students must take courses for which they are not yet prepared and they may fail. It still continues because it is efficient. It is easier to schedule students in blocks than as individuals. Students are often tracked by overall achievement test scores and the achievement tests are blamed, but achievement test subscores could as easily be used to provide the basis for subject ability grouping.

Subject ability grouping has many advocates, but many feminists advocate **heterogeneous grouping,** *the practice of mixing high- and low-ability students altogether in one class.* The rationale is that high-ability students will assist low-ability students learn, and high-ability students will profit from their experience teaching others. The results are not yet clear whether heterogeneous grouping or subject ability grouping is best for students. It is clear that heterogeneous grouping becomes increasingly difficult as students get older and the gaps among students become wider. Instruction and assessment are easier in ability-grouped classes because everyone is studying the same content at the same level, but ease of assessment is not a particularly important criteria for deciding which approach to use. Benefits to students is the paramount concern. Heterogeneous grouping is often described as an educational innovation, but it is in some respects a return to 19th-century schooling practices. Nothing could be more heterogeneously grouped than the one-room schoolhouse.

▨ CURRENT REFORMS: NATIONAL TESTS AND AUTHENTIC ASSESSMENT

If one picks up any newspaper today, the topic of education and educational assessment is likely to appear on the editorial pages. One hot topic is national tests. Educators who are politically in the middle of the road tend to favor national examinations. They want to make sure each school district and each private school is giving its students equal opportunities for advancement through education. Educators on the political left tend to be suspicious of standardized tests, while those on the political right are suspicious of anything that is national. Although national tests remain controversial, more and more states are requiring basic literacy tests before students can move from middle school to high school and exit examinations before awarding high school diplomas.

The other controversial assessment issue is authentic assessment (Worthen, 1993). Many of today's educators, like the Progressives and feminists before them, dislike the limitations of paper-and-pencil tests. Moderates in this controversy say tests should authentically measure the goals of instruction, and they note the limitations of multiple-choice tests in measuring many educational goals. For example, if you want to know whether a child can write a coherent essay, have the child write an essay, not complete a multiple-choice grammar quiz. That essay need not be written in a 30-minute timed situation. Likewise, scientific problem solving is very difficult to capture on a timed, multiple-choice test. Moderates, however, allow that traditional testing has legitimate uses in education. More radical approaches would abolish all traditional tests and grades, replacing tests with performance assessments such as journals, group projects, and individual research, and replacing the gradebook and letter grades with portfolios of student work and teacher narratives.

Tensions in American education about assessment are likely to be with us for a long time because, as this brief sketch of assessment history has indicated, they have been with us for a long time in one form or other. The approach taken in this text is not extreme on any issue. The approach of this text is that a variety of assessment approaches enhances assessment and that a balanced approach is the best one.

Questions for Reflection

1. Contact someone you know from a previous generation of students, such as a grandmother or older neighbor. Ask them to describe the different kinds of tests they had in school. Ask them about elementary school, middle school, high school, and, if they attended, college. Ask them to tell you what they thought was fair or not fair about testing. Ask whether testing made them feel good or bad about themselves.

2. Go to the library and find either an old (published before 1940) textbook on testing or educational psychology, or an article on testing in an old education journal. Find the section that describes the author's general orientation to testing/assessment. Summarize it and then explain how we may differ in our attitudes today. Alternatively, you may want to search international Web sites to find out about current practices elsewhere in the world today.

3

Goals and Objectives

*O*ne of my favorite courses in college was art appreciation. It was organized historically, from ancient Greece through modern art. We read a heavy, expensive textbook filled with illustrations, discussions of the lives of individual artists, and the changes in techniques and subject matter of art over 3,000 years. In class the professor put two slides on the screen in the front of the room, discussed them, and showed what they had in common and what distinguished them. I learned about artists and how to look at paintings, sculpture, and architecture. The lectures and readings were stimulating, and I think the course genuinely lead me to appreciate art.

But when the time came for tests, they always consisted of 20 slides. We had to name the work, give the artist, the date of its execution, the materials it was made of, and its current location. That was it. One point for each fact.

I remember a year or so after I took the course, I was eating lunch with the professor, and I asked him about the tests in the class. What did learning all those details about several hundred paintings, sculptures, and buildings have to do with appreciating art? I distinctly remember his reply:

"I never thought about that," he said. "That's just the kind of test I had when I was a student. Anyway, they're easy to grade."

▣ INSTRUCTION, LEARNING, AND ASSESSMENT

All too often in the past, assessment was thought of as something separate from learning and instruction. When I was getting certified to teach in the elementary school, I took four courses: *The Elementary School Curriculum*, in which we learned about the sequence of learning goals for each subject in each grade level; *Instruction*, in which we learned techniques of teaching; *The Elementary School Student*, in which we learned about how students learn and how they develop over the elementary school years; and *Tests and Measurements*, in which we learned to construct paper-and-pencil tests and learned about standardized tests. There was very little integration among these topics. When I began to teach, it occurred to me that teaching was not compartmentalized into these four areas, but a whole, inseparable act. What you want students to learn depends on what they have already learned, what they are capable of learning, and what they will learn next. What students know and their developmental level will determine how you teach them. How you teach them determines how you assess their progress. What you learn from the assessment about what they learned will determine what you teach next and how you teach it. Learning, curriculum, instruction, and assessment were one thing: teaching. We call this seamless teaching.

> *Teaching begins by thinking about two things at the same time. First, we often begin by thinking about what we as teachers will do. But the second thing is really the more important: What do we want students to be able to do at the end of instruction that they cannot do at the beginning. When we focus on what students will learn to do, rather than on what we as the teacher will do, the integration of learning, curriculum, institution, and assessment becomes much clearer.*

Let's say we are going to teach the novel *Pinocchio*. One of our first considerations would be to look at it in terms of where it fits in the context of the overall curriculum and to look at the characteristics of the students we are going to teach. When we have those things clearly in mind, the changes in student behavior are likely to become evident. If I were to teach the novel to third-grade students, I might focus on the plot. The book is too difficult and long for children at this age to read independently, so I might read them the larger part of it. Children in the third grade are studying aspects of plot such as how one event affects later action. After reading them a part, I would have the students discuss why certain events took place, as they relate to past events in the story. I would also encourage students to guess what would happen next, so that they could learn to apply the logic of plot. I may well be interested in having children learn how Pinocchio's decision not to go to school led him to encounter bad companions, which led to his adventures. I want to focus on the sequence of events.

If I were going to teach this book to sixth-grade students, I might focus on the moral of the plot, and how that moral is embodied in the central image of a boy of wood becoming a real boy. Children at this level can read the book independently; I would give home reading assignments, but still read parts in class followed by class discussion. The discussion would focus on the meaning of the actions and the imagery. I would assume that the students could understand most of the plot relations.

If I were going to teach the novel to undergraduate students in a course on children's literature, I would want them to analyze the plot and understand the imagery and moral. I would also ask them to analyze the problems they would encounter in using this book in a classroom. I would want them to develop ways of teaching it to children at different ages. I could expect college students to read the work at home in a few nights. I would probably spend a little time on the moral and imagery and little or no time on understanding the plot.

I took an intermediate Italian course a few years ago and read a part of *Pinocchio* where the emphasis was on learning vocabulary and a literary past tense. We read two to three pages a night and translated a page or two every day in class. Each class began with the teacher asking us very simple questions about the plot, both to check that we had done our homework and to make sure we understood it. Then we read the new material out loud, with the professor correcting our pronunciation and asking us questions to see if we understood the material. We also had some grammar lessons in English, which helped us understand the material.

The same book can be used in many different places in the curriculum, and the way we teach it depends on the level of the class and the expectations we have about student learning. The way teachers will assess students' learning will also depend on the level of the class and the expectations they have for them.

1. For the third-grade students, I may ask them to complete a summary of the book to see if they understand how the main parts of the plot are connected. The summary might be written, but it might also be a series of drawings or a play written by a group of students. Along the way, I might also give some traditional tests for vocabulary and spelling words.
2. For the sixth-grade students, I would probably elect to have them write individual essays on the meaning of the book, but I would probably have spelling and vocabulary tests, too.
3. When I have taught this book as a part of a teacher preparation class, I have had students write a set of lesson plans showing how they would use it for a particular group of students. To make sure that students actually read the book (rather than rely on their memory of the distinctly different Disney movie version), I also gave factual quizzes on its content.
4. In my Italian class the main test was about vocabulary and grammar. We had to demonstrate our knowledge of the grammar and vocabulary by filling out a question-and-answer worksheet in Italian. We also had an oral examination based on the worksheets.

This example emphasizes that learning, instruction, and assessment are integrally tied together. The compartmentalization of teaching can have a negative effect on students. For example, many books for children come with teacher guides. Some of these teacher guides are excellent, but others come with rather limited activities for students and test items geared to one purpose, age, or ability group of students. These activities and test items are useful for stimulating teacher thinking, but the way one teaches content and assesses student learning depends upon the reason a teacher includes it for a specific group of students. Adopting another person's activities and tests is like my art teacher saying he tested us because that's the way someone else had done it and because it was easy.

▨ GOALS VS. OBJECTIVES

When we teach, our expectations for students can be stated in goals and objectives. **Goals** are *general expectations of student outcomes.* Often goals are lofty and somewhat vague, the kinds of statements politicians and school administrators make. The *Elementary and Secondary School Act* of 1957 stated that the goal of public education is the creation of informed citizens. That sounds great—few people would disagree with it as a goal of public education—but what does it mean, exactly? Certainly it means students should be literate and know something about their government. But it does not specify much. On the other hand, an **objective** is *a statement of what the student should be able to do as a result of instruction.* To state the obvious, an objective is much more objective than a goal. For example, we may now believe that in order for students to be informed they should have the ability to find a variety of information resources via the Internet. We may expect students to be able to describe the checks and balances among the executive, legislative, and judicial branches of government; we may want students to be able to define terms like *republic, democracy,* and *legislature.* Objectives are smaller than goals; they are the specific pieces of the goals.

Teaching units often begin with goals. For example, many middle schools now engage students in a project related to the stock market. A group of students is given a sum of imaginary money with which to buy stock. Depending on the background of the students, they may research their companies, and sometimes they are allowed to buy and sell stocks, learning about sales fees, dividends, etc. They follow their stock portfolio over several months. The goal for such a unit might be to learn how the stock market works. This goal is very general and does not guide the teacher on what to do on a day-to-day basis. We need to break down this goal into objectives. Let us assume here that we are dealing with sixth-grade students who come from a low-income community and who may have learned very little about the stock market at home. We will have to teach this unit from scratch. The children may have no idea what a corporation is, let alone stock.

1. Our first effort might be to explain to students how corporations form and how they issue stock to raise capital. We will also explain to them about dividends. The *Wall Street Journal* has a number of video and print materials that can help students understand the basics.
2. We may have students learn to read the stock market reports in the newspaper.
3. We explain sources of information about stocks. Because of the background of these students, we may rely on a relatively simple source of information, such as the business pages of *USA Today.*
4. We give students an imaginary $2,000 each to invest in stocks. For a month we follow the stocks every Monday, charting each stock's productivity. After a month we allow students to sell their stocks and purchase others based on the previous month's performance.

5. For three more months we track the record of the students' portfolios. (This activity should take place over at least three months, so that students learn about dividends.)

6. Finally, we have each student produce a report about their portfolio's performance.

After completing these activities, we may feel we have attained our goal of helping students learn how the stock market works. We would be more secure in our feeling, however, if we have specific objectives for each activity. For example, under activity 1, how much do we expect our sixth-grade students to really comprehend about corporate structure? We now take into consideration our students' backgrounds and prepare a list of specific objectives that we are going to have for the students.

In Table 3.1, we have translated our steps into objectives. We have one objective for each of the steps above, except that step 4, as we thought about it, is actually two steps, and so we have two objectives here. We have consciously stated each objective in terms of student behavior: What will the students be able to do and have they learned what we expected?

We are now in a better situation to know whether the students have met our goals because we have specified the behaviors we want them to be able to demonstrate. There are still other steps necessary before we can assess how well individual students met our objectives. For example, Objective 4 says: Based on their research, students will select a portfolio of two or three stocks and determine how to invest $2,000. How will we determine whether a child based his selection on his research or whether he just picked the

TABLE 3.1   LEARNING OBJECTIVES FOR A UNIT ON THE STOCK MARKET

1. Students will define the basic components of a corporation: *stock, capital, investor, share*, and so on.

2. Students will demonstrate their ability to read the Saturday stock market weekly report by finding information about specific stocks in an actual weekly report.

3. Students will research five publicly-traded corporations in groups and prepare a written report of their findings, including what the company does and what its recent earnings have been.

4. Based on their research, students will select a portfolio of two or three stocks and determine how to invest $2,000. Students will determine after one month whether they wish to retain their portfolio or reinvest their money based on the previous month's performance of their stocks and the stocks of other students in the class.

5. Students will track the weekly performance of their portfolio using a histogram, including stock price and dividends.

6. Students will prepare a written report of their portfolio's performance and present it to the class orally.

names of two stocks at random? Objective 6 says that students will write and orally present a report on their stocks' performance, but how will we distinguish an excellent report from a merely acceptable one? What standards of written and oral presentation will we expect, and will the written and oral presentation be included in the unit grade?

We have accomplished the major task here by converting a vague goal (to learn about the stock market) into a set of behavioral expectations for a specific group of students. This is the first giant step in the process of teaching and assessment.

▨ MEASURABLE VS. NONMEASURABLE OBJECTIVES

Putting goals into behavioral language is our first major step, but for the purposes of assessment, we must be sure our behavioral language is measurable. *Write a report* is a behavior, but it is not measurable in much detail: We can only distinguish those who wrote a report from those who did not. Suppose we have these two final reports from the stock market unit:

John's Report

I invested in Dupont and USX. I made some money, and I'm pretty happy with the results.

Susan's Report

My initial investment was in DuPont and USX because of the long-term productivity of both stocks. I invested $1,000 in each company. On the basis of the first month's performance, I sold my USX stock for $954 and reinvested the money in Dow Chemical. At the end of the four-month period, my stocks were worth $2,142.34 and I had received $39.15 in dividends. This means that I had earned $181.49. If I had put my money in a 3 percent savings account, I would have earned only $15. I earned the equivalent of 36 percent per year.

Most teachers would say that Susan demonstrated more learning than John, but since our objective states only that the students would prepare a report on their stocks' performance, both students met the objective.

An easy fix would be to change the objective so that we say *writes a report of 100 words*; although this is measurable, the mere length of the report is not our real focus: We want to know if the students understand the stock market. If we were to consider Susan's report as ideal, we could rewrite our objective thus:

Students will prepare a written report that will include (1) the reason for their initial stock purchases and reinvestments; (2) a specific statement of earnings; (3) and a comparison of the portfolio's earnings with a standard investment over the same time period.

Susan's paper meets all three objectives, while John's does not meet any of them. We now have an objective against which we can compare student work.

Other objectives are so intangible we cannot tell whether they have happened or not. One of the often-stated objectives of the whole language approach to teaching language arts is to get students to like reading and writing. How would we go about measuring this objective? We could ask our students if they like reading and writing, but this is unsatisfactory. We could have a free time built into our day, and we could note the number of children who choose to read and write compared to those who listened to music or put puzzles together. All this would really tell us is that some children prefer to write rather than to put puzzles together or to listen to the music we have in the classroom. Liking is a very hard objective to measure. So are other important objectives such as appreciate, value, and respect. This does not mean we should not try to get our students to appreciate art, or value other children's property, or respect the symbols of our country. It does mean, however, that we will have less tangible evidence that we have accomplished these objectives than other goals such as remembering facts, applying formulae to solve problems, or analyzing the components of a poem.

▣ LEVELS OF SPECIFICITY

Teachers (and education students) are often dismayed by the task of writing objectives. Coming up with a unit idea and developing the sequence of activities is fun, creative work. We can imagine ourselves in the classroom leading a group of interested students in a discussion about investments. Writing objectives is time-consuming, analytical, and often a little boring. We have to think about the material from the point of view of the child, and that is harder to do than thinking about ourselves.

Another reason writing objectives is a hassle is that sometimes writing objectives tells us our creative ideas need fine tuning. Let us go back to the *Pinnochio* example. We have decided to give children the option of showing their understanding of the plot of the novel by producing a picture book of the plot. What do we do when a child produces a book of drawings of each of the main characters, but there is no action and no sequence of events shown? Perhaps this was because our objectives were not specific enough (as well as our instructions to the child based on our objectives). We may need to introduce an intermediate step in which we have each child construct the book and then write captions for each page before he begins drawing, telling what action will be represented on the page. This extra instructional step suggests we write at least one more objective in our unit.

When I teach assessment to current and future classroom teachers, they often say, "You don't really mean we have to write three or four objectives for every subject every day, do you?" My response is a disconcerting, "Yes". There is a consolation: Like every skill, it starts off slowly and deliberately and gets easier and more automatic. Writing objectives is like driving a car. If you can remember your first hour behind the wheel—it was probably difficult, you felt like your mind was on overload, and you made a lot of mistakes. Now you can listen to the radio, have a conversation with a friend, and plan what you will say to your spouse when you get home, as you weave in and out of rush hour traffic on the interstate. Writing your first full set of objectives may be time consuming, and you may get a lot of negative feedback from your professor or your supervisor. But if you practice, over several weeks you will get very good at it.

Students then ask, "So, tell us, what's the form of an objective?" For years I resisted answering this question because the real answer is that there are many forms, and a teacher will eventually find one which fits his or her temperament and level of teaching. Now I give an answer. If you are reading this book in the context of a course, your instructor may tell you to disregard what follows next and provide you with another form. But here are my five rules for writing an objective:

1. *Write the objective with a potential substitute teacher in mind. Be specific enough that he or she will know what to do and why he or she is doing it.*

This rule is a useful notion that will serve you both in a preprofessional course and in a classroom after you have taught for 15 years.

If you tell a substitute teacher to go over pages 15–19 of the text, you need to let her know whether she is dealing with facts—and which ones—or whether you want some higher-level learning to take place. "Go over" is not very helpful. If you tell her students will have to remember word definitions, recall the basic facts, give their reaction to the reading, or apply a previous concept to understanding the material, she will have a much better idea of how to teach your class than if you just jot down the pages to be covered.

2. *Think about the verb in your objective. Objectives are about behavior and the behavior is embodied in the verb.*

Do you want students to repeat, recall, recognize, apply, analyze, draw, sing, write? Avoid verbs that are vague, like *learn*. We can learn things in very many ways and show our learning in many ways. Describe the behavior through which the child will exhibit his learning. The more specific the verb, the better the objective. What specific behavior will the child engage in when you assess whether she has learned the behavior? *Outline* is better than *organize*. *List* is better than *remember*. *Draw a series of pictures depicting the plot* is better than *show*.

3. *Begin your set of objectives with a general stem and then begin each objective with the verb.*

The student will:
- *write a paragraph describing the reasons for the origins of the Civil War.*
- *include a topic sentence and a concluding sentence.*
- *include at least three reasons for the Civil War.*
- *cite pages in the textbook for their reasons.*
- *use a spell-checker to make sure all words are correctly spelled.*
- *use complete, grammatical sentences.*

Even the most inexperienced substitute teacher should be able to help students meet these objectives.

4. *Don't go crazy.*

Suppose that you want children to know the definitions of the 15 key words in the *Wall Street Journal*'s unit on the stock market. You do not need to list all 15 words. Simply indicate where these words can be found. It might be useful to list the words if you substantially add to or subtract from a list, not only for the substitute teacher, but for yourself when you do this unit again next year, or for a colleague who was impressed with your unit and wants to try it with his class. But if you hand your colleague five pages of heavily detailed objectives, he might pass on your good idea.

5. *Avoid premature quantification.*

Some approaches to writing objectives include quantitative criteria.

The student will:
- *write a paragraph of 200 words describing the reasons for the origins of the Civil War.*
- *include a topic sentence and a concluding sentence.*
- *include at least three reasons for the Civil War.*
- *cite pages in the textbook for their reasons, at the level of 80 percent accuracy.*
- *use a spell-checker to make sure all words are correctly spelled at a 95 percent level of accuracy.*
- *use complete, grammatical sentences, at the level of 90 percent accuracy.*

There are more numbers here than in the previous versions of these objectives, but these numbers seem to me to give the illusion of quantification rather than help. What really happens if the child writes a paragraph of 14 sentences and there are grammatical errors in two of them (below the 90 percent accuracy criterion)?

■　■　■

This chapter is intended mostly as a general introduction to goals and objectives. The nuts and bolts of the process are given in Chapters 10, 11, 12, and 13 for traditional tests, and Part III for performance assessments.

Teachers should try not think of objectives as their enemies or as time-consuming, bureaucratic hurdles they have to jump over. The writing of objectives is one of the best ways for teachers to think through their teaching. We have each been in a classroom where one of two questions has popped into our head: Why are we doing this? or What am I expected to do? If your teacher had genuinely thought through her objectives, we would probably not have either of these questions. A few minutes spent thinking through these issues will make our teaching more deliberate and more intregrated with past and future learning.

Writing objectives is not some sort of secret teacher behavior. Sharing goals and objectives with students is a good idea, even with very young students. Telling the students on day one of the unit on the stock market that they have to concentrate on definitions in order to understand the stock market is useful. Even if the students do not grasp every part of the process, they may someday be able to invest their money in a way that will help them live more comfortably.

Questions for Reflection

1. Somewhere on all college and university Web sites will be a set of goals and objectives for the teacher education program. Find these objectives and see whether they meet the criteria for good objectives. Are they written in terms of student behaviors? Do they specify what the teacher education students will be able to do so that you can tell how they will be assessed? Are there both goals and objectives? Pick two objectives you think are clearly and objectively written. Find two objectives you think may be more difficult to assess and tell why.

   You may also want to find the curricular goals and objectives for the grade level in the state in which you are teaching or intend to teach. Most states have such objectives and post them on a Web site. You may easily locate them by using the terms *department of education* and the state name on your search engine.

2. At the beginning of your college catalog you will find a goal statement or mission statement. Often these statements are written in grand, eloquent language, which is hard to pin down. Write three specific objectives for the first three goals you find. Your first objectives should reflect what you think the goal really means. The second objective should be something you think would appeal to a lazy student. For your third objective write something outrageous, but something that you think could genuinely cover the goal. For example, "Students will be firmly embedded in their culture and be able to appreciate other cultures" is an interesting goal.
   a. Students will read and take objective tests on *Moby Dick* and *Crime and Punishment*.
   b. Students will be able to decribe an episode of *Friends* and an Italian soap opera.
   c. Students will write an essay contrasting the American Communist Party with the Chinese People's Party.
3. Critique the goals and objectives on your course syllabus.

4

Reliability

*A*bout a month before I started to write this chapter my bathroom scale broke. For two years when I got on it, it showed my depressing rise in weight from 180 to 190 pounds. Then one day I stepped on the scale and it said 127. I got back on: 144. One of the springs in the scale had broken. In the language of assessment, my scale had become unreliable.

▧ RELIABILITY IN CLASSROOM TESTS: TRUE/FALSE TESTS

There is an analogous situation in the classroom. Suppose two children know nothing about the material you are going to test them on. You decide to give them a 10-item true-false quiz. Both students guess and give the following answers:

	MATT	LEIGH	CORRECT ANSWERS
1.	T	T	T
2.	F	T	F
3.	T	F	T
4.	F	F	T
5.	T	T	T
6.	F	T	F
7.	T	F	F
8.	F	F	F
9	T	T	T
10.	T	T	F

Both Matt and Leigh followed a pattern. Leigh scored 50 percent and Matt scored 70 percent. You can make up your own correct answer list and see the grades Matt and Leigh would earn. In the way most middle school tests are graded, Leigh almost passed, and Matt earned a C−. We started with the assumption that neither student knew anything about the topic.

When used in the way they are given in most classrooms, true-false tests are very unreliable. Because students have a 50–50 chance of getting an item correct by guessing, true-false tests almost always overestimate what a student knows. After the spring broke, my bathroom scale always underestimated what I weighed. If you gave the same test again the next day and the students used a different guessing strategy, they would get a different grade, but it would almost never be zero. Yet, we started with the assumption that the students knew nothing about the material.

Reliability is *the extent to which an assessment accurately measures what it was designed to measure.* Put another way, reliability is *the extent to which error is eliminated from the assessment process.*

Please note that an assessment can be reliable but not useful in a particular sitatuation. A well-functioning bathroom scale accurately measures my weight, but if I want to know whether I should wear a short-sleeve shirt or a sweater, knowing my weight does not help: I need to consult a reliable outdoor thermometer. A computation test may be a good measure of a student's mastery of factual material about multiplication but the scores on the computation test are of little help if we are interested in higher-order goals like understanding where multiplication is useful and where it is not. This problem is called *validity*, and it is the topic of the next chapter.

We have talked about reliability as extent because no test is completely reliable. There will always be error. As hard as you may try, you will make errors in assessing students' work. Even on something as straightforward as grading multiple choice tests, teachers routinely make 1 to 2 percent errors.

While 1 to 2 percent seems like a lot of error, true-false tests introduce **systematic error,** *which is inherent in the assessment process.* Because of the nature of true-false tests, students will always earn a lot of credit on items they do not know.

We want to do what we can to reduce systematic error (or increase validity). For example, on a true-false test we could encourage students not to guess. On a 10-item quiz, you could tell students they will get 10 points for a correct answer, negative 10 points for a wrong answer, and 0 points for a blank. In this case Leigh would get a zero (5 right = +50 points; 5 wrong = −50 points) while Matt will get a 40 (7 right = +70 points; 3 wrong = −30 points). By using this scoring a teacher can reduce systematic error, although not completely eliminate it.

▣ RELIABILITY OF PERFORMANCE ASSESSMENTS

The example of true-false tests shows that reliability is a problem on traditional paper-and-pencil tests, but systematic error is even more of a problem when we move to other kinds assessment. In this section we briefly discuss some issues of reliability on assessments of writing, oral reports, and group work.

Writing

More than 30 years ago the critic Leslie Fielder (1964) wrote an essay on the difficulty of grading freshman composition essays in college. He made a clever distinction between two qualities of an essay: *cow,* which was the knowledge base the student had about the topic, and *bull,* which was the ability of a good writer to disguise the fact that he did not know much about the topic. Fielder seemed perplexed because he tended to award higher grades to high-bull, low-cow essays than to low-bull, high-cow essays.

When we sit down to assess a stack of student writing, we are always in danger of awarding higher grades to more interesting papers and lower grades to less interesting ones. Elementary and secondary school teachers are at an advantage over college faculty in this regard because they have been trained to recognize the differences between skills (bull) and content (cow). In a reading lesson the teacher has been trained always to be aware of whether the primary objective of the lesson is developing reading skills or developing content knowledge. We should be equally aware of whether the primary function of a writing assignment is about learning to write better or expressing content knowledge through writing. Of course, we want our students to become better writers and learn the content, but when we are dealing with elementary and middle school students, we know writing is a struggle for almost all of them, and it is usually better to focus students on either writing skills or content.

Assessment in writing, like assessment in general, always returns to the instructional objectives. If we give a writing assignment with clear objectives, we will know better how to assess it than if we have vague objectives. Table 4.1 lists four objectives, two about writing process and two about content. The first objectives in each category sound good, but they both turn out to be vague. The second objectives are more precise and more easily assessed.

Consider the following essay on apples written by a third-grade student (with spelling corrected):

> I like apples. Some are red, some are bright green, some are yellow. Some are sweet and some are sour. Some are for making pies. Some are for making applesauce. Some are for making vinegar. Some are just for eating. In my hometown there are many apple orchards, which are farms with trees, not animals. I would like to play there, but bees like to live there, too, so it is a little dangerous.

TABLE 4.1 WRITING OBJECTIVES FOR A THIRD-GRADE UNIT
ON APPLES

Writing Process

1. Students will write a well-organized paragraph about apples using descriptive adjectives.

2. Students will write a paragraph, beginning with a clearly defined topic sentence about apples, followed by several supportive statements using information learned in the unit, and concluding with a summary statement.

Content

3. Students will demonstrate their knowledge of apples in a well-crafted paragraph.

4. Students will demonstrate their knowledge of apples by listing apple-based products and discussing the economic impact of apples.

This is a very entertaining paragraph, showing a lot of bull ability for a third-grade student. Under the vague objectives, a teacher may (or may not) give this student a very high mark. For example, under Objective 1 (Students will write a well-organized paragraph about apples using descriptive adjectives.) teachers could disagree on whether or not the paragraph was well-organized: The thesis, evidence, and conclusion we normally expect in a well-organized paragraph are about different topics (the thesis is about liking apples; the evidence is about kinds of apple products; the conclusion is about bees in local orchards). The student has, however, used a good number of descriptive adjectives very nicely. Under more specific Objective 2 (Students will write a paragraph, beginning with a clearly defined topic sentence about apples, followed by several supportive statements using information learned in the unit, and concluding with a summary statement), the student's work is somewhat deficient. "I like apples" is not a topic sentence, nor is the sentence about bees a summary.

The essay is much more acceptable under the specific content Objective 4 (Students will demonstrate their knowledge about apples by listing apple-based products and discussing the economic impact of apples). The writer mentions products and begins to develop the idea of economic impact—at an appropriate level for a third-grade student. Objective 3 (Students will demonstrate their knowledge of apples in a well-crafted paragraph) is not only vague (What does *well-crafted* mean?), but it mixes content with skills.

One way of understanding reliability in writing is to think about a particular kind of reliability called **interrater reliability,** or *the percent of agreement between two readers.* On an objective test this is not an issue. Usually two teachers will give the same grade on the same test, but on a written response different readers can have different opinions. As an experiment for writing this chapter, I gave this essay to 12 experienced elementary-school teachers,

TABLE 4.2 12 TEACHERS' GRADES ON AN ESSAY WITH FOUR DIFFERENT OBJECTIVES

OBJECTIVE	GRADES		
1	A	D	B
2	C	C	C
3	A	C	D
4	A	A	A

giving one objective to three teachers and asking them to give letter grades. The results are shown in Table 4.2.

There was high interrater agreement for the specific objectives (2 and 4) and low agreement for the vague ones (1 and 3). You should also note that while there was agreement among the teachers on Objectives 2 and 4, there was no agreement between the two objectives. As we discussed above, the paragraph lacks important organization properties, so the teachers all gave it a C on Objective 2. It meets the content objectives, so all the teachers gave it an A on Objective 4.

Normally, a teacher will not have another teacher grade all his tests to supply interrater agreement information. Sometimes a teacher, particularly an inexperienced one, will ask another teacher to independently grade a few essays to check the reliability of her scoring. More often, teachers will regrade some essays to see if they give the same grades on a second scoring. Usually, the use of a checklist will help increase reliability in such cases. Suppose we make a checklist based on the objectives in Table 4.2 and have two teachers evaluate the same essay. Table 4.3 reports the results of a little experiment I conducted with two experienced teachers who were asked to rate the apple essay on page

TABLE 4.3 TWO TEACHERS' RATINGS OF THE APPLE ESSAY

T1	T2	STUDENTS WILL:
3	1	_____ write a well-organized paragraph.
3	3	_____ use descriptive adjectives.
1	1	_____ begin with a clear topic sentence about apples.
3	3	_____ have several supportive statements using information learned in the unit.
1	1	_____ conclude with a summary statement.
1	1	_____ list different uses of apples.
1	1	_____ know the economic impact of apples.

30. Here the two teachers (scores on the left) agree in 6 of the 7 categories (86 percent agreement). They completely disagree on the other one (3 = Excellent; 2 = Good; 1 = Poor), so this is pretty good agreement. Because there was no agreement on item number 1, it would be a good idea to eliminate it (that is, the checklist will become more reliable).

Oral Reports

Assessing an oral report is even more complicated because it involves two separate sets of skills: composition and delivery. If we are primarily interested in assessing content, a student's grade may be influenced by the organization of the material and the student's skills in making a presentation. Consider this transcript of a student's oral report on apples:

> Today I'm going to tell you about, um, apples, yes, and um, what I want to tell you is about the many things that people make out of apples and how important apples are. I mean, how important they are to farmers who raise them. Apple farmers are called orchardists. My uncle Bob raises apples. He's my mother's brother, um, and he, um raises . . . [shuffles notes for 25 seconds, clearly lost] . . . yes, my uncle Bob raises three kinds of apples. He has a cider press and he makes vinegar and um, he also sells apples to a big company—I forget the name—for apple sauce and canned apple pie filling. And I think some of the peels are used to make fertilizer. My uncle makes a lot of money doing this and he employs three people full-time and over forty people during picking season.

Suppose now we are only interested in assessing the content of this student's understanding of apples, using Objective 4 (Students will demonstrate their knowledge of apples by listing apple-based products and discuss the economic impact of apples). If we listen to this child rambling and become uncomfortable when he gets lost, we may lose track of the content objectives he meets: He lists apple-based products, and he discusses the economic impact of apples.

We can make our evaluations more reliable by using a checklist based on the objectives and making checks as the student makes the presentation. Here the objectives are:

_____ lists apple-based products

_____ discusses the economic impact of apples

We could use this checklist to learn whether the student accomplished each of the two objectives and get three possible scores:

2	Excellent	Met both objectives.
1	Good	Met one objective.
0	Poor	Met neither objective.

TABLE 4.4   CHECKLIST FOR A CONTENT ASSESSMENT ON A PRESENTATION ABOUT APPLES

Lists apple-based products	Economic impact
_____ None (0)	_____ None (0)
_____ 1–2 products (1)	_____ One impact (1)
_____ 3 or more products (2)	_____ Two or more impacts (2)

We could further differentiate our checklist with levels for each objective. (See Table 4.4.) Our student's speech mentions five apple products (vinegar, fertilizer, cider, apple pie filling, apple sauce) and three impacts (orchardist, full-time, and temporary employees). He would get a score of 4 out of 4.

We may not be primarily concerned about content. We may be interested in overall organization or in oral presentation skills. In those cases we would develop a much different kind of checklist. Our ultimate goal is for students to be able to give well-organized, well-presented, high-content oral reports. But all of that may be too much to expect of young students at one time. Assessing oral reports is the topic of Chapter 21.

Group Work

Group work always poses problems about reliability because we are always concerned about **authorship,** or *who is responsible for the work?* A problem of reliability arises if a student receives an excellent grade when he did little work, achieved little or no mastery of the material, or gained no competency in group skills because he was assigned to a group where others did excellent work. When we assign a grade to an individual member of a group, we want that grade to reflect something about his behavior. Parents will insist on this, but they are not likely to frame the issue as reliability!

To make their assessment of group work more reliable, teachers will often include measures of individual work as well as a grade for the group product when assessing group work and include a measure of group participation. The teacher who taught the unit on apples included a group book on apples. All the students in a group participated in producing the book, but she also gave a quiz at the end of the chapter to test students' knowledge. She also had each student rate each other student's participation, using a series of three happy faces. One face was broadly smiling (worked extra hard); one was smiling a little (worked pretty hard); and one had a straight line for a mouth (needs to work harder). The book counted 50 percent of the students' grades, the quiz counted 30 percent of the students' grades, and the evaluation by group members counted 20 percent. In a group with an excellent book, those who participated at lower rates and learned little would have their grade dropped. In a group with books that were rated lower, students who learned a lot and participated a great deal would have their assessments raised. Assessing group work is covered in Chapter 22.

▓ THE RELIABILITY OF STANDARDIZED TESTS

For those who develop and use standardized tests the question of reliability is fundamental. A test that is not reliable has no use. Standardized tests address the issue of reliability in four ways: (1) test-retest reliability, which is analogous to stepping on and off a scale to see if it gives the same reading both times; (2) alternate form reliability, which is analogous to checking the accuracy of a scale by comparing a reading on it to another scale, the same rationale, in many respects, as interrater agreement; (3) split-half reliability, which is similar to alternate form, except that it is done at the same time, like putting one foot on one scale and one on a second scale to see if they both register half of your weight; and (4) internal consistency, which has no direct analogy to the bathroom scale.

Test-Retest Reliability

For classroom teachers **test-retest reliability** is an intuitively useful idea, although they will rarely use it. On a test that is free of systematic error, *scores ought to be the same on two separate administrations of a test if no learning takes place.*

Table 4.5 is an example of scores on a fill-in-the-blanks quiz given at the end of a unit. Scores range from 10 percent to 100 percent. Two weeks later the same quiz was given again after the students had moved on to a new unit, and column 2 reports the scores on the second administration.

TABLE 4.5   TEST-RETEST RELIABILITY OF A RELIABLE TEST

	TIME 1	TIME 2	CHANGE
Allison	10	20	+10
Betty	20	30	+10
Charles	30	30	0
Davis	40	30	−10
Ellen	50	50	0
Fran	60	60	0
George	70	80	+10
Hiram	80	70	−10
Isaac	90	80	−10
Jennifer	100	100	0

The scores of these students are relatively stable. Charles, Ellen, Fran, and Jennifer did not change scores from one administration to the next. Allison, Betty, and George have scores that go up 10 points. (Maybe they were more relaxed when the scores did not count.) Davis, Hiram, and Isaac have scores that went down 10 points because they forgot some of the content. Although the scores change a little, most of the students are in the same relative position on the first administration as they are on the second. (In column 2 only George and Hiram change places.) If we forget about the signs, the average score changes only 6 points (60/10).

Table 4.6 represents scores on a true-false quiz where guessing significantly affected student performance. Here the scores at Time 1 and Time 2 are not very closely related; the test has very low test-retest reliability. Many students change their relative place, and if we disregard the sign of the change in scores in column 3, the average test score changes 32 points.

In Chapter 7 we will describe a statistical test called the correlation coefficient, which is useful in describing how reliable a test is using the test-retest procedure. In the first example the correlation coefficient is .92—a high coefficient (1.00 is as high as it gets). In the second example the reliability is low: the correlation coefficient is .26 (0.00 is as low as it gets). Standardized tests usually have test-retest correlation coefficients of .85 or higher. When classroom tests are examined for reliability they are often found to have lower reliability coefficients, but we would not want to use a test which had a reliability coefficient much below 0.70.

Alternate Form Reliability

Sometimes a test can be administered only one time. For example, a student might remember the answers from the first administration on the second ad-

TABLE 4.6   TEST-RESTEST RELIABILITY OF AN UNRELIABLE TEST

	TIME 1	TIME 2	CHANGE
Allison	10	80	+70
Betty	20	30	+10
Charles	30	70	+40
Davis	40	30	−10
Ellen	50	20	−30
Fran	60	30	−30
George	70	80	+10
Hiram	80	30	−50
Isaac	90	80	−10
Jennifer	100	40	−60

ministration. This might be the case on a timed test where you had a computation problem; the second time through the student might remember the
item and not have to take the time to recompute it. We want to have two
forms of the same test, and we want to demonstrate that the scores on one
test are very close to being the scores on the second test. Again, we would
use the correlation coefficient to find the reliability.

Teachers often need an alternate test. If you recycle students through a
unit and then want to test to see if they have mastered the material, you may
need to develop a second test. If you have a student who missed a test, you
may decide you need an equivalent test to give, particularly if you have
given the first test back to other students with the correct answers. The
make-up test should not be appreciably harder or easier than the original
test. Corresponding items on the second test could be different from each
item on the original. On a test of presidents, you might ask who was the
fourth president on one test, and who was the sixth on another. (Asking who
was the first president would be too easy!) This alternate form is called a
parallel form, *where each item on one test has an equivalent question on the other.*

Alternate form reliability is *the degree to which scores on two tests designed
to be equivalent are the same.* The same logic used with test-retest reliability
pertains, except we have two tests instead of one test administered on two
occasions.

Split-Half Reliability

Split-half reliability has no real equivalence for classroom teachers, but it is
important for some kinds of standardized tests. Sometimes, on a standardized test you actually have two items to measure each objective, like putting
two parallel form tests together to compute the correlation coefficient for the
two halves of the test. Other times the items are quite different. Split-half reliability is used sometimes when it is impossible to get test-retest reliability,
and it approximates the reliability of the test. If you are looking at a standardized test to see whether you might want to use it, a split-half reliability
above 0.85 indicates the test is reliable, and a lower score should be a red
flag that the test might not be reliable.

Internal Consistency

The full consideration of internal consistency, a technical kind of reliability,
is beyond the scope of this handbook. Internal consistency asks the question
about the relation of all items to each other, and it is important when we
want to know whether the assessment measures one thing or a variety of
things. Technically, it is the average of all possible split-half reliabilities and
is either estimated by a formula or computed on a computer.

Think about an arithmetic test that includes both computational problems (2 + 7 = ?) and word problems. If you were taking an Italian arithmetic
test, you might get all of the computation problems correct and all of the

word problems incorrect. The same issues might occur in an English arithmetic test in which some of the problems involved difficult vocabulary. (If you paid 55 pence tax on a litre of gasoline, how much tax in dollars would you pay on 14 gallons of gas?) A test that measures both arithmetic skills and vocabulary would have a low internal consistency.

If you are reading about a test, you may encounter KR-20 or KR-21 formulae, which estimates this correlation. Again, scores above 0.85 are good, while those much below 0.85 suggest the test is not reliable.

Questions for Reflection

1. Think about grading a stack of essays written by students at the level you hope to teach. Even if you plan on teaching kindergarten, you may have students compose an essay, which you will write down for them. List at least 10 things that may influence your grading, besides the actual content of the essay. Compare your answers with another student's in the class.
2. We assess test-retest reliability on two occasions when no learning has occurred on those items between the two administrations. Why can no learning occur?
3. Make a list of those kinds of assessments you think will have high reliability and a list of those kinds of assessments where you think low reliability may be a problem.

5

Validity

*J*n the previous chapter we used the example of a bathroom scale to demonstrate the concept of reliability. Suppose you have a reliable scale and you want to use it to measure whether your suitcase meets the weight limits imposed by an airline. The suitcase weighs 12 pounds. The limit is 14 pounds. The scale validly answers the question. You are okay.

But suppose you want to know if you packed the right clothes for a trip to Alaska in January. The bathroom scale is not a valid instrument to answer this question. There is some relation between the question and the scale's reading because warm clothes are usually heavier than summer clothes, but the answer "12 pounds" is not really helpful. Too often in the past, teachers and others who used educational assessments felt that a reliable test can be used for almost any purpose. **Validity** refers to *the extent to which a test accomplishes a specific goal.*

First, let me give you an example from standardized testing. The Scholastic Aptitude Tests (SATs) predict fairly accurately how well a student will do during his or her freshman year in college because they measure general verbal and mathematical ability.* Most freshmen have to take freshman English, math, and other courses that rely heavily on verbal and quantitative abilities. After the freshman year students get into their majors. Some majors, like art, music, and drama, rely less on the skills measured by

---

* Some people will disagree with this statement. At highly competitive colleges and universities where all students do very well on the tests, SATs are not as helpful as they are at colleges that admit students with a wider range of ability. At open admissions colleges the SATs are very predictive: A person with a combined score of 750 is going to have a much tougher time than someone with a score of 1,400. At competitive colleges no one does really poorly on the test. A person who scores 1,400 will not have much advantage over a person who scores 1,350. The difference will depend on how hard the students work and what courses they take.

the SAT, so in those majors the SAT does not predict achievement very well after the freshman year. For English, history, and foreign language students, the SAT-Verbal test is still useful; for other students, in engineering, mathematics, and economics, the SAT-Quantitative test is still useful. The SAT is valid for some uses and not valid for others. While reliability is a quality of a test regardless of its use, tests are valid for some uses and not for others. Just because a test is valid for a particular use does not mean it is valid for other purposes.

Let me follow this up with an example from classroom teaching. A few years ago I was with a school district that was having a summer program for creative students in science. Teachers were asked for nominations. Most teachers went to their grade books and nominated students with the highest grades in science. While this procedure picked out some creative science students, most grades in science courses are based not on original thinking in science, but on learning the facts. There is a difference between learning the facts and being creative. Many of the students nominated by this procedure turned out not to be original thinkers. Science grades are not a valid way of picking out creative science students.

In this chapter we discuss four kinds of validity: One is crucial for classroom assessments; three are of primary use in standardized testing. The three basic forms of validity all begin with the letter C: content, criterion, and construct. There is a fourth kind of validity, face validity, which is not really a kind of validity at all, but it is an important quality of a test.

▨ THE VALIDITY OF CLASSROOM ASSESSMENTS

Content Validity

Classroom teachers need to be primarily concerned with content validity when it comes to developing their own assessments. **Content validity** *measures the outcomes of the instructional objectives in the assessment.* All too often tests used by teachers do not measure the objectives very well, including objective paper-and-pencil tests or oral reports, group projects, or writing exercises. An extended example from a student teaching experience I supervised a few years ago will make the point. The student teacher developed a unit on China mandated by the state standards of learning. The standards of learning stated that:

> Children will explore aspects of ancient Chinese culture to learn that other cultures exist with different standards of behavior, customs, and cultural products.

The student teacher taught the unit using cooperative learning groups. At the end of the unit, each group made a presentation of their research. The student teacher used two checklists to evaluate the students, in keeping with school district standards that used an excellent/good/needs improvement grading system for second-grade students. The first checklist (Table 5.1) measured how well individual students worked in the group.

TABLE 5.1   CHECKLIST EVALUATING GROUP PARTICIPATION

_____ 3. **Excellent.** Took a leadership role in the project; helped make decisions

_____ 2. **Good.** Contributed to the group; asked questions; did assignments

_____ 1. **Needs Improvement.** Did not contribute to the group

The second checklist (Table 5.2) was for the presentation. All students in the group got the same rating.

The two ratings were averaged together for the individual student's grade for the project.

As we watched the six presentations, most of which were very good, the student teacher and I rated the presentations on the second checklist. At the end we had exact agreement for each presentation. The student teacher and the cooperating teacher, likewise, had come to unanimous agreement on the individual participation checklists. These agreements indicated that the two checklists were highly reliable. But as I sat and discussed the unit with the student teacher, she felt that the grades did not accurately (i.e., validly) reflect students' learning.

"Doria, for example, got two Excellents, [3.0]" the student teacher said, "but I'm not sure she understands anything about how the Chinese were different from us, while Peter got a Good for the group presentation and a Needs Improvement in participation [1.5], and he was the student who got the most excited by the project, and I think he learned the most."

"What was the problem?" I asked.

At first she thought the checklists were too rigid, but after some discussion she realized that she had only measured process and not content. Doria's group had given an excellent presentation on how Chinese people grew rice, but they made no comparison to America. Peter's group had made a presentation on Chinese lanterns. They made constant comparisons to American customs of lighting, but as they really didn't understand electricity, their presentation was less slick. Peter became engrossed in his own research and failed to be a big contributor to the group.

We developed a simple content checklist (Table 5.3), which reflected the content of the objective. The student teacher decided that 50 percent of the

TABLE 5.2   EVALUATION OF GROUP PRESENTATION

_____ 3. **Excellent.** Organized presentation; used pictures and/or products; interesting

_____ 2. **Good.** Lacked one of the qualities above

_____ 1. **Needs Improvement.** Lacked two qualities; laughed and giggled; long pauses

TABLE 5.3   CONTENT CHECKLIST FOR GROUP PRESENTATION
ABOUT CHINA

_____ 3. **Excellent.** Compares and contrasts cultures.

_____ 2. **Good.** Explains American and Chinese traditions without direct
comparisons.

_____ 1. **Needs Improvement.** Only tells about Chinese culture.

grade should be content and 25 percent each for group participation and
group presentation. This meant that Doria got a 2.0 and Peter got a 2.25. Because working in the group and giving a good presentation were also goals
of the unit, she felt this was a reasonable solution to her concerns.

Content and Level of Understanding   We need to decide whether we
are primarily measuring process or content goals. If we are measuring content, we need to examine the level of content understanding we expect from
students. For example, if we are teaching a unit on early exploration of the
United States, we could have the following goals for students:

1. Know the names of explorers' ships (e.g., be able to match Francis
   Drake with *Golden Hinde*).
2. Restate material given to them about the reasons for early exploration
   (e.g., be able to say that Spanish explorers wanted to find gold and sil-
   ver and convert the Native Americans to Christianity).
3. Read complex material and extract ideas on their own (e.g., be able to
   read a selection from the diary of Cortez and explain his reasons for
   coming to the New World).
4. Relate new material to early learning (e.g., explain how exploration of
   the New World was similar to and different from the reasons for undertaking the Crusades, which had been studied in an earlier unit).

Content validity is also concerned with the level of understanding
we expect from students. In the example of the unit on China, second
graders were only expected to note differences between ancient China and
contemporary America. They were not expected to relate this to differences in religion, technology, or agricultural practices, as we might for an
older group of students. A content objective always contains reference to
the knowledge and the level of understanding expected. In Chapter 8
we use Bloom's Taxonomy of the Cognitive Domain to examine one common way in which knowledge objectives are differentiated in terms of
level of understanding. At this point, however, it will be useful to think
about three different levels of knowledge: (1) Facts, (2) Applications, and
(3) Analysis. These levels relate to three basic questions: what? how? and
why?

As we ask young students to learn about China, we may focus on what the ancient Chinese did. Somewhat later we may ask how that was different from the way we do things. For older students we may hope that they understand why we and the ancient Chinese did things differently. This represents a development in thinking: What comes before how; how comes before why. Younger children are better at what-thinking than how-thinking, and older children are better at why-thinking. As we learn about any content area at any age, we begin with facts, go on to applications, and then to analysis.

Assessments that ask questions at the wrong level of understanding lack content validity. If I have taught a unit on early exploration on the level of fact, and then ask why questions on an examination, my assessment lacks content validity. Likewise, if I have taught it at the level of analysis and ask just factual questions, my assessment lacks content validity.

As we develop an assessment instrument, we need to go back to the objectives to see the level of understanding we expect from students. Often the verb in the objective (what we want students to be able to do) is the most important clue to level of understanding:

An objective such as "students will be able to match early explorers with their ships" clearly defines the level of understanding on the factual level. Because we included the verb *match*, it defines the kind of test item we might expect to find. An objective such as "students will be able to use multiplication or addition in story problems requiring multiplication or addition" is an application objective, cued by the verb *use*. Again, we know what kind of assessment item to use: word problems, some of which require addition and some requiring multiplication. An objective such as "students will be able to demonstrate their understanding of the importance of religion in forming American and Chinese culture through oral and/or written reports" suggests that we are at an analysis level, although the objective specifically allows for different methods of demonstrating this knowledge.

Poorly written, indefinite objectives make the job of assessment difficult. Consider the objective "students will learn to appreciate good literature by studying the novels of E. B. White." While no one would argue that a goal of the language arts curriculum should be to help students to appreciate good literature, this kind of objective will cause us no end of problems when we come to assess it. How would we know if this objective had been met? What do students do to demonstrate their appreciation of good literature? Too often, teachers with these noble (though vague) goals will do one of two things: They will test on the facts, with a general idea that if you haven't read the material you certainly can't appreciate it; or they will come up with an equally vague assessment activity such as to "keep a daily journal about your reactions to *Stuart Little*." When the teacher collects and reads the journals, she is not looking for anything specific, so she will make comments back to the students or correct the grammar and spelling.

There are two important points to be made here. First, like instruction, good assessment begins with good objectives. A carefully thought-through objective should guide the teaching and assessment process. A hastily constructed objective will provide very little guidance for either activity. Usually a carefully developed objective will be more specific than a less carefully prepared one, but specificity is not the point. We could write a very specific objective about *Stuart Little*. We could demand that students remember the details of each chapter; we could ask students to illustrate a specific episode from the book which would include a list of details we supply; or we could ask students to commit a portion of the text to memory. But if we are trying to help students appreciate good literature, these objectives might not help us approach this goal. Objectives that focus on how E. B. White develops character, uses point of view, or develops the main plot and subplots might be more in keeping with our goal, although they would be more difficult to write.

Second, I believe that instruction and assessment are not two separate processes but two parts of teaching. What binds them together is the curriculum, which is specified by the objectives. Instruction focuses on what the teacher does; assessment focuses on how the students have changed because of the instruction: Have they developed new knowledge and skills that will carry them along the curricular path?

✳ VALIDITY ISSUES PRIMARILY ASSOCIATED WITH STANDARDIZED TESTS

Criterion Validity

Criterion validity measures *the extent to which a test predicts another performance—the criterion*. There are two kinds of criterion validity: **concurrent,** *measuring the criterion immediately*, and **predictive,** *measuring the criterion in the future*.

A standardized test is often developed to find a simple assessment which will predict a more complicated criterion. The Metropolitan Readiness Test is often administered to students in kindergarten or first grade to determine their needs in language arts instruction (basic prereading, sight word skills, or reading basal readers). The few items on the MRT were validated against hundreds of other skills. The basic process is developed in the example following, which relates to predictive validity.

When I was studying to be an elementary school teacher one of my professors insisted that it was unnecessary to give students elaborate reading readiness tests in kindergarten. He asserted that if a child could throw and catch a ball and could hop on one foot five times without falling, she was ready to learn to read. I do not recommend this as a substitute for more standard assessment, but one year I decided to determine whether this method was useful. I gave this assessment to all 22 children in my kindergarten. Then I spent four weeks giving all of them basic reading instruction. At the end of the four weeks I gave all of the students a sight reading test of ten

TABLE 5.4 PREDICTIVE VALIDITY OF THE HOP-AND-CATCH TEST. (THE NUMBERS REPRESENT THE NUMBER OF SIGHT WORDS CORRECTLY IDENTIFIED OUT OF 10.)

CAN'T HOP AND CATCH	HOPPERS	CATCHERS	HOPPERS + CATCHERS
2	3	3	9
1	3	3	8
0	2	1	7
0	1	1	7
0	0	0	5
		0	3
Mean 0.6	1.8	1.3	6.5

words we had been working on. Five students couldn't jump or catch; five students could just hop; six could just catch; and six could hop and catch. Table 5.4 shows the results.

Without applying any fancy statistics, these results tell us that those who could hop and catch learned two-thirds of the words; those who couldn't hop or catch knew about 10 percent of the words. I would conclude that this is a reasonably valid assessment. Because my criterion was collected four weeks after my test, I established predictive validity. (Usually, the criterion is determined months or years later.) If I had collected the test and criterion data at the same time, we would say that I had used a concurrent validity procedure.

Construct Validity

The third kind of validity, **construct validity,** is *used only with standardized tests.* For example, before we could call a new test an IQ test, we would have to show that the new test results are similar to results obtained from a recognized IQ test. We would do this in a manner similar to what I did to establish the predictive validity of the hop and catch test. Instead of comparing my new test to a criterion behavior, I would compare it to scores on an established test. Let's say I compared the hop and catch to the Metropolitan Readiness Test. (I didn't.) I could imagine, however, getting the results shown in Table 5.5.

Students who score 0 on the hop-and-catch test average a score of 12 on a standard readiness test; those who score 1 (hop or catch) score an average of 19; and those who score 2 (hop and catch) average 37. I would be justified in calling my test a readiness test because the scores on my test closely match the results on a well-established readiness test. We elaborate on this technique, correlation, in Chapter 7.

TABLE 5.5   CONSTRUCT VALIDITY OF THE HOP-AND-CATCH
READINESS TEST

CAN'T HOP AND CATCH	HOPPERS	CATCHERS	HOPPERS + CATCHERS
20	30	27	44
11	31	30	51
8	24	12	43
10	10	14	38
8	5	11	25
		8	21
Mean 11.6	20.0	18.7	37.0

Face Validity

The final form of validity is not technically a validity. **Face validity** refers to *whether the people who use or take tests believe the tests have validity.* This issue became important early in testing when IQ tests, which were developed for children, were first being used to assess adults. One of the first items on the Stanford-Binet Test is to have the examinee tie the shoe of a doll. Some adults thought that this task was silly, so they treated the whole test in an unserious manner. We would expect that if an examinee did not try hard, it would affect both the reliability and validity of the results of the test.

Face validity is important in education. Sometimes teachers do not believe in standardized tests. When they give their students tests like the Stanford-9 or the Iowa Test of Basic Skills, the teachers' attitudes are subtly conveyed to the students, and the students do not try as hard. Some minority groups believe standardized tests are biased against them, and they may not try as hard.

Teachers may need to realize that some parents will question the validity of teacher-made tests. Many parents who were brought up on paper-and-pencil tests question some authentic assessment techniques, particularly group work. The parents' attitudes may influence the children to try less hard on certain kinds of activities.

Questions for Reflection

1. Think back over your educational experiences and recall an assessment you think did not validly reflect the objectives. Describe what you think the objectives were and what the assessment was like. Try to determine why it was not valid. Come up with a valid form of assessment.
2. With three or four other people in your class, write down your SAT-Verbal and SAT-Quantitative scores on a piece of paper. Then write

down your grades in your freshman English class and your freshman math class. Also write down your current GPA. Don't put your names on the papers. Now see if the SAT-Verbal scores predicted your freshman English grades; your SAT-Quantitative scores predicted your freshman math grades; and if either predicts your GPAs. You can do this by rank-ordering the SAT scores and seeing if the grades fall in roughly the same order:

SAT-V	FRESHMAN ENGLISH	GPA
640	A	3.05
590	A−	3.40
550	B	3.15
500	B	3.25

In this case SAT-V did predict freshman English, but not GPA.

3. Go to the library and look up information on the validity of a standardized test. One simple way of doing this is to go to the ERIC index and enter the name of the test and the keyword *validity*. This will get you an abstract of a research article. Most likely the articles you find will be about criterion validity. What was the criterion used in this study? What did the authors conclude about the validity of the test to predict this criterion?

CHAPTER

6

Descriptive Statistics

*T*he term *statistics* in the title of this chapter may cause some of you to panic and others of you to stop reading. You shouldn't; we use statistics every day. In this chapter we will develop a few, simple procedures which will help us talk about the many numbers teachers have to deal with in assessing their students.

A college mathematics department often has three levels of statistics based on arithmetic, algebra, and calculus. Statistics based on calculus is difficult because calculus is difficult. Statistics based on algebra is less difficult, but still abstract, because algebra is abstract. In this chapter and throughout this book, when we need to develop a statistical concept, we will use arithmetic to do so. You learned the mathematics we will use by the end of the sixth or seventh grade. Sometimes we will use formulae that look like algebra, but the ideas will always be from arithmetic.

A **descriptive statistic** is *a number that represents a group of numbers*. For example, we may say that in the last election, 57.2 percent of the people voted for Republicans and 42.8 percent voted for Democrats. These percentages are statistics because they represent a summary of all the votes cast. You may tell a student he has a test average of 89.0, which is easier to understand than a simple list of his test scores. The test average is a statistic.

We divide statistics into two major classifications: **descriptive statistics,** *which summarize larger groups of numbers*, and **inferential statistics,** *which are decision rules to help us make decisions about groups of numbers*. This chapter is only concerned with descriptive statistics.

Any group of numbers can be summarized sufficiently if we know three things about it:

1. its size
2. its center (a measure of central tendency)
3. the way the numbers cluster around the center (a measure of dispersion)

Size is easy; we are familiar with measures of central tendency. Only measures of dispersion should give us any difficulty.

▦ SIZE

The statistic for size (N) is completely straightforward: How many numbers make up the group? If you give 10 tests in a grading period, your sample size is 10. If you throw out the lowest test score, the sample size is 9. If you want to find out your class average for social studies final examinations and there are 23 students in your class, the sample size is 23. There are no tricks here. Sample size can be for a single student (10 tests) or for a class (23 students).

▦ MEASURES OF CENTRAL TENDENCY

We have used measures of central tendency since middle school when we learned to average. Now we must stop using the word *average* because there are many different kinds of averages. For classroom testing statistics, we need to know four averages: the unweighted mean, the weighted mean, the median, and the mode.

The Unweighted Mean

We normally call the **unweighted,** or **arithmetic, mean** the average. If we take 10 quizzes (and they all count the same), we compute the mean by the following two steps:

1. We add up our scores.
2. We divide by 10.

Perhaps you can remember that we can write "we add up our scores" by using the symbols Σx. Σ (read sigma) means "sum up what follows"; x refers to the test scores; and *sigma x* means "add up the test scores."

We also know that in step two we divide by the number of items, which we defined as N in the previous section. The formula for the unweighted mean is $\Sigma x/N$ (*sigma x* divided by N).

Suppose a student earned the following 8 quiz scores: {2, 4, 3, 3, 4, 4, 5, 2}; what is her unweighted mean score?

First, find Σx: $2 + 4 + 3 + 3 + 4 + 4 + 5 + 2 = 27$.

Then, divide by N (in this case 8) $= 27/8 = 3.375$. (Means should always be expressed to at least one decimal place.)

The Weighted Mean

But suppose in addition to 8 quizzes in the example above, this teacher also gives two tests, and tests count more than quizzes. Can she compute a mean then?

Of course, but since some numbers will be weighted more than others, she will have to use a **weighted mean.** We promised only to use arithmetic in this chapter, and we will avoid the complex algebraic notation and use the arithmetic way of computing a weighted mean.

Suppose the teacher wants a test to count three times as much as a quiz. Then she writes down each test score three times, but she also has to increase N so that it is the number of scores she added to obtain the sum. Our student received these quiz scores: {2, 4, 3, 3, 4, 4, 5, 2}; and she received these two test scores: {82, 88}.

We have a problem. The quiz scores were on a scale of 0 to 5; the test scores were on a scale of 0 to 100. We have to change the quiz scores into the same scale units as the test scores (0 = 0, 1 = 20, 2 = 40, 3 = 60, 4 = 80, and 5 = 100).

Now we can add the scores together:

40 + 80 + 60 + 60 + 80 + 80 + 100 + 40 + 82 + 82 + 82 + 88 + 88 + 88 = 1,050

$\Sigma x/N = 1{,}050/14 = 75.0$

Note: We divide by 14 because each of the 8 quizzes count as one score and each of the 2 tests count as 3 scores, or 8 + 6 = 14.

No wonder teachers grumble when they have to compute grades. Fortunately, for only a small amount of money, you can purchase an electronic gradebook program for your classroom computer. When you use these programs, every time you enter a score you give it a weight. At the end of the semester, all you need to do is hit the return key, and all of your grades will be averaged for you. Some teachers don't like technology, but if you get one of these programs and spend an hour learning how to use it, you will save yourself hours and hours of computations every grading period for the next 30 years of teaching.

The Median

The **median** is *the middle score in a ranked set of numbers.* After you put all the numbers in order, you count and find the score in the middle. Suppose you gave 7 quizzes and a student got the following scores:

{1, 4, 3, 4, 5, 2, 4}

First, you must put the numbers in order, from lowest to highest:

{1, 2, 3, 4, 4, 4, 5}

Then count to the middle number:

{1, 2, 3, **4,** 4, 4, 5}

Four is the middle score. Because it is an actual number, not the result of division, we do not use a decimal point unless there was a decimal point in the original score.

Some of you are ahead of me and are asking what happens if there is an even number of scores. We can look at the problem by using the scores from the previous example:

{2, 4, 3, 3, 4, 4, 5, 2}

After putting them in order, {2, 2, 3, 3, 4, 4, 4, 5}, we notice that the middle score is between the 3 and 4. We take the two middle scores and average them together, giving us 3.5. If the middle two scores were 4 and 9, then the median would be $(4 + 9)/ 2 = 13/2 = 6.5$.

The Mode

The mode is the easiest of the measures of central tendency. It is the most frequently occurring score. In our two examples, the mode for {2, 2, 3, 3, 4, 4, 4, 5} is 4, and for {1, 2, 3, 4, 4, 4, 5} it is also 4. The only tricks about the mode are (1) not every group of scores has a mode: {1, 2, 3, 4, 5}, does not have a mode; and (2) some groups, have more than one mode {1, 2, 2, 2, 3, 4, 4, 4, 5} has modes of 2 and 4. Many groups of scores are bimodal. Some are trimodal, etc.

Different Uses for Different Measures of Central Tendency

In classrooms we almost always use weighted means to compute students' grades, unless all grades count the same and we use the unweighted mean. We use a median to compute the average when we expect one or a few extreme scores to influence our results unduly. For example, a few years ago the University of North Carolina computed the average salaries of its graduates for one year by major, and, much to its surprise, found that sociology majors had the highest earnings. Michael Jordan was a sociology major and was earning $50,000,000. There were about 100 sociology majors, and his salary inflated the mean by about $500,000 over the median of $32,000.

There is no particular reason why classroom teachers might not want to use a median as a method of calculating grades. Suppose a student has five grades: 75, 72, 75, 78, and 48. The mean for this group of grades is 69 (a D by most standards), but the student has a median of 75 (a C). Four of the student's grades were Cs, which might suggest he was a C student. One problem with using the median is that it not only cuts down the influence of a low grade, it also cuts out the influence of a high grade. If the student had earned {75, 72, 75, 78, and 100}, the median is 75 (a C), but the mean is 80 (a B−). Usually, teachers are more willing to eliminate the effects of one low grade (everyone can make a mistake from time to time) than to eliminate the effects of one high one, because teachers are in the business of encouraging students to work hard, even if particular students do so only occasionally. Teachers usually use the mean, sometimes throwing out the lowest grade.

The mode has few practical uses for classroom teachers, but elsewhere in this book it can help us understand other statistics.

▣ MEASURES OF DISPERSION

Two measures of dispersion are useful to teachers: the **range,** which is *the lowest to the highest score,* and the **standard deviation,** which is *the average distance scores are away from the mean.* The range is more useful on a day-to-day basis for classroom teachers, but the standard deviation is important in helping us understand what scores on standardized tests mean. Standard deviation is important in Chapter 7, in developing the correlation coefficient.

Range

Suppose you have two students who earn the following test scores:

Bill: {75, 76, 77, 78, 79}
Joe: {57, 67, 77, 87, 97}

Both students had a mean of 77, but Bill's range of scores is smaller than Joe's.

There are two ways of reporting the range. One is to state the highest and lowest scores. The other is to subtract the highest from the lowest score. Thus, we can say, "Bill had a range of test scores of 4 points, from 75 to 79; Joe had a range of 40 points, from 57 to 97."

The range is important to teachers because it tells us how stable students' scores are. In Bill's case he earned five scores that were very close together. We can assume he is a C student in this subject. Joe's scores range so widely (He earned an A, B, C, D, and F), we may be more reluctant to call him a C student. Potentially, he's an A student because, at least once, he earned an A.

You can also look at the range for a whole class. Suppose you look at the scores on a test you have just administered and the mean grade is 70—a pretty disappointing performance. If most of the students scored in the range (e.g., 65 to 76), your best bet is to reteach all or part of the lesson to everybody. If the scores went from 60 to 95, you know that some students mastered the unit, and others need to have remedial instruction.

The range is also useful in showing parents where their children's strengths and weaknesses lie, which is helpful in getting parents to agree to have their child evaluated for special education. Saying to a parent "Your son always gets 60s in math" is not as effective as showing that he is consistently at the bottom of the class range of scores. If you just say, "Your son always gets 60s in math," the parents can come back and say, "Your tests are too hard." By showing where their son falls in the range of scores, you can help his parents understand his difficulties (Rose, 1998).

You can show parents their children's location in the class by using a stem-and-leaf plot. In this procedure you make a stem by a scale and put leaves on it for each student. In the graph below the scale ranges from 60 to 100, and each x represents one student in that range. There is, for example one student between 95 and 100, three students between 90 and 95, and so on in the distribution of scores:

10	0	x
	5	xxx
9	0	xx
	5	xxxx
8	0	xxxx
	5	xxxx
7	0	xx
	5	xx
6	0	x

The stem-and-leaf plot can tell parents a great deal about their child's performance relative to other students in the class.

The Standard Deviation

Before we discuss the standard deviation, we need to know what a deviation is. Any score in a group of scores can be rewritten as its distance and direction from the mean. If you got a 90 on a test, and the mean score for the class was 80, your deviation score is +10. If you got a 75, your deviation is −5. To find a **deviation score** you subtract the mean from that score:

$d = x - M$ (The deviation [d] is the raw score [x] minus the mean [M].)

We would now like to find the average deviation. If all of the deviations are small, then the average deviation will be small. If there are quite a few large deviations, then the average deviation will be bigger. A small average deviation would indicate that all the scores were packed closely together. As the number gets bigger, the scores become more spread out.

There's a problem here, because if we just calculated the mean of the deviation scores, we would always get zero. In other words, if we add up all the deviations higher than the mean and all the deviations lower than it, those two sums are the same, except one is positive and one is negative. When we add them together we always get zero. Because we are taking the arithmetic approach, we can work a few simple problems:

Begin with the set of numbers {1, 2, 3, 4, 5}. These are five quiz scores, which we will call raw scores.

The mean is $(1 + 2 + 3 + 4 + 5)/5 = 15/5 = 3.0$.
Now find the deviation scores:

RAW SCORE	DEVIATION SCORE (RAW SCORE MINUS MEAN)	
1	$(1-3) =$	-2
2	$(2-3) =$	-1
3	$(3-3) =$	0
4	$(4-3) =$	$+1$
5	$(5-3) =$	$+2$

When we add up the deviation scores, we get zero.

Begin with the set of numbers $\{1, 2, 3, 4, 5, 5\}$.
The mean is $(1 + 2 + 3 + 4 + 5 + 5)/6 = 20/6 = 3.33$.
Now find the deviation scores:

RAW SCORE	DEVIATION SCORE (RAW SCORE MINUS MEAN)	
1	$(1-3.33) =$	-2.33
2	$(2-3.33) =$	-1.33
3	$(3-3.33) =$	-0.33
4	$(4-3.33) =$	$+0.66$
5	$(5-3.33) =$	$+1.66$
5	$(5-3.33) =$	$+1.66$
	$\Sigma d =$	0

Again, when we add up the deviation scores, we get zero.

We get rid of the pesky negative signs by squaring the deviation scores. Remember a square always gives us a positive number: $\Sigma d^2/N$.* After we have computed this formula, we take the square root, giving us the **standard deviation**. Technically, the standard deviation is *the square root of the sum of the deviation scores, divided by* N: $\sqrt{\Sigma d^2/N}$. There are six steps in this procedure:

---

* Usually, some students will suggest that we might just find the mean of the absolute values of the deviations. That's a very good idea, and there actually is a statistic that does just that. But the slightly more complex standard deviation has some mathematical properties that make it far more desirable. For further developments with the standard deviation, see Chapter 25.

1. Find the mean.
2. Find each deviation score by subtracting the mean from each raw score.
3. Square each deviation score.
4. Add up all the squared deviation scores.
5. Divide this sum by N.
6. Take the square root of this number.

Let's work through the simple example of the set of numbers $\{1, 2, 3, 4, 5\}$:

1. Find the mean:

   $(1 + 2 + 3 + 4 + 5)/5 = 3.0$

2. Find each deviation score:

RAW SCORE	DEVIATION SCORE (RAW SCORE MINUS MEAN)	
1	$(1-3) =$	-2
2	$(2-3) =$	-1
3	$(3-3) =$	0
4	$(4-3) =$	$+1$
5	$(5-3) =$	$+2$

3. Square each deviation score:

RAW SCORE	DEVIATION SCORE (RAW SCORE MINUS MEAN)		d^2
1	$(1-3) =$	-2	**4**
2	$(2-3) =$	-1	**1**
3	$(3-3) =$	0	**0**
4	$(4-3) =$	$+1$	**1**
5	$(5-3) =$	$+2$	**4**

4. Add up the squared deviation scores:

RAW SCORE	DEVIATION SCORE (RAW SCORE MINUS MEAN)		d^2
1	$(1-3) =$	-2	**4**
2	$(2-3) =$	-1	**1**
3	$(3-3) =$	0	**0**
4	$(4-3) =$	$+1$	**1**
5	$(5-3) =$	$+2$	**4**
			$\Sigma d^2 = $ **10**

5. Divide this sum by N.

    $10/5 = 2$

6. Take the square root of this number.

    $\sqrt{2} = 1.414$

The Meaning of the Standard Deviation

There are two ways of explaining the meaning of the standard deviation. First look at the formula $SD = \sqrt{\Sigma d^2/N}$ and notice that if we removed the square and the square root signs, we almost have the average of the deviation scores that we wanted in the first place: $\Sigma d/N$. The standard deviation is an approximation of the average deviation.

Second, as we will see throughout the section on standardized testing, the standard deviation has some remarkable properties. Most important is that if we set a range around the mean using the standard deviation for many groups of numbers we will know what percentage of the scores to expect:

- If we set a range of one standard deviation above the mean and one standard deviation below the mean, we will include about two-thirds of the scores; this means that on a test with a mean of 75 and a standard deviation of six, two-thirds of the students will score between 69 and 81.
- If we set a range of two standard deviations above the mean and two standard deviations below the mean, we will include about 95 percent of the scores.
- If we set a range of three standard deviations above the mean and three standard deviations below the mean, we will include about 99 percent of the scores.

We can also look at test scores from the perspective of the individual score. Let's say we know that on an IQ test the mean is 100 and the standard deviation is 15. If you got a score of 130, your score was two standard deviations above the mean. That tells us that you scored higher than 99 percent of the others who took the test. We develop these ideas in the chapters which follow.

If this doesn't make sense to you, you might want to check out another elementary exposition of statistics, like the one usually found as an appendix in introductory psychology textbooks. When students do this they are often confused by one point. In the mean and standard deviation formulae the denominator may be $N - 1$ rather than N. For technical reasons, when you are doing research with samples, you use $N - 1$. When you are finding statistics for the entire group (e.g., all of a student's tests) you use N.

If you think learning to compute simple statistics is a waste of time, consider this: The National Council of Teachers of Mathematics (NCTM) wants elementary and middle school teachers to teach statistical concepts to their students. The material in this chapter and the next may be as common in your classroom teaching in ten years as finding the area of a rectangle or learning to estimate.

Questions for Reflection

1. You have been elected the local education association's representative to the school board, and you are going to make the case that teachers need a raise. You teach at a small elementary school with ten teachers, some of whom teach summer school. One of those teachers is the lead teacher (number 9), and one is the principal (number 10). Here are their salaries, with and without summer school pay:

REGULAR SALARY	SUMMER SCHOOL
1. $32,000	
2. 29,000	
3. 29,000	
4. 31,000	3,000
5. 34,000	
6. 27,000	
7. 34,000	4,000
8. 29,000	
9. 43,000	4,000
10. 83,000	

The school board contends that the average teacher salary at your school is $38,200. Use the statistics measures developed in this chapter to give them a better picture of teacher salaries.

2. John is a student in your class; you give weekly spelling tests. During the last four weeks of the eight-week grading period, John has had a bad case of bronchitis, which has affected his work. His test scores are 92, 94, 90, 94, 76, 78, 60, and 68. What might be a fair average for his spelling grades?

3. Just for fun, calculate the standard deviation for John's grades in Question 2. Compare your work with another student's.

7

Correlation

Suppose you are a fourth-grade teacher and you have two students who have been doing poorly. Your principal comes to you at the end of the year and asks whether they should be retained, promoted, or put in summer school. Stan is a student who tries very hard, but he still has difficulty decoding words in reading, struggles with basic addition and subtraction, and has difficulty when asked to work with others, make oral reports, and do projects involving reading, writing, or even drawing. Brenda seems not to care about school. She does well sometimes, but she rarely does homework. She has many friends, and her friends seem to be her priority. How do you make a decision about these students?

One way of solving this dilemma is to promote the student who tries hard. You may reason that if he tries hard he has a good chance of catching up. Or you may want to reward effort. Another is to find out if there is any pertinent research literature on elementary school children. If Stan is only reading at a second-grade level, what is the probability of his success in fifth grade? There is research that might help you guide your decision. As for Brenda, how stable are the attitudes she exhibits toward school? There is also research that might help you make this decision.

If we look in the research literature about reading ability and attitudes, we find that reading ability at one grade strongly predicts reading ability at the next grade level, while positive and negative attitudes toward school among elementary school students change. We expect Stan's reading problems to be more likely to persist into the fifth grade than Brenda's negative attitudes. Fourth- and fifth-grade reading scores are highly correlated; fourth- and fifth-grade school attitudes are less strongly correlated.

When we use information at one time to predict outcomes at another, we often use the correlation statistic. **Correlation** is *the mathematical extent to which two sets of numbers are related to each other*. The **correlation coefficient** (**r**) tells us how the sets are related. Let us start by looking at sets of quiz scores for 10 students so that we can get a feel for what this means.

Table 7.1 reports the number of correct answers that students earned on two quizzes about health. When we line up the students on the basis of quiz one, from highest to lowest, their test scores on quiz two also line up from highest to lowest. Because of this relation, we say that these two sets of quiz scores are highly correlated. Typically, students who do well on one assessment will usually do well on another in the same subject area. We can predict the scores on quiz two on the basis of the scores on quiz one (and vice versa). One important use of the correlation coefficient is the ability to predict one set of scores from another.

The mean on quiz one was 6.0 and the mean on quiz two was 5.0. We can rewrite these scores as deviation scores, as we did in Chapter 6. The deviation score (d) is the student's raw score (x) minus the mean (M); hence ($d = x - M$). Remember that the deviation score tells us how far away from the middle each score is by the number. (Anthony's score of 10 is 4 units away from the mean.) The $+$ or $-$ sign tells us whether the scores were above the mean ($+$) or below the mean ($-$). Anthony's score is above the mean; his deviation score will be positive. Table 7.2 reports the deviation scores for these ten students.

It is important to notice here that most of the positive scores on quiz one are matched with positive scores on quiz two, and negative scores matched with negative scores, except for Ellen and Frank. Not only are positive scores matched with positive scores, but the largest positive deviation scores in one set of quiz scores are matched with the largest positive scores in the other set. The largest negative deviation scores in one set of quiz scores are matched with the largest negative scores in the other set. In the formula for the correlation coefficient, to get the top term, we multiply the deviation

TABLE 7.1   STUDENTS' RAW SCORES ON TWO QUIZZES

	QUIZ ONE	QUIZ TWO
Anthony	10	10
Brenda	9	8
Carl	9	7
David	8	6
Ellen	7	5
Frank	6	4
Greg	5	4
Harry	4	3
Ivan	2	2
Joe	0	1

TABLE 7.2 DEVIATION SCORES FOR THE QUIZ GRADES REPORTED IN TABLE 7.1

	QUIZ ONE	QUIZ TWO
Anthony	+4	+5
Brenda	+3	+3
Carl	+3	+2
David	+2	+1
Ellen	+1	0
Frank	0	−1
Greg	−1	−1
Harry	−2	−2
Ivan	−4	−3
Joe	−6	−4

scores for each student and then add them. As you can see from this example, we have positive numbers multiplied by positive numbers and negative numbers multiplied by negative numbers (which gives a positive result), so the sum of these numbers will be positive. *When the high numbers match high numbers in raw scores,* we have a **positive correlation** because we have mostly positive numbers multiplied by positive numbers and negative numbers multiplied by negative numbers in the top term of the formula for the correlation coefficient.

Suppose something strange happened and we got the results in Table 7.3. In this case, we have used the same numbers, except we reversed the numbers from quiz two, and the student who scored the highest on quiz one got the lowest score on quiz two. The student who scored second highest on quiz one got the second-lowest score on quiz two, and so on. This is not likely to happen in a real classroom, but it represents an important point in understanding the correlation coefficient. Can we still predict scores from one set to the other? Yes! If you scored high on quiz one, I predict you scored low on quiz two—and I'd be right. Because we can predict from one to the other, we still say the scores are correlated; but this time when we write out the deviation scores, we see that positive scores on quiz one are paired with negative scores on quiz two, and vice versa. If we multiply these numbers together, we get mostly negative numbers. We have a negative correlation. (See Table 7.4.)

There are a few examples of negative correlations that make sense. The number of correct items on a test is negatively correlated with the number of incorrect items. If you were trying to diet, the number of calories of fat you ate would be negatively correlated with the number of pounds you lost. But most of the time in classroom testing we are interested in positive corre-

TABLE 7.3   EXAMPLE OF A NEGATIVE CORRELATION

	QUIZ ONE	QUIZ TWO
Anthony	10	1
Brenda	9	2
Carl	9	3
David	8	4
Ellen	7	4
Frank	6	5
Greg	5	6
Harry	4	7
Ivan	2	8
Joe	0	10

TABLE 7.4   DEVIATION SCORES FOR THE QUIZ GRADES REPORTED IN TABLE 7.1

	QUIZ ONE	QUIZ TWO
Anthony	+4	−4
Brenda	+3	−3
Carl	+3	−2
David	+2	−1
Ellen	+1	−1
Frank	0	0
Greg	−1	+1
Harry	−2	+2
Ivan	−4	+3
Joe	−6	+5

lations. The point to remember is that a high correlation is one that is near either + 1.0 or −1.0. A low correlation is one that is near 0.0.

Let's now graph these two examples. First, in Figure 7.1, we have graphed Frank's quiz grades. You may remember that the horizontal axis is called the x-axis and the perpendicular axis is called the y-axis. We put the first quiz on the x-axis and the second on the y-axis.

Now we will put everyone's test scores on the graph in Figure 7.2. This graph is characteristic of a high, positive correlation. If the correlation is high, the grades will more or less line up. If the correlation is positive, the line of grades will go from the lower left to the upper right.

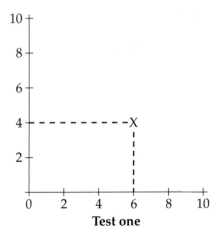

FIGURE 7.1   FRANK'S QUIZ GRADES (6, 4)

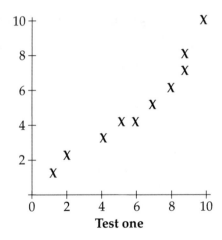

FIGURE 7.2   CLASS QUIZ GRADES

Figure 7.3 shows the class grades when we had the negative correlation. Because the correlation is relatively high, the scores tend to fall in a straight line, but because the correlation is negative, the scores go from the top left to the bottom right.

Let's consider some examples of things that are correlated and things that are not.

Are height and weight correlated? Well that depends. If we look in a fifth-grade classroom, where we have some very tall children and some not-so-tall children, yes. We can predict that a child who is four and a half feet tall weighs more than a child who is three feet tall. In kindergarten, where the children are all near the same height, we can't predict as well.

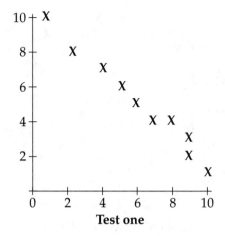

FIGURE 7.3 CLASS QUIZ GRADES (NEGATIVE CORRELATION)

Are shoe size and height correlated? Yes, at least a little. Very tall people have longer feet than do short people.

Is height in centimeters correlated with height in inches? Exactly. The correlation is +1.00. If we were to graph this relationship, the pairs of scores would fall exactly along a straight line.

Are height and IQ correlated? Not at all. Knowing someone's height tells us nothing about his or her intelligence. Table 7.5 compares height and IQ in our class. We see that the rank of height and the rank of IQ are not related. Figure 7.4 graphs this lack of relation. There is nothing like a straight line in this graph.

TABLE 7.5 RELATION BETWEEN HEIGHT AND IQ

	HEIGHT	HEIGHT RANK	IQ SCORE	IQ RANK
Anthony	62"	1	95	8
Brenda	61	2	115	4
Carl	60	3	125	2
David	59	4	90	9
Ellen	57	5	100	7
Frank	56	6	130	1
Greg	55	7	105	6
Harry	54	8	110	5
Ivan	52	9	85	10
Joe	50	10	120	3

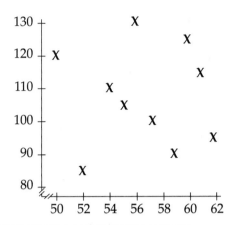

FIGURE 7.4 SCATTERGRAM OF HEIGHT AND IQ

Before we go to the actual computation of the correlation coefficient, I want to reiterate some of these findings:

1. A correlation of +1.00 is perfect and positive. If I know the scores on one measure, I can absolutely predict the scores on the other. Because it is positive, high scores predict high scores. Very few times in statistics do we get a perfect correlation.

2. A correlation of −1.00 is also perfect, but it is also negative. We can absolutely predict one score from the other, but the relationship is negative: High scores on one measure predict low scores on the other. Think about being on a highway that is 100 miles long with a city at either end. If you know you are 10 miles from city A, you are 90 miles from city B; if you are 80 miles from city A, you are 20 miles from city B. This is a perfect relationship, but as your distance from city A gets greater, the distance from city B gets smaller.

3. A correlation of 0.00 indicates no relationship between two measures.

4. As the correlation coefficient goes from 0.00 to +1.00 or −1.00, the two measures become more and more related. Correlations from −0.30 to +0.30 are said to be small. We normally treat such relations as the equivalent of a 0.00 correlation. Correlations between −0.30 and −0.70 and between +0.30 and +0.70 are moderate: We know something about one measure by knowing the other. Shoes size and height would be in this range. The relationship between SAT scores and freshman GPA are in the range. The relationship between a standardized test in reading and performance on a specific unit might be in this range because reading ability is only part of how well a student does on the unit. Scores between −0.70 and −1.00 and between +0.70 and +1.00 are high. The number of pounds an adult is overweight and the number of calories eaten on a typical day are in this range. Scores on standardized tests from one year to the next are also in this range.

▦ COMPUTING THE CORRELATION COEFFICIENT

It is not necessary that every teacher become an expert in computing the correlation coefficient. In your developmental psychology course you learned that children learn mathematics best by hands-on experience. So do adults. Actually working a few correlation coefficients will give you a better understanding of what the numbers mean than if you just read about the correlation coefficient. After you understand what the number means, you can use a computer or a statistical calculator to compute correlations.

The **correlation coefficient** *measures the degree to which two sets of numbers are related.* There are several different formulae for computing correlation (Edwards, 1976). We will use one that is not commonly used by mathematicians but that does help us understand the meaning of correlation coefficient.

The **denominator** of the equation we will develop is *the total variability in both sets of numbers of the equation.* As we described in the previous chapter, the best way of measuring variability is with the standard deviation. In this case we multiply the two standard deviations together and multiply this by the number of pairs of numbers. We call one set of numbers the x-values and the other set the y-values. Our denominator is $N(SD_x SD_y)$, or the number of pairs (N) times the standard deviation of the x-scores (SD_x) times the standard deviation of the y-scores (SD_y). This number may not make sense when you first begin to use this statistic, but you can think about it as the total possible variability. This number will always be positive.

The **numerator** is the *portion of the variability that the pairs of numbers contribute (e.g., how much they share in common), and it is the sum of the deviation scores multiplied together* ($\Sigma d_x d_y$). As we have already seen, if high scores go with high scores and low scores with low scores, then this number will be large and positive. If high scores go with low scores, then the number will be large and negative. If there is little relationship between the scores, then the number in the numerator will be small because you will have some positive numbers multiplied by positive numbers, some negative numbers multiplied by negative numbers, and some positive numbers multiplied by negative numbers. The correlation coefficient is a comparison between the amount of variability among pairs compared to the total variability. The total formula is:

$$r = \frac{\sum d_x d_y}{N(SD_x SD_y)}$$

This turns out to be simple, if you adopt the following.

r = the correlation coefficient

x = the scores on test 1

y = the scores on test 2

N = the number of pairs of scores

M = the mean of a set of scores $(\Sigma x/N)$

d_x = a deviation score from test 1 $(d = x - M_x)$

d_y = a deviation score from test 2 $(d = x - M_y)$

$\Sigma d_x d_y$ = the sum (Σ) of the products of each pair of deviation scores

SD_x = the standard deviation of the x scores $(\sqrt{\Sigma d^2/N})$

SD_y = the standard deviation of the y scores $(\sqrt{\Sigma d^2/N})$

Here is a simple example of how we can work this. We begin with the actual scores on two tests, and we use a table to keep our computations in order.

STUDENT	x	y	d_x	d_y	d_x^2	d_y^2	$d_x d_y$
Anne	50	10					
Beth	60	8					
Charlie	70	6					
David	80	4					
Elise	90	2					
Σ	350	30					

We do not need to have the tests on the same scale in order to compute a correlation coefficient. Please note that the scores on test one go from lowest to highest, and the scores on test two go from highest to lowest. We expect the correlation to be negative. Also, we note that the scores in both sets go in order, so we would expect this to be a high correlation.

Now we compute the means. Notice at the bottom we have already computed the sums of the x and y scores.

$M_x = \Sigma x/N = (50 + 60 + 70 + 80 + 90)/5 = 70$

$M_y = \Sigma x/N = (10 + 8 + 6 + 4 + 2)/5 = 6$

To get the deviation scores, we subtract the appropriate mean from each number:

STUDENT	x	y	d_x	d_y	d_x^2	d_y^2	$d_x d_y$
Anne	50	10	−20	+4			
Beth	60	8	−10	+2			
Charlie	70	6	0	0			
David	80	4	+10	−2			
Elise	90	2	+20	−4			
Σ	350	30	0	0			

Next we square each of our deviation scores and add up the total at the bottom of the column. Note that when we added up the deviation scores, we got zero. If you forget why this happens, you can refer back to the last chapter under the standard deviation. Remember, this will always happen.

STUDENT	x	y	d_x	d_y	d_x^2	d_y^2	$d_x d_y$
Anne	50	10	−20	+4	400	16	
Beth	60	8	−10	+2	100	4	
Charlie	70	6	0	0	0	0	
David	80	4	+10	−2	100	4	
Elise	90	2	+20	−4	400	16	
Σ	350	30	0	0	1000	40	

Our final step is to compute the cross products of the d scores ($d_x d_y$), then we will have all the numbers we need to plug into the formula. Note that we are multiplying the d scores, not the d^2 scores.

STUDENT	x	y	d_x	d_y	d_x^2	d_y^2	$d_x d_y$
Anne	50	10	−20	+4	400	16	−80
Beth	60	8	−10	+2	100	4	−20
Charlie	70	6	0	0	0	0	0
David	80	4	+10	−2	100	4	−20
Elise	90	2	+20	−4	400	16	−80
Σ	350	30	0	0	1000	40	−200

First we compute the standard deviations using the sum of the d^2 column:

$$SD_x = \sqrt{\Sigma d^2/N} = \sqrt{1000/5} = \sqrt{200}$$

$$SD_y = \sqrt{\Sigma d^2/N} = \sqrt{40/5} = \sqrt{8}$$

The denominator is $5(\sqrt{200}\sqrt{8}) = 5\sqrt{1600} = 5(40) = 200$. The numerator is the sum of the final column $= -200$; $r = -200/200 = -1.00$. (We usually report correlation coefficient to two decimal places.)

This is a very simple example. If you are not sure of this procedure, you might want to try the following two examples. In the first one, we would expect a correlation of +1.00 because the scores in both cases are the same. In the second example we would expect a somewhat lower correlation because two of the test scores have been changed. The math here is very simple.

STUDENT	x	y	d_x	d_y	d_x^2	d_y^2	$d_x d_y$
Anne	1	1	—	—	—	+4	—
Beth	2	2	—	−1	—	—	—
Charlie	3	3	—	—	—	—	—
David	4	4	—	—	+1	—	—
Elise	5	5	—	—	—	—	—
Σ	—	—			—	—	10

Final result: $r = +1.00$

STUDENT	x	y	d_x	d_y	d_x^2	d_y^2	$d_x d_y$
Anne	1	1	—	—	—	—	—
Beth	2	3	—	—	—	0	—
Charlie	3	2	—	—	—	—	—
David	4	4	—	—	—	—	—
Elise	5	5	+2	—	—	—	—
Σ	—	—			—	—	—

Final result: $r = +0.90$

▣ CAUSALITY

The correlation is the basic statistical procedure used in assessment. It is used in describing the reliability and validity of standardized tests, and it is used in research on all kinds of assessment. At minimum, all teachers should have an intuitive grasp of what different correlation coefficients mean if they want to be able to read the professional literature on assessment. There is one strong caution. A high correlation coefficient only means that two sets of test scores are related, it does not tell us why they are. Let me give a classic example: The more you smoke, the more likely you are to develop lung disease. Most people interpret this finding to mean that smoking causes lung cancer, but on the basis of correlations only, we could conclude:

Smoking causes lung cancer.

Lung cancer causes smoking.

Something else causes both.

Scientists are now finding that there are genes which may make some people likely to develop lung cancer, and these same genes may be related to making some people find smoking pleasurable and others find it distasteful. It may well be that people who smoke also engage in other unhealthy behavior.

Much educational research is based on correlations. Let's go back to our original examples from the beginning of the chapter. We would expect Stan's low reading achievement to be correlated with low reading achievement the following year. Perhaps Stan has a reading disability. That disability influences his ability one year and also the next. Yet there may be some other factor that influences his low ability. Maybe he has an undetected vision problem. If it is detected, then we would not expect him to continue at that low level.

Research indicates a much lower correlation for Brenda's attitude problem. But her problem may be due to a problem at home, which will continue next year.

Reliability

In Chapter 4 we talked about several kinds of reliability. Inter-rater reliability is the percentage of agreement between two raters. Usually, we will not use correlation to compute this kind of agreement—simple percentage agreement is often enough. Internal consistency requires a special statistic. But both alternate form reliability and test-retest reliability use the correlation coefficient.

Alternate Form Reliability   If you were to compute the alternate form reliability of a test, you would begin by administering two tests that you designed to measure the same material. You would give the tests at the same time: Each student would have scores on test A and test B. Then you would compute the correlation coefficient between test A and test B. If the correlation is high (above +0.80), the two forms of the test are *equivalent.* You could use either test as a substitute for the other.

Why would you want to do this? The answer is that in the course of routine teaching, you will probably have only rare occasions to need to substitute. But let us suppose that in your curriculum you have a particularly crucial assessment you might want to give twice. For example, before introducing multiplication, you want to be sure each child understands addition and subtraction. You give test A and 75 percent of your students pass and begin multiplication. You reteach addition and subtraction to those who do not pass and again want to assess whether children are ready to begin multiplication. If you give the exact same test again, students might recall the items on test A. You could determine that your two tests are equivalent and use them again, year after year. It may be worth the effort.

Here's another example: Suppose you are moving into performance assessment, but you have a group of parents who want you to give traditional tests. You might want to show that your performance assessment yields equivalent scores to traditional tests. You give both and find that the correlation is +0.85. You might even find that most students do somewhat better on the performance test than on the traditional test (you might not, however). You could then explain the equivalency of the two tests to your students' parents, which may allay their suspicions of the new way of assessing.

Test-Retest Reliability   A teacher will rarely need to compute the test-retest reliability of a classroom test. This form of reliability is used only when no instruction has occurred between the two administrations of the test. You can either administer the same test twice before instruction or the same two tests after instruction. Then you can compute the correlation coefficient between scores on the two assessments.

I'll give you an example of how a teacher actually used this process to defuse a problem in her classroom. This sixth-grade teacher was moving toward group work in her classroom, and, as part of student grades, she had included student ratings of each other's performance as members of the team. Two parents strongly objected to this process, even though the ratings were only 10 percent of the final grade on the project. The teacher thought that the parents might be right, and she reasoned that if the students' ratings of each other were not reliable, she would drop the ratings.

The teacher had used two ratings, one she designated *leadership* and the other she designated *cooperation*. The leadership rating was:

4 was the leader of the group all the time

3 helped keep the group going; was a leader sometimes

2 made useful suggestions; was a leader once in a while

1 did his or her part but wasn't a leader

0 didn't help the group

The teacher asked the children to make the same ratings two weeks after the first ratings. She found that the test-retest reliability of the leadership rating was low (about .40). The rating on the cooperativeness scale, however, was very high (about .80). She found the inter-rater reliability of cooperativeness was also high. (All students in a group tended to give high or low ratings to the same members of the group.) The teacher met with the two parents and showed them the results. She told the parents that perhaps sixth-grade students who had little experience in group work were not yet able to rate leadership reliably. But they seemed able to rate cooperativeness reliably. She also showed the parents that all of their children's peers had rated them low. She assured the parents that these ratings would not damage the children's grades substantially, and that the low ratings on cooperativeness were a signal to her to help the students learn group skills. One parent was convinced, the other was not. When the unconvinced parent met with the principal after the teacher had shared her statistics with him, the principal strongly backed her up.

Validity

Content validity does not use the correlation coefficient and construct validity is beyond the scope of this text. (See Sternberg in Wainer & Braun 1988.) Criterion-related validity uses the correlation coefficient and may be useful on occasion for classroom teachers. You may recall from Chapter 5 that criterion-related validity is the extent of the relation between an assessment and some outside criterion. For example, SAT scores are correlated between .40 and .60 with freshman grades. This is a moderate correlation, but it suggests that SATs have a moderate level of criterion-related validity with respect to freshman GPAs. We expect reliability scores to be in the high range (0.70 to 1.00), but we can say that an assessment is valid if the scores are in the moderate or high ranges.

I worked with a teacher a few years ago at a school where many children were having difficulty passing the state writing competency exam. Passing this test was necessary for a student to go from middle school to senior high school. This teacher was very interested in teaching writing and also interested in her students passing the competency exam. The content of the exam was a closely guarded secret, and the teacher felt frustrated in deciding what to teach her students. She had four writing assessments for each child, one involving a structured paragraph, one involving a description, one involving a science experiment, and one a narrative. She correlated the children's scores on these writing assessments with the children's scores on the competency exams, and she found that the structured paragraph, science experiment, and narrative exams were correlated with the competency exams, but the description was not. She used this information to restructure her writing curriculum. The next year the percentage of students passing the writing competency rose from 55 percent to 85 percent.

Questions for Reflection

1. Make a list of things you think are highly correlated, moderately correlated, and not correlated. Share your list with another student and see if you can agree how they are correlated. That is, which causes the other, or are some third issues related to both of them?
2. Suppose you have a principal who was a former mathematics teacher. At the end of the year, he shows you the correlations between the grades you gave your students in reading and mathematics and the state exams. The correlation for reading was only .42, while the correlation for mathematics was .63. What would you say to him? What would you say if one of the scores had been −.22?

PART II

■

Traditional
Teacher-Made
Tests

$\mathcal{I}$n the previous section characteristics of all forms of assessments were discussed. Assessment was viewed as an integral part of the whole act of teaching; all assessments were seen as based on objectives; and the necessity that all assessments be reliable and valid was developed. A brief historical overview of assessment was provided, as well as some basic descriptive statistics useful in describing assessments.

In this section we discuss traditional paper-and-pencil classroom tests. There are those who would advocate eliminating these kinds of assessments from the schools in favor of performance-based assessments, but there are reasons why a teacher still needs to know how to construct a traditional test and should want to do so.

First, a traditional test often remains the most authentic way of measuring objectives. For example, eventually students need to be able to spell. Spelling tests remain an excellent way of assessing spelling knowledge. Factual and conceptual knowledge is often efficiently assessed by traditional tests.

Second, many school districts require traditional tests. Several years ago I was invited to participate in workshops in a school district that was committed to moving toward portfolio assessment. At the middle school level, although the district wanted all teachers to use portfolios, there remained a requirement for six-week tests, which would count 33 percent of the students' grades in each subject area.

Third, tests remain an important part of our culture, and practice with tests and learning test-taking skills are an important part of education. As mentioned in Chapter 2, the United States is perhaps the least test-dependent industrialized country in the world. We used homework, worksheets, projects, lab reports, book reports, essays, speeches, drawings, and many other ways of assessing student knowledge in elementary and middle schools long before the authentic assessment movement. SATs remain only a part of getting into college in the United States; in countries as varied as Colombia, Bulgaria, Japan, and Great Britain, standardized tests are the sole criterion for college admission. Students wanting to work for the government have to take civil service exams, and entry into professions as diverse as law, medicine, psychology, teaching, and hairdressing involve passing traditional tests.

In this section we begin by examining one system for writing objectives, the taxonomic approach of Benjamin Bloom and his associates. We then consider converting objectives into test questions, using a table of specifications, which is related to the idea of content validity. We then look at particular item types (true/false items, multiple choice items, matching items, fill-in-the-blank items, short answers, and essays) and their strengths and weaknesses in assessing specific objectives. We give some attention to grading systems and methods of determining grades. We look at item analysis and conclude the chapter with consideration of modifications of traditional tests for students with identified handicapping conditions.

8

The Taxonomy of Instructional Objectives

*T*have great admiration for teachers who help students learn very complex skilled behavior. A former student of mine is now a talented gymnastics coach. I have watched her work tirelessly with five- and six-year-olds in her beginners' classes, rolling and somersaulting and tumbling in a pile of soft foam bricks. The youngest children's efforts are amusing: They rarely get a move right, but they are learning to be aware of their bodies, to take chances, and to right themselves when they land. In the intermediate class the teacher's behavior becomes more demanding, and the students bring with them what they learned in the beginners' classes and physical maturity. They are able to complete maneuvers that approximate the tricks of real gymnastics. They still work on soft surfaces because they fail as often as they succeed, but some have real talent. In the advanced classes the teacher expects perfection: not only a true landing after a walkover, but a graceful landing, followed by a flourish that demonstrates confidence. Gone are the foam bricks—a missed trick can cause a stinging landing on the mat and a bruised leg.

This teacher is successful because she has analyzed the steps leading to the final goal of gymnastics. Intermediate levels of skill are based on basic levels of accomplishment, and advanced performances are built on mastered intermediate steps. Reading, understanding science, and appreciating or producing a work of art is like gymnastics.

The material in this chapter is among the most important in this book, a basic skill for developing assessments. The chapter describes the various steps in the curriculum. It is a way of deciding, after we have analyzed where we are in a skill development process, what we want our students to be able to do to demonstrate they have advanced in their learning.

In this chapter we discuss the taxonomy of instructional objectives. This is sometimes called Bloom's taxonomy, after the educator Benjamin Bloom, who oversaw a project in the 1950s and early 1960s that developed a simple procedure to write objectives. There has been some tinkering with the system, but most educators are reasonably happy with the results. It is certainly a good place to begin thinking about writing objectives.

▨ WHAT IS A TAXONOMY?

A **taxonomy** is a *hierarchical classification system.* We are all familiar with taxonomy in biological classification, where we begin with simple plants and animals and proceed to higher forms of life. We classify together things which are similar. For example, *simian* combines various monkeys and apes. Simians are higher than other mammals; mammals higher than reptiles; reptiles higher than worms; worms higher than single-celled animals, and so on. In a taxonomy we classify and order.

Bloom's taxonomy is a classification and ordering of behavior. It is about behavior, because an educational objective describes what we want the child to be able to do after instruction. If we begin to think about a complex behavior, we can see that the behavior is built on less complex behaviors. Think about a fairly standard high school essay test question, the compare and contrast type, technically a synthesis-level objective. In a social studies class we might ask students to compare and contrast democracy with socialism. Before you can compare and contrast these two forms of government, you first have to analyze each form independently. We can only analyze each if we know the definition of a large number of concepts, such as government, free elections, central planning, capitalism, and so on. Complex intellectual activity is based on less complex thinking; lower-level thinking is based on factual knowledge.

Bloom's taxonomy divides objectives into three areas or domains. The first is the **psychomotor domain.** *This domain refers to movement and thinking.* The root of the word is *motor,* which refers to the fact that we are primarily interested in performances that use muscles: speaking, using our hands and feet and body. The prefix *psycho* refers to the fact that the muscular performances are guided by thinking. Learning to pass a soccerball to your teammate requires footwork and knowledge of strategy. Writing a word requires coordinating the action of your hands with the representation of the word that is in your head. The coordination of thought and muscular behavior is the psychomotor domain.

The second domain is the **cognitive domain.** *This domain has to do with knowing and thinking.* If you were to take a course in cognitive psychology, you would study memory, logic, classification, and problem solving. This is the domain of primary interest to most teachers. We will spend most of our time in this chapter and in the rest of this book on the cognitive domain.

The third area is the **affective domain.** *This domain has to do with feeling.* Here we are interested in students' values and emotional responses. In this domain we specify what behaviors show that students accept responsibility for their role in group work, appreciate art, or value democratic government. This is perhaps the area in which we have the most trouble. Affective objectives are hard to write and measure, but valuing and liking are important objectives, so we should try to write them, even if they are difficult.

⬚ THE PSYCHOMOTOR DOMAIN

The most basic kind of learning involves motor behavior. We want young children to be able to tie their shoes and to have legible handwriting. We want children to pronounce English words correctly. We want them to be able to use the keyboard proficiently on a word processor. We want children to be able to dribble a basketball. We may want children to be able to play a musical instrument or manipulate art materials appropriately.

The first step in the psychomotor domain (Simpson, 1972) is to pay attention to the activity that will be required. It is a necessary first step in writing for children to understand what writing is: what kinds of behavior produce writing and what writing looks like. The same goes for playing soccer or learning to pronounce a foreign language. Then the steps in the psychomotor domain move from general large movements to fine, specific movements. We begin first-grade writing, for example, by having students learn to make circles and sticks. Then they put together these two basic patterns to form individual letters. Eventually we elaborate on these elementary printed letters to form cursive writing. You will also notice in this example that we work from activities which require very little thought guiding the action to more thought. We get students to makes circles and sticks comfortably, and only then do we begin to teach them to make letters and to associate the letters with the sounds of English. Later the thought will be more automatic. When you write the word *instructional*, you do not think of it stroke by stroke or even letter by letter; rather, you think automatically of the whole word. We would teach soccer in this way. First just kick the ball. Then kick the ball in a specific direction. Then kick the ball to your teammate. Then go on automatic and kick the ball to your teammate in an actual game. For most children, these four general principles will work in the psychomotor domain:

1. You must pay attention to the behavior before you can begin to learn it.
2. Gross motor behavior (kick the ball, make circles and sticks) comes before finer behavior (kick the ball to your teammate, write whole words).
3. Little thought (just make circles, just kick it) comes before more thought (make letters, kick it to the left).
4. We move from highly controlled thinking (make letters, kick it to the left) to automatic performance (write words and sentences, play a game of soccer).

For children with physical or mental handicaps, you will need to specify much smaller steps. In this case you may need to become more familiar with the steps and substeps of the psychomotor domain. A more detailed discussion of the taxonomy of the psychomotor domain is included in Chapter 21.

▓ THE COGNITIVE DOMAIN

Cognitive objectives involve recognizing, recalling, stating, applying, analyzing, comparing, and evaluating.

> *Please Note: The term "evaluate" in the cognitive domain does not refer to how much you like something, but to how you evaluate it intellectually. It involves applying a standard to some complex material. It is very much like the idea of evaluation in teaching. You do not look at a student's test and say: Neat! Rather you evaluate it against your expectations of their work. In my experience, confusing a cognitive evaluation with giving an opinion is the most common mistake students make in understanding the taxonomy.*

The Six Levels of the Taxonomy

Bloom, Englehart, Furst, Hill, and Krathwohl (1956) described six levels of cognitive objectives:

1. Knowledge
2. Comprehension
3. Application
4. Analysis
5. Synthesis
6. Evaluation

It will be useful to memorize these classifications in order (because they are hierarchical). You can remember them by the sentences that my students developed: <u>Know</u> <u>comp</u>letely the <u>application</u> of <u>analysis</u> to <u>sin</u> and <u>evil</u> or <u>K</u>atie <u>C</u>ouric <u>A</u>sks <u>A</u>naly<u>t</u>ical <u>S</u>entences <u>E</u>very day. Let me give a definition of each level and then give an example of each:

1. **Knowledge** involves nothing but rote memory.
2. **Comprehension** involves memory and a demonstration to help you understand what the fact means.
3. **Application** involves using facts in a new context, either by providing an original example or by using your information to accomplish something.
4. **Analysis** involves dividing a complex idea into its component parts.
5. **Synthesis** involves putting together several ideas to form a new idea.
6. **Evaluation** involves judging a complex idea against a criterion.

Examples

Knowledge   My favorite example of this is day one of foreign language instruction. About eight years ago I started to take Japanese. When we entered the class the teacher said to us: *"Ohaio gozaimasu."* We sat for a moment in stunned silence. Then she repeated her greeting and waited. We then repeated what she said. She shook her head and said: *"Ohaio goziamasu, sensei."* (Good morning, teacher.) When we had said this correctly, she went on to other activities, but she expected us to remember that greeting for subsequent classes, although we did not fully comprehend what we had said for several weeks. This is just rote memory.

Comprehension   While we occasionally want students to remember a fact or a phrase, usually we want students to understand what the fact means. You may memorize the definition of a test as "a sample of behavior produced under standard conditions." If you say this I might ask you to restate it in a way that demonstrates to me that you really understand what *sample, behavior,* and *standard conditions* mean. When we ask students to demonstrate factual knowledge, sometimes they merely repeat—sometimes in a sing-song fashion—the words in the textbook. We might suspect that the students do not really understand what they are saying. For example, after a month my Japanese teacher wanted us to tell her that *ohaio* meant morning; *sensai* meant teacher; and *gozaimasu* was a term that implied politeness.

In actual use in the classroom, it is often difficult to distinguish Knowledge from Comprehension. If a third-grade child recalls that Columbus discovered America in 1492 we do not often ask questions to determine whether he really understand the idea of 1492. If he says, "500 years ago," he may be only repeating something else he has heard and does not really understand, or he may really understand what 1492 means. Sometime the distinction between Knowledge and Comprehension is useful, but other times it is very difficult to make a meaningful comparison between these two levels of the taxonomy. This is a distinction that should not get you bogged down. But when it comes to writing items, you may need to decide whether to use the exact words in a definition (to test for Knowledge) or to paraphrase (to test for Comprehension.)

Application   There are two ways of demonstrating application: giving an original example and using knowledge and comprehension to complete a task. In the first case, the example must be original, not one remembered from class. On a test in a course in educational evalution, perhaps I will ask you to give an example of a synthesis-level objective. Having read this chapter so far, if you said "students will be able to compare and contrast democracy and socialism," you will be merely recalling the text material. You would have to give another example to show Application learning.

As for using information, think about children who have been studying electric circuits. As a test you give them a battery, several wires, a switch, and a light and then ask them to set up a circuit so that the switch turns the light off and on. They are translating book learning to performance. On a traditional paper-and-pencil test, you might also give students a slightly different circuit diagram than the one they studied and ask them if it will work. That, too, would be Application.

Analysis   Analysis involves getting to the logical basis of something fairly complex. One of the most common ways of doing this on a traditional test is to ask students to give the basic components of a complex idea. Outlining is a good example of this. If you have given the children the outline and they are just recalling what you told them, then the item is Comprehension, not Analysis. They have to come up with the outline, not recall your outline.

Suppose you have been studying paragraph organization. You now want to determine whether students can recognize (1) the topic sentence; (2) evidence; (3) the conclusion; and (4) irrelevant information. You give students the following paragraph and ask them to identify these components:

> Today is my birthday. I have always assumed that everyone celebrates birthdays, but I have learned this is not the case. In Japan, for example, everyone's official birthday is February 20th. In the United States there are religious groups, such as the Jehovah's Witnesses, that do not observe birthdays. Even my mother doesn't always want to celebrate her birthday. When she turned 40, she asked us to ignore her birthday. She turned 40 two years ago. I'm glad I belong to a group that celebrates birthdays, but I have learned that it is not a universal custom. I hope I get a new bicycle.

We have deliberately modified a student paragraph to see if children can analyze its logical structure. Children who assume the first sentence is always the topic sentence and the last is always the conclusion will not correctly analyze this paragraph.

Synthesis   Synthesis involves combining elements in a new, unique manner. Writing a story to demonstrate that one understands the elements of narrative is an example from language arts. When I taught eighth-grade English, I was required to teach an abridged version of the *Odyssey*. One of the interesting structural elements of the *Odyssey* is that the narrative begins in the middle and the first part of the story is told about halfway through in a long flashback. While I could have had students define flashback or the technical term *In media res*, I wanted them to struggle with putting together a narrative that begins in the middle. I had them write a two-page story that included a flashback to the beginning of the plot.

Evaluation   It has always seemed to me that Evaluation was a particular kind of synthesis. In this case we take a complex idea or document or object and we ask students to apply a specific standard to it. We could ask students to determine whether the paragraph on birthdays above met the criteria for a good paragraph, provided children have been given a criterion for a good paragraph. Most often, Evaluation is an objective for advanced students.

In studying art we could ask students to evaluate a painting using a particular artistic criterion. If you had studied Jefferson's writing on architecture, you could ask your students to say what Jefferson would say about their own school building. In studying education we might ask you to critique a teaching unit from a particular criterion. After you have written a science unit, your teacher, asking you to apply Dewey's ideas from *Democracy and Education*, might say, "Imagine that John Dewey is your teacher. What kind of feedback would he give you on your unit?" It is clear that we have to analyze the writing, art work, or unit; analyze the criterion; and then compare and contrast the two.

The Verb Method of Writing Objectives

Often the process of writing objectives is reduced to lists of verbs which more or less match the various levels of the taxonomy. This method is not perfect, but it is a good place to start the process. Here is a short list of verbs that match the various levels of the cognitive domain taxonomy. This list represents behaviors we want students to demonstrate on a paper-and-pencil test. In a few instances we have used the same verb in more than one level. One can explain an idea at a basic or advanced level and the level of explanation will determine whether it is Comprehension or Evaluation.

- Knowledge: recall, remember, match, recognize, select, compute, define, label, name, describe
- Comprehension: restate, elaborate, say in one's own words, identify, explain, paraphrase, summarize
- Application: use, give examples, apply, do, solve problems using, compute, manipulate, prepare, predict, produce, operate, modify
- Analysis: outline, break down, divide into its parts, draw a diagram, illustrate, discriminate, subdivide
- Synthesis: compare, contrast, construct, categorize, write, organize, explain, generate, design
- Evaluation: evaluate by, support, interpret, explain, criticize

Elaborating the Verbs

Getting the right verb is only the first step. We now must write the actual objectives.

There are many different forms for writing objectives. Your school system or course instructor may require a specific format or leave this up to you. My own preference is to be as simple as possible. I like to use the stem, *students will be able to,* and then list objectives underneath, beginning with the verb. I like to group objectives by their level. I do not specify the criterion level (at 80 percent accuracy), but some teachers do. I do not usually list every fact. (Remember definitions of democracy, totalitarianism, republic, constitutional monarchy, absolute monarchy, dictatorship. . . .) Instead I write a general description. (Remember definitions of types of government.)

Here is the set of objectives I have for students in my evaluation class for the first part of this textbook:

The student will be able to:

Define key assessment terms	Knowledge
Recognize major historical developments in testing	Knowledge
Describe in their own words different kinds of reliability and validity	Comprehension
Interpret a correlation coefficient	Comprehension
Differentiate between traditional and performance assessments	Application
Compute the mean, median, mode, range, and standard deviation of groups of numbers without the formula	Application
Compute the standard deviation with the formula provided	Application
Differentiate reliability from validity	Analysis
Develop an assessment method for an original unit	Synthesis
Critique a classmate's unit assessment for reliability and validity	Evaluation

Normally, I would not include the levels on the right column, although this may be a good idea when you are beginning to write objectives.

▣ THE AFFECTIVE DOMAIN

There are five levels of the Affective Domain (Krathwohl, Bloom, & Masia, 1964):

1. Receiving: Students become aware of an idea or behavior.
2. Responding: Students engage in a simple behavior with respect to this idea or behavior, but the students' behavior does not necessarily indicate any commitment to it.
3. Valuing: Students indicate that they have a commitment to the idea or behavior.
4. Organization: Once a student has accepted a new value he or she may have to see if this newly valued behavior or value fits into their total value system. The new value may eventually be rejected or modified or other exisiting values with which it conflicts may need to be rejected or modified.
5. Characterization by a Value or Value Complex: After a while the value may become an integral part of the person's value system and actually characterize that person.

I am going to quote a student's essay from one of my measurement classes in which she described her own change in teaching orientation:

How I Am Becoming a Group Teacher

In many of my education courses I listened attentively to ideas about group work. I had taught fifth grade for four years and had never really used this approach to teaching. I had many reservations about the approach, but I listened and learned. That was my *receiving* experience.

In this course I was required for the first time to design a unit involving group work. I took a unit that I was about to teach, with no real intention of actually teaching it as a group unit. I selected that unit because it would be easy for me to write the objectives. I wrote the unit and got a A− on it. I engaged in the behavior, but I had little commitment. This was my *responding* phase.

Right before I was going to teach the unit, I witnessed an incident on the school grounds involving my students. I have a practicum student from a local university. She took my class out onto the playground and told them to form two teams and play kickball. After 35 minutes of arguing about who would be on which team and what position each person would play, they had still not come to a conclusion when it was time to return to the classroom. I had two reactions to this. First, I thought the students learned something from the process of trying to form groups and assigning roles, but, second, I was embarrassed that my students had so few group organization skills. I organized everything for them. I value a smooth running classroom. I decided to pull out my group unit and try it out. I guess I had come to *value* group skills in my students.

The unit I had developed was on contagious diseases. I put students into groups of four and had each group do research on one disease: colds, flu, measles, and chickenpox. The students needed to write a group paper and make a group oral report. I found that I was nervous about this, because while I was working with one group, the others were "working" on their own. I like more order in my classroom than was exhibited at times during the group process. I wanted to be in control of everything, but I found I could only be in control of a part of my class. I didn't like the fact that sometimes one or another group seemed to be wasting time, talking about something other than what I wanted them to learn about these four diseases. I began to see that if I moved to more group work, I was going to have to change some of my ideas about the classroom. This was my *organization* phase. This was the hard one. This made me realize that changing values was a tough experience. One of the most important things I learned was that I was not only teaching about contagious diseases, but I was teaching students to work together. I really had to rethink the idea of wasting time, when the kids were working on organizing the task, but not learning something about the topic.

I haven't lived with group work long enough to say that I can be *characterized* as a group teacher. But the students began to come up with wonderful ideas in their groups. Their final products were amazing. I still couldn't give up on individual assessment completely, so I gave a test, and I had very high scores on that test, so I am going to do more group work. Maybe in another year group work will become second nature to me.

Questions for Reflection

1. Take an idea that you would like to teach students someday (e.g., the Mona Lisa or evaporation) and write an objective at each of the levels of the cognitive domain. Write at least one affective domain objective on this subject and identify its taxonomic level.
2. Take a common everyday task (making bread, mowing the lawn, brushing your teeth) and write a series of cognitive domain objectives for it. You are not describing how to do it, but the learning that underlies it. Why, for example, do we knead bread; or why do we brush our teeth?
3. Write a series of objectives for this chapter. Include at least one objective at each of the cognitive levels and one objective for each of the affective levels.

9

Developing a Table of Specifications

I vividly remember making up my first test. Unlike most current first-time teachers, I had taken no professional education courses in which I learned how to make a test. After graduating from college I signed up to be a substitute teacher to make money while I got ready to go to graduate school. I thought I would go from one classroom to another with a day or two in each. After a month of filling in one or two days at a time, I was offered a two-month position while an eighth-grade science teacher had an operation.

Most of my students were working at a basic level; I had no difficulty with the material, even though I had not been a science major. I found that I could lecture and lead discussions. The labs were set out for me in my teacher's guide, and the students did pretty well on them. At the end of my second week, the head of the science department came down to my classroom and handed me a test. "You can use this one or develop your own," he said, "but it's time for the six-week test." I did not know what the former teacher had taught, but I looked at the test and realized that what I had taught and what the test covered were very different. I thought if I gave that test my students would do poorly because I had not gone over much of the material on the test. Today I would analyze that problem by saying I had taught at the Application level, and the test was at the Knowledge level. The test asked many detailed factual-level questions. I had stressed only those facts that would help the students understand the labs. I decided to throw out the multiple choice and matching test in favor of an essay test that I thought would capture the students' higher-level learning.

Unfortunately, the students were expecting a fact-based test and were dismayed by my essay questions. The department head gave me a piece of advice that has always stuck with me: "Make sure the students know how to deal with the test as well as know the material."

The department head gave me a little book by Robert Mager (1962) called *Preparing Instructional Objectives,* which opened me up to the idea of instruction and assessment grounded in well-thought-out objectives. By my second six-week test I had done my job better, and the students were able to demonstrate their grasp of the material.

▨ A TABLE OF SPECIFICATIONS

There are many ways of connecting objectives (curriculum), instruction, and assessment. A table of specifications is only one possible way of doing so. And there are many different ways of constructing a table of specifications. The format I describe here is the method I have found useful in teaching kindergarten, elementary, and secondary students. Teachers should feel free to modify this basic approach. In this chapter we are primarily interested in constructing a paper-and-pencil test. A table of specifications is also useful in developing performance assessment and even an integrated approach in which paper-and-pencil tests and performance assessments are used together.

A **table of specifications** is *a graphic showing the relation between objectives, instruction, and evaluation.* The process of developing a table of specification involves several steps:

1. Developing a set of instructional objectives
2. Translating those objectives into instructional activities (e.g., daily lesson plans)
3. Teaching the unit
4. Refining the objectives for a test based on the experience of what was taught and what needs assessment
5. Determining the weight for various objectives
6. Writing items

To exemplify the process we will go through these six steps for a short unit in social studies.

1. *Developing a Set of Instructional Objectives.* The process of developing a table of specifications begins with describing a unit of instruction in terms of behavioral objectives. The objectives for a unit on early exploration for seventh-grade social studies are shown in Table 9.1.

These may not be your own ideal objectives for this unit, but this is an actual set of unit objectives that a practicing teacher developed for a seven-day unit on this topic. In developing these objectives the teacher used information about what the students knew and what the students would need to know later in the year. This was their second time through American history; before this unit most of the material in their social studies class this year had concentrated on Native American cultures. Students needed to know where different national groups were located in order to understand the French and Indian War, the Louisiana Purchase, the Texas War, and so on.

TABLE 9.1   BEHAVIORAL OBJECTIVES FOR A SEVENTH-GRADE UNIT ON EARLY EXPLORATION

After instruction the student will be able to fulfill the six levels of cognitive objectives:

Knowledge

1. Recognize explorers' nationalities
2. Match explorers with the names of their ships

Comprehension

3. List four reasons for early exploration
4. List the advances in navigation which permitted exploration
5. Write a complete sentence giving the main contribution of each explorer

Application

6. Label a map with the areas explored by different explorers
7. Construct a time-line of early exploration

Analysis

8. Tell what all nations involved in exploration had in common

Synthesis

9. Discuss the different nations' specific reasons for exploration
10. State why you would or would not want to be a member of an expedition to the New World

Evaluation

11. After reading John Kennedy's speech establishing the objective of putting a man on the moon, explain what early exploration had in common with recent space exploration

---

It is useful, particularly for beginning teachers, to order the objectives in terms of the taxonomic levels. In Table 9.1, I have grouped the objectives under the six levels of the cognitive taxonomy. With practice, this attention to detail may not be necessary.

2. *Translating Objectives into Instructional Activities.* The next step toward developing a table of specifications would be to develop a sequence of activities through daily lesson plans. I am not going to reproduce the daily lesson plans in their entirety, but the general plans are shown in Table 9.2.

3. *Teach the Unit.* The next step is to teach the unit. Now we are ready to use the objectives to develop a table of specifications and then use the table to develop a test.

4. *Refine the Objectives.* We cannot go directly from the objectives we imagined before we taught the unit directly to making the test. We must determine which of the objectives need to be measured by the test and which should not be measured by the test. In the process of actually teaching the unit, the teacher felt that she had not really emphasized Objective 2 enough (Match explorers with the names of their ships) to include it on the test

TABLE 9.2 SUMMARY OF DAILY LESSON PLAN ON A SEVENTH-GRADE UNIT ON EARLY EXPLORATION

Day 1. Prince Henry the Navigator. Brainstorm reasons for early exploration. Read pages 34–38 for homework in text.

Day 2. Columbus. Watch Columbus video. Draw Columbus' voyages on individual students' maps. Begin to construct a time line, both as a class activity and as an individual activity.

Day 3. Magellan. Lecture. Discuss flat/round world theories. Look at globes and maps. Read pages 39–43 for homework.

Day 4. Ponce de León. Lecture on the exploration of Florida. Class discussion of how de León was similar and different from Columbus and Magellan. Tie in this activity with reading Hawthorne's "Dr. Heidegger's Experiment" in language arts class.

Day 5. English exploration: Drake, Cabot, the "Lost" Colony, Jamestown. Read pages 44–48. Add to map and time line. Discuss differences between Spanish and English motivation in exploration.

Day 6. Dutch and French exploration. Short lecture. Read pages 49–51. Complete worksheet on explorers' ships and areas each explored.

Day 7. Space. Watch video of JFK speech. Read JFK speech for homework. Discuss JFK's reasons for going to the moon.

---

fairly; she decided to eliminate this objective. She also decided that the objective of constructing the time line had already been covered by the act of making the class and individual time lines, and she did not want students to spend time memorizing the specific dates, so she eliminated Objective 7. Finally, she decided that she wanted to make Objective 10 (State why you would or would not want to be a member of an expedition to the New World) an out-of-class essay rather than part of the test. She decided this was an objective that was best assessed by a nontimed activity. By eliminating three objectives, she had eight objectives to measure rather than 11:

1. Recognize explorers' nationalities
3. List four reasons for early exploration
4. List the advances in navigation that permitted exploration
5. Write a complete sentence giving the main contribution of each explorer
6. Label a map with the areas explored by different explorers
8. Tell what all nations involved in exploration had in common
9. Distinguish among the different nations with regard to specific reasons for exploration
11. Explain what early exploration had in common with recent space exploration

5. *Determine the Weight of Various Objectives.* This is the most subjective of the six steps. We now need to determine how much to count each of the objectives. Let us suppose we want a 100-point, final-unit grade. We will also include the student's time lines and their essays on why they might want or not want to be part of an early expedition as part of that 100-point total.

One way of doing this is to estimate the amount of time spent on each objective. Let's say that we spent 15 percent of our time on the time line and we expect students to spend about 10 percent of their total time on this unit on the essay. We could then assign 15 percent of the total score to the time line and 10 percent to the essay, leaving 75 percent of the unit to be evaluated by the test. Our test would then count 75 points. Now we can assign those 75 points to the eight objectives that will be measured by the test. The teacher who taught the unit made the following estimates of her emphasis on the remaining objectives:

OBJECTIVES	PERCENTAGE
1. Recognize explorers' nationalities	10
3. List four reasons for early exploration	5
4. List the advances in navigation which permitted exploration	5
5. Write a complete sentence giving the main contribution of each explorer	10
6. Label a map with the areas explored by different explorers	15
8. Tell what all nations involved in exploration had in common	5
9. Discuss different nations' reasons for exploration	10
11. Explain what early exploration had in common with space exploration	15

For example, Objective 11 (Explain what early exploration had in common with space exploration) took up one whole day of a seven-day unit. It would be reasonable to think this might be one-seventh of the total unit (15 percent).

6. *Write the Test Items.* Table 9.3 lists the objectives, their taxonomic level, and the points on the test that will be measured by each objective.

- For Objective 1, we need to write Knowledge-level questions that will ask students the nationality of the explorers. We can do this by asking five matching items. Our objective is to recognize, and we will use a method like multiple choice or matching. Students do not need to produce the answer, only recognize the correct one.
- Objectives 3 and 4 ask students to list material learned in class. Presumably, we gave the students the list of material and told them to recall it (because they are Comprehension items). The appropriate kind of item here is a produce-short-answer item, so we decided to use a fill-in-the-blanks type item.

TABLE 9.3 TABLE OF SPECIFICATIONS

LEVEL	OBJECTIVES	PERCENTAGE
Kn	**1.** Recognize explorers' nationalities	10
Co	**3.** List four reasons for early exploration	5
Co	**4.** List the advances in navigation which permitted exploration	5
Co	**5.** Write a complete sentence giving the main contribution of each explorer	10
Co	**6.** Label a map with the areas explored by different explorers	15
An	**8.** Tell what all nations involved in exploration had in common	5
Sy	**9.** Distinguish among the different nations' reasons for exploration	10
Ev	**11.** Explain what early exploration had in common with space exploration	15

- Objective 5 asks for a sentence on each explorer. Of course we do not have to ask for a sentence about each explorer, only a sample of them.
- Objective 6 asks for students to label a map. We want students to know where the English, Spanish, French, Dutch, and Portuguese explored. This is an Application item, so we actually want the student to label a map. The teacher decided to put a map on the test and have students label it.
- Objectives 8, 9, and 11 are higher-order objectives. Usually these require essay responses on a paper-and-pencil test. Here is a sample test. The points have been slightly changed.

Early Exploration Test   75 points   Name _____

1. Matching (2 points each) (You may use answers more than once.)

_____ Henry Cabot	**a.** Dutch
_____ Christopher Columbus	**b.** Spanish
_____ Prince Henry	**c.** Portuguese
_____ Francis Drake	**d.** English
_____ Ponce de León	**e.** French

2. Short Answers

A. List three reasons for early exploration (2 points each):

1. _____

2. _____

3. _____

B. List three improvements in navigation which led to early exploration (2 points each):

1. _____

2. _____

3. _____

C. Write a complete sentence describing the main contribution of each explorer (2 points each):

Vespucci _____

Prince Henry _____

Hernando Cortez _____

Henry Hudson _____

3. Label the map below by the areas explored by the English, French, Spanish, Portuguese, and Dutch (3 points each).

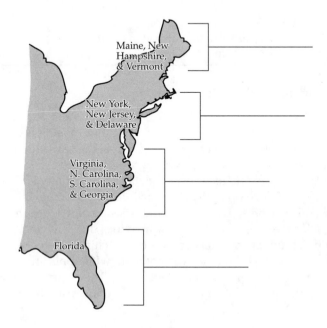

4. Essay Questions (one paragraph each)

   A. What reasons for exploration did the English and Spanish explorers have in common? (5 points)

   B. What were the differences between the Spanish and Dutch explorers? (10 points)

   C. What did the early explorers have in common with space exploration? What was different? (15 points)

We can now complete our table:

LEVEL	OBJECTIVE	POINTS	ITEMS
Kn	1. Recognize explorers' nationalities	10	1a–e
Co	3. List four reasons for early exploration	6	2A
Co	4. List the advances in navigation which permitted exploration	6	2B
Co	5. Write a complete sentence giving the main contribution of each explorer	8	2C
Co	6. Label a map with the areas explored by different explorers	15	3
An	8. Tell what all nations involved in exploration had in common	5	4A
Sy	9. Discuss the different nations' reasons for exploration	10	4B
Ev	11. Explain what early exploration had in common with space exploration	15	4C

Let us summarize the major steps again:

1. *Develop a Set of Instructional Objectives.* The foundation of teaching is knowing what you want students to know after the unit is completed. The more specific the objectives, the easier all the subsequent steps will be. Chapter 8 will be useful in writing the objectives.
2. *Translate Objectives into Instructional Activities* (e.g., daily lesson plans). The process of developing teaching activities to promote the learning described in the objectives is beyond the scope of this text, but the level of the objective is often a clue to the activities that will go on in the classroom. Students can master facts by watching videos, reading text, listening to lectures, etc. They can come up with applications by using hands-on experiences or by brain-storming. They learn to analyze by watching the process of analysis their teacher uses and by working with

others to understand the structure of ideas. They synthesize and evaluate by questioning and playing hunches.

If we want students to read maps, we should give them experience with maps. We must not assume that if there is a map in their textbook they will pay attention to it and learn what it means. If we want students to understand a complex idea, such as Kennedy's reasons for committing the country to going to the moon, they need to hear the speech, read the text, discuss it, and write about it. If we want students to make connections between early exploration and space exploration, we need to plant ideas that will serve as springboards for their own thinking; and we want to provide them with specific opportunities to think about these connections.

3. *Teach the Unit.* Teaching is a rewarding and occasionally exasperating profession because every time we teach a unit, our students surprise us. For beginning teachers these surprises are often overwhelming. You may begin a lesson you have carefully thought out, only to have students raise their hands and tell you they did this activity last year. You may begin with a discussion to see what students know about a topic, and they seem to know nothing about it, have no thoughts about it, and have no interest in it. Or you may bring up what you consider a mundane side topic and have it spark a heated discussion. The actual process of teaching will affect what you assess. I am often bewildered by some of my university colleagues who spend their summers revising their courses and their tests. I cannot imagine making up a test until the classes have actually been taught.

4. *Refine the Objectives for a Test.* Sometimes in the process of teaching a unit, you will abandon an objective. Sometimes you will need to step back on a higher-order objective and make it a Comprehension or Application objective when you had hoped that your students would be addressing the content at the Analysis or Synthesis level. Sometimes you will go the opposite way: You had planned on factual-level teaching, but your students were more sophisticated than you had expected, and you were able to push the learning to a higher level. Only after teaching the unit do we know what kinds of learning we expect from our students.

5. *Determine the Weight for Each Objective.* As mentioned above, this is the most subjective of the steps, but after time teachers get a feel for this process. The objective you spend the most time on should have more weight than others. If it is assessed by other activities, then its weight on the test should be reduced, as the paper-and-pencil test is only part of the total assessment strategy.

6. *Write Items.* Now we have what we need to construct the test. We may need to measure a Knowledge-level objective in a way which will count five points on a test. This might suggest five matching or fill-in-the-blanks items. Perhaps we have spent a great deal of time on Applications.

We may include several items on map-reading, if this is our application objective. The weights determined in the last step suggest how many items we need. The taxonomic level of the objectives suggests the items. Chapters 10, 12, and 13 can help you determine the items useful in meeting various levels of objectives.

7. *Summarize the Process in a Table of Specifications.* All of the steps above can be put into a table like that above. If you are preparing for student teaching, your supervisor will be impressed. If you are a probationary teacher, your principal will be impressed.

Questions for Reflection

1. Use one of the sets of objectives you wrote for the previous chapter, or create a set of objectives for a short unit. Use those objectives to create a brief set of lesson plans. Use the lesson plans to create weights for different objectives, and write an outline of what your test might look like. (You need not write actual items.)
2. List as many reasons as you can why you might want to give more weight to one objective (and less to others) even if you spent the same amount of time on both.

CHAPTER

10
Objective Items

*I*t is fashionable now in education to look down on instruction that involves facts and testing that assesses students' factual knowledge. As we discussed in Chapter 8, students learn from the specific to the general. If we are going to teach students about any topic, we must begin with facts. We should be cautious of instruction that never gets beyond the factual level or tests that only assess facts. There is room in the curriculum for children to learn state capitals, to spell words correctly, and to memorize addition and multiplication tables. Students need to know which chemicals are acids and bases in order to understand basic chemical reactions. Learning to read music opens students to an understanding of music that is not possible without this basic skill. Learning the color wheel is an important step in being able to express one's ideas through paint. Students are shortchanged when their education goes no further than facts. Students are likewise shortchanged when they are given no factual base on which to build higher-order thinking skills.

In this chapter we discuss **objective items:** *No subjective judgment is required to score them.* The kinds of items discussed are (1) true-false items, (2) multiple-choice items, (3) matching items, and (4) fill-in-the-blank items where the teacher provides students with an answer bank. We include fill-in-the-blanks items where answers are not provided in Chapter 12 on subjective items. Even in this simple form some teacher subjective decision-making is necessary. For example, if you asked the question: "The president of the United States during the Civil War was ———," a subjective judgment is necessary to decide whether to count "Honest Abe" as a correct answer, a partially correct answer, or an incorrect one.

Perhaps it would be better to describe the items in this chapter as recognition items. It is useful to describe assessments in terms of student demands rather than scorer demands, and in each case the student needs to recognize the correct answer, rather than recall or provide an answer.

While it is quite plausible that these items can be used to measure Analysis, Synthesis, and Evaluation objectives, most often these items are used to assess Knowledge, Comprehension, and Application objectives. Each type of item has particular strengths and weaknesses, various modifications a teacher may consider, and different demands on students. We discuss each type of item by providing a series of suggestions for their use.

▨ TRUE-FALSE ITEMS

In Chapter 4, my dislike of true-false items is clear. As a measure of what a student knows, true-false items will overestimate student learning because the student has a 50-50 chance of getting the item correct just by guessing. That is one way of saying that true-false items are highly unreliable. If you take a true-false test in a language you cannot read, you will get some of the items correct just by guessing. When I gathered sample tests from 100 teachers in preparation for writing this book, 84 teachers included at least some true-false items somewhere in their assessments. True-false items can be quite contentious. Consider this example:

T F   1. A test is a sample of behavior.

Is this answer true or false? One interpretation is that it is true. There is nothing incorrect in this statement. But according to our definition of a test from Chapter 1, a test is a sample of behavior given under standardized conditions. The statement is incomplete. But is it false? If you ask these kinds of true-false questions, and count an incomplete answer as a false one, you will get arguments from your students.

You may get another argument if you include many facts in a question, only one of which is false. Consider this question:

T F   2. Lewis Terman adapted Binet-type items for American students in his test, the Stanford-Binet, first published in 1937, although, unlike Binet, his interest was in identifying gifted students, not those with mental retardation.

All of the information in this question is correct, except that it was the second edition of the Stanford-Binet, that was published in 1937, not the first. Such long strings of facts are likely to provoke complaints that the item was unfair. I would not say this is an unfair item, but it certainly is a very hard one, and it seems intentionally designed to make a lot of students miss it. Usually when we write items for a test, we are interested in finding out what students know, not tricking them into getting the answer wrong.

The Use of True-False Tests

If you are not scared away from true-false items because of their lack of reliability and their potential for provoking argument, here are five practical suggestions for writing good ones:

1. *Test One Fact at a Time.* We could make the question about Terman six separate questions:

T F 3. Lewis Terman developed the Stanford-Binet Intelligence Test.
T F 4. The first edition of the Stanford-Binet was published in 1937.
T F 5. The Stanford-Binet uses items similar to those developed by Alfred Binet.
T F 6. Terman was interested in identifying gifted students.
T F 7. Binet was interested in identifying students with mental retardation. (This could be contentious because the term *mental retardation* had not been invented at the time.)
T F 8. The Stanford-Binet was developed for use with American students.

One-fact-at-a-time is an important principle for using true-false items with younger children or children with learning disabilities. I would not recommend ever using true-false items with children before fourth grade. By sixth grade you might include two facts. By eighth, you might include three. I see no reason for ever including more than three facts in a true-false item, even with graduate students.

Using several facts strains the memory resources of students with a learning disability, particularly if the item is going to be administered to them orally. They will remember the information at the beginning of the statement and at the end. Six separate questions will find out better what they know than two questions with three facts in them. (If the student has been diagnosed with a memory problem, such questions might even be *illegal* because long questions will test their memory, not their knowledge of the subject matter. It is illegal to penalize a handicapped child because of his or her disability.)

I had a teacher one time whose false questions were always longer than her true ones. One-fact-at-a-time prevents students from using such clues to make better guesses. In looking over the true-false items on the tests that the teachers sent me, most long questions were false.

2. *Correct for Guessing.* In order to increase the reliability of a test, if you give one point for a correct answer, a zero for a blank, and a minus one for a wrong item, you will decrease guessing. Of course, you should tell students before they take the test that you will be using this procedure. (See Chapter 4 for more information on this technique.)

3. *Avoid "Nots."* Young children, children with disabilities, and children with poor reading skills will often be tripped up by negative sentences:

T F 8a. The Stanford-Binet was not developed for French students.

Here the answer "Yes, it wasn't," is a very confusing response for many children. Children whose first languages are Asian or Eastern European will find these questions even more difficult than English-speaking children. In Japanese and Slavic languages, the response "No" to the question "Don't you want to go downtown?" means "I want to go downtown." Even children whose first language is English may have difficulty with such questions if their parents are not native English speakers.

 4. *Correct False Questions.* Once children are in middle school, a useful strategy on true-false items is to have students correct the false statements:

                                                   American
  T F   **8b.** The Stanford-Binet was developed for ~~French~~ students.

Usually this would result in additional credit for the correction, and we have now ventured beyond recognition items by asking students to provide additional information. This is not a bad thing, but such a practice must square with the objectives. Students should not get credit for merely inserting a *not* into the sentence:

                                       not
  T F   **8b.** The Stanford-Binet was⟋developed for French students. (*no additional points*)

 I recall once having a professor who gave a false test, where every statement was false, and we had to make such corrections. This is an interesting alternative for advanced students.

 5. *Use True-False Items for Application Objectives.* While I believe that Knowledge and Comprehension objectives are better measured by multiple-choice and matching items than for true-false items, Application objectives can sometimes be neatly assessed by true-false questions. Suppose in a science lesson you have taught the distinction between deciduous and conifer trees. On the test you bring in five samples:

1. A branch of a maple with dried leaves
2. A pine with its cones
3. A magnolia in full leaf
4. A spruce
5. An elm about to sprout leaves

 You could then provide students with a quiz sheet that asks:

  9. The following are deciduous trees (T or F):
  1. _____   2. _____   3. _____   4. _____   5. _____

What you would be asking students to do here would be to apply their definitions of deciduous trees and notice that in case one all leaves are dying at the same time, in case three the leaves are large and rounded, in case five, there is a uniform blooming with no residual leaves, etc.

 In another context students may have been studying about electric circuits. On the test you provide them with diagrams they have never seen before.

  T F 10. This circuit will light the bulb when the switch is thrown.

Here again is an excellent opportunity to ask students to correct the false response. If the switch will not light the bulb, students can alter the diagram so that it will.

I suspect teachers use true-false items because they are easy to make up, certainly easier than multiple-choice items. You can look through your textbook and copy statements directly for true questions and change one detail to produce a false one. But as I have stated elsewhere, teacher ease is not the primary criterion for developing particular assessment strategies.

▣ MULTIPLE-CHOICE ITEMS

Standardized tests have long relied on multiple-choice items. One reason for their popularity is that they are easy to score by computer. Another is that guessing is not as large an issue as it is for true-false items.

I believe teachers should get their students used to multiple-choice items. Many so-called high stakes assessments use them: achievement test batteries on which school systems are evaluated; competency tests which will determine whether students pass on from junior to senior high school; the Scholastic Aptitude Tests for college admission; civil service examinations to gain government jobs, etc. Students who have had more practice with these kinds of items do better on these tests than students who have had little practice.

Good multiple-choice items take time to prepare. Many of the multiple-choice items from the teachers' tests I have collected were not very carefully prepared. Sometimes even the multiple-choice items that come with textbook series are not particularly well-crafted. Here are eight rules for making better multiple-choice items.

1. *Distracters should be reasonable.* We call the *wrong answers in a multiple-choice item* **distracters.** The first rule of creating a multiple-choice item is that the distracters should be possible answers. Most teacher-made multiple-choice items are less than excellent in this area. Suppose we have decided we want the students to learn the first seven presidents of the United States in order. Here's a bad item:

> **11.** The third president of the United States was:
> **a.** Leontyne Price
> **b.** Mick Jagger
> **c.** Bruce Willis
> **d.** Thomas Jefferson

Here the students need only recognize that one of these is a president and the others are not. It does not tell us whether the child knows the order of the first seven presidents. If you want students to learn the first seven presidents in order, the best way to assess it is to ask them to list them, but that is not a recognition item. If you just want recognition you need to include more of the first seven presidents in this item.

Although we rarely use multiple-choice items in testing arithmetic, they can be used very skillfully to test students' knowledge and at the same time diagnose students' problems if we use good distracters. For example, when testing whether students can add three three-digit numbers, there are a number of common problems. If the distracters each measure one of these problems, we can tell what mistake the child is making. For example, for this problem:

$$309$$
$$217$$
$$+\underline{502}$$

the correct answer is 1,028. What are some common errors? One is simply not to carry, which would give us 1,018. Another is for a student not to begin with the third place. When she adds $5 + 2 + 3 = 10$, she puts down 1, so we include 128. Another common error is for students to assume that you have to carry in all columns, so the student carries from the 10's place to the 100's place: 1,128. We have thereby created three likely distracters:

12.	309	**a.** 1,018	**c.** 128
	217	**b.** 1,028	**d.** 1,128
	+502		

2. *For beginning students, three choices are enough.* Sometimes we will introduce children to the idea of multiple-choice tests as early as first grade using pictures as answers. For example:

13. A wheel is

a.   b.   c.

We may begin to introduce whole-sentence questions as early as third or fourth grade. During these years, as students are beginning to be comfortable with this format, three possible answers are enough to measure their recognition knowledge. True, with only three items, the student has one chance in three of getting the right answer, but if we started off with five items, the demands of the question would prove too difficult for many—particularly if we follow the first rule and all the distracters are reasonable. So three choices will overestimate the students' knowledge, but five may underestimate it. Four choices are probably good for fifth and sixth graders, but the standard five might be adopted by seventh grade.

Teachers should not feel as if they must make all multiple-choice items have the same number of responses. If there are only two alternatives, just use them:

> **14.** In the story, the explosion took place _____ the train wreck.
> **a.** before
> **b.** after
> **c.** at the same time as

Adding some clearly wrong distracters will not make this a better question.

3. *Don't give context clues.* Here is a bad item:

> **15.** The main character in the story bought an _____ painting.
> **a.** French
> **b.** German
> **c.** American
> **d.** Dutch

The student does not need to have read the story to get the correct answer here; she only needs to know that *an* goes before a vowel. There are many other context clues which students can use (plurals, parts of speech), examples of which are given below.

Of course we want students to learn to use context in such activities as reading, but well-crafted objective tests, such as the high-stakes tests described above, will not have them. If we let our students think that they can figure out such tests by context clues, we will have done them a disservice.

4. *Don't connect items.* We can all remember tests where three or four items are related, so that if you miss the first item, you will miss all of the subsequent ones. Technically, these items are not bad ones, but you could underestimate what your students know if you use them. (They might know the answer to the second question, but miss it because they got the first one wrong.) Consider this example:

> **16.** The fourth president of the United States was
> **a.** John Adams
> **b.** Thomas Jefferson
> **c.** James Madison
> **d.** James Monroe

17. His wife's name was
   a. Abigail
   b. Martha
   c. Dolley
   d. Elizabeth

Students really hate these connected items. If you want to make sure that students know that James Madison's wife was named Dolley, ask it in a separate question and move it away from this question so that the student does not pick up the correct answer from the context between the two of them.

5. *Stop and think long and hard before using options such as "all of the above," "none of the above," "both a and b," etc.*

We have all encountered questions such as this:

16. A criterion-referenced assessment has
   a. a passing grade
   b. scores reported in percent of items passed
   c. a standard score that tells you how well you did relative to other test takers
   d. all of the above are true
   e. A and B are true
   f. A and C are true
   g. B and C are true
   g. None of the above are true   (The answer is e.)

A question like this will baffle elementary and most middle school students. This question is actually asking an Analysis-level question. It requires what Piaget would call formal operational thinking, which is not typical in students until ninth or tenth grade.

You might want to prepare students for this kind of question but in a much easier context:

17. At the very beginning of the story, Pinocchio
   a. is made of wood
   b. has a long nose
   c. both is made of wood and has a long nose

Here the answer is a. Only later, after he lies, does his nose grow.

These five rules will certainly not answer all problems in developing multiple-choice items, but they are a good start. Here are three rules for constructing and using multiple-choice *tests*:

6. *Don't use patterns of answers.* Many students believe that they can figure out the correct answers to multiple-choice tests by looking for patterns. On five-response tests, some think that *a* and *e* are less likely than b, c, and d. Sometimes teachers will deliberately have 2 a's, 2 b's, 2 c's, 2 d's, and 2 e's. That is another kind of context clue which students will soon pick up on.

Sometimes students will think that if there are three b's in a row, it must be a mistake. On high-stakes tests, using such ideas will hurt students, so as you construct your tests, try not to fall into such patterns.

7. *Pay attention to class patterns.* In the next chapter we discuss item analysis, a formal way of determining whether your items are good items. Classroom teachers only occasionally use this system, but there is always a possibility that an item you have written with the goal of one correct answer really has two (or none). If you ask a question and most students miss it, there are three possibilities:

a. It was a tough question, although a good one.
b. You did not teach the material well enough.
c. There was something wrong with the item.

Whenever you find that many students are missing an item, you should try to figure out which of the three possibilities is working.

8. *Teach students how to approach multiple-choice items.* If one of your objectives is for students to become better test takers, you should help them develop skills in approaching different kinds of test items. Three strategies seem essential for taking multiple-choice tests:

a. *Eliminate all the answers you know to be wrong, and then guess.*
b. *Skip items you know nothing about. Return to them after you complete the rest of the test.*
c. *When you feel uncertain about an item, mark it, and come back to it.* Some students believe that if you are considering changing an item, you should always go with your first inclination. Research shows that this is wrong—usually your second choice is the right one.

Teachers may also want to have students occasionally use scantron sheets so that they get used to them. Even if your school does not have a card reader, you can make a key by punching out holes over the correct answers on a blank scantron sheet and score the student' sheets quickly. This can save you time, and help your students practice a useful test-taking skill.

▒ MATCHING ITEMS

Matching items are particularly useful in assessing Comprehension and Application objectives. They are helpful in making sure a student understands concepts which are interrelated. They are not particularly useful in testing isolated facts. Here are some guidelines for making up successful matching items:

1. *Use matching for at least four items that go together.* Items that are related are usefully assessed by matching. Choose either items which share the same base of information (Comprehension) or which test to see whether students can apply a concept (Application).

Consider the following three sets of matching items. In the first we have a set of interrelated facts. In the second we have a set of isolated facts. In the third we are testing to see whether students can apply a concept:

18. Match the following items:

_____ the first president of the United States

_____ wrote the *Declaration of Independence*

_____ wrote many of *The Federalist Papers*

_____ built Monticello

_____ was president during the Louisiana Purchase

_____ negotiated the Louisiana Purchase as Ambassador to France

a. Thomas Jefferson

b. John Adams

c. James Monroe

d. George Washington

e. James Madison

(The answers are d, a, e, a, a, and c)

19. Match the following items:

_____ was the first president of the United States

_____ the name of Jefferson's house

_____ period of time from Washington to J. Q. Adams

_____ book supporting the ratification of the Constitution

_____ emperor of France from 1801 to 1815

a. Monticello

b. Napoleon

c. George Washington

d. *Federalist Papers*

e. Federalist

(Answers are c, a, e, d, b)

20. Match the following student activities with the level on Bloom's cognitive taxonomy:

_____ Students write French equivalent of English words

_____ Students draw an illustration of a story they have read

a. Knowledge

b. Comprehension

_____ Students sight sing an unfamiliar melody from standard musical notation

_____ Students outline a story they have read using headings Exposition, Narrative, Climax, and Denouement

_____ Students construct a new experiment to demonstrate a vacuum

_____ Students critique each others' objectives according to the standards provided in Mager's *Preparing Instructional Objectives*

c. Application

d. Analysis

e. Synthesis

f. Evaluation

(The answers are a, b, c, d, e, and f)

The first set of questions all revolve around facts concerning the first five presidents. Students cannot use context cues in answering them because some answers are used more than once, while others are not used at all. (Jefferson is the answer to three questions, Adams is not an answer to any.) This is simply an efficient use of testing. This series of matching items could be all constructed as six multiple-choice items, where the six questions were each followed by the same five options.

The second set can almost be completely answered by context cues because the answers consist of a house, two people (an American president and a French emperor), an adjective, and the title of a book. Here we would be better off constructing individual multiple-choice items or even true-false items. Unfortunately, many teacher-made matching tests look like this.

The third set asks student to demonstrate their conceptual knowledge of Bloom's taxonomy to new examples. This assesses an Applications objective. This is not a very skillfully laid out set of matching because there is a one-to-one correspondence between the questions (stems) and answers. Usually I would recommend:

2. *Do not have a one-to-one correspondence between stems and answers.* If you give matching items so students can eliminate answers each time they are used, you will overestimate what students know. I would recommend that you include some answers that are not used and some that are used more than once.

For younger children one-to-one correspondence is a good way of helping them learn how to take matching tests. Matching tests can be used as early as kindergarten to test sight words:

21. Draw a line between the word and its picture

book	a.	
cat	b.	
cap	c.	
tree	d.	

3. *Do not use more than 15 items in a matching cluster.* I have seen matching clusters of 25, 40, and even 50 items in elementary school tests. I would suggest no more than seven for primary school children, ten for upper elementary students, and never more than 15, even for graduate students. The purpose of matching items is to allow students to demonstrate that they understand factual knowledge of interrelated ideas or concepts. Putting huge numbers of items together does not measure those ideas and knowledge, but how well a student takes tests.

4. *Make sure all your answers are of the same class.* The problem with item number 19 on page 104 is that it combines a book, people, and adjective, and the name of a house. Matching items work best when all of the answers are similar: all people, all books, all adjectives, all taxonomic levels, all political parties. This is another way of saying, *eliminate context cues.*

Unless, of course, you are trying to measure context cues, which leads us to the final type of objective items, answer-bank fill-in-the-blank tests.

▓ ANSWER-BANK FILL-IN-THE-BLANK TESTS

Many of the tests I have collected from elementary teachers appeared to be fill-in-the-blank tests, but the teacher provided an answer bank. An answer-bank fill-in-the-blank test is a modification of the matching test. This kind of test has become very popular in the language arts and has the benefit of letting students write the correct word, thereby practicing correct spelling, rather than merely check a letter.

The above suggestions on matching tests all apply here, with one exception. In the language arts we are often interested in teaching students to use context cues and assessing their ability to use context cues. Many of the tests I have collected seemed to use context cues deliberately. Consider this quiz on the Japanese fairy tale *Momotaro*:

ANSWER BANK

peach	dog	islands
old woman	monsters	green

1. The person who found Momotaro was the _____.
2. She found him floating on the river inside of a giant _____.
3. She made Momotaro a _____ suit.
4. A _____ joined Momotaro on his journey.
5. He went to the _____ to fight the _____.

By the process of elimination, you can answer all of these questions without knowing anything about the story. This is an excellent strategy if you are interested in assessing whether students can use cues to answer questions. It is not as useful if you are trying to assess Knowledge, Comprehension, and Application objectives. Again we return to the primary issue of assessment: What are your objectives? If we are interested in factual knowledge, we might want to include more options in the answer bank:

peach	dog	pheasant	apple
old man	old woman	islands	boat
green	blue	yellow	red
monsters	cats	monkeys	towns

Questions for Reflection

1. Obtain a teacher-made test that includes objective-type items. See whether you can improve the items using the guidelines above. If you cannot get a teacher-made test, work with a partner and make a test with the same content. Critique each other's tests.
2. Make up a 10-item matching test that assesses students' understanding of the material in this chapter. Exchange your test with another member of the class, and after she takes the test, have her explain how she answered the items: Was she able to answer some questions using the context cues alone, for example?
3. Find an objective test from a college-level course. Take the first 10 items, and see whether they could be strengthened.

CHAPTER

11

Item Analysis

*B*efore we discuss the topic of item analysis we have to recall two of the purposes of testing referred to in Chapter 1, norm-referenced and criterion-referenced tests. Norm-referenced tests locate an individual's position within a group of peers, and criterion-referenced tests tell how much of the material a student has mastered. Norm-referenced tests are most useful in a selection process. Criterion-referenced tests are most useful in judging whether individual students have mastered instructional objectives.

The SATs (Scholastic Aptitude Tests) are an example of norm-referenced tests. Their main purpose is to rank students in terms of the likelihood of excellent performance in college. A college of nursing may use SAT scores to help them select the most promising members for a freshman class. The scores on the SAT do not tell you how much of the material a student got right, but where a student fell relative to the other students taking the test. A score of 500 on the Verbal test of the SAT indicates that you were approximately at the mean for college-bound students. Each 100 points up or down from the mean represents a standard deviation (or z-score*) unit. Table 11.1 shows how to interpret SAT scores. Perhaps the most meaningful scores are the **percentile scores.** A percentile score indicates *the percentage of students you did better than.* It is not the percentage of items you got right. Thus a person with a 400 on the Verbal test on the SAT beat 14 percent of the students who took the test. A person who got a 700 beat 98 percent of those who took the test.

---

* A z-score is the number of standard deviations above (+) or below (−) the mean. A +1.5 z-score indicates you were 1½ standard deviations above the mean. The letter z is used because the statistician who invented the terminology was German, and the word for standard deviation begins with a z in German.

TABLE 11.1 REPRESENTATIVE SAT SCORES, Z-SCORES, AND PERCENTILE SCORES

SAT SCORE	Z-SCORES	PERCENTILE SCORE
300	−2 Standard Deviations	2nd
400	−1 Standard Deviation	14th
500	Mean	50th
600	+1 Standard Deviation	86th
700	+2 Standard Deviations	98th

Although nursing schools want to select the best students for their fresh-man class, at the other end of education there are often tests to determine if each student has mastered the material necessary for entry into a profession. Usually these tests are criterion-referenced. The nursing boards are an example of this kind of test. Here we are not interested in who has the best scores, but whether each person knows an acceptable amount of the required material. In a very good class, everyone might pass. In another year everyone might fail. In most years there will be some who pass and some who do not. We do not want to certify someone to be a nurse unless we are reasonably certain that he or she has the knowledge and skills to be a competent nurse. We want to compare their knowledge against an objective criterion. If a person cannot tell the differ-ence between a virus and a bacterium, stitch up a simple wound, or compute a volume/body weight ratio for administering a drug, we do not want them to be practicing nurses, even if they got the best score on the test that year.

Teachers can use tests in a norm-referenced way or a criterion-referenced way. At the beginning of a school year a teacher administered a reading test to all of her third-grade students in order to make reading groups. If she rank-ordered the students and selected the top third for her high reading group, the next third for her average group, and the bottom third for her re-medial group, she used the test as a norm-referenced assessment. If she did not preselect the number in the reading groups, but instead grouped the stu-dents on their **grade equivalent scores,** *which equate each student's perfor-mance with the average student at each grade level,* and put all those reading at the fourth-grade level or higher in the high level, those who were reading at the third-grade level in the average group, and those reading at a second-grade level or lower in her remedial group, she would have used the test in a criterion-referenced way. *Norm-referenced* and *criterion-referenced* are terms that normally denote how the test was developed, but the terms can also be used to describe how the test was used. When we preselect the number in our advanced group, we are selecting students by their rank, which is a norm-referenced technique. When we group according to student achieve-ment on tests, we are using tests in a criterion-referenced manner. Most of what follows refers, however, to how the tests were developed.

▨ NORM-REFERENCED AND CRITERION-REFERENCED TESTS

Items on Norm-Referenced Tests

Classroom teachers are often against the notion of rank-ordering students, but there are occasions in which teachers are called upon to make such ranking. For example, a third-grade teacher may be asked to nominate the two best spellers in her class for the National Spelling Bee Competition. In doing so the teacher could consult her grade book, but more than likely, the teacher will realize that the students who are in the spelling bee competition are expected to be able to spell words beyond those on the third-grade spelling list. In order to select students for this kind of competition, most teachers will use different words, and they will be harder words.

The items on a norm-referenced test must be difficult, but not too difficult. An item that all students (or most students) get correct does not help us rank-order students. Likewise, an item that all students (or most students) get wrong does not help rank students. The ideal item will be passed by 50 percent of students.

The development of items for a norm-referenced test is an arduous process. First, a large list of items must be developed that are related to what we are trying to assess. Then these items are administered to a large group of students. Items are selected for their difficulty, throwing out those which are too easy and those which are too hard. They are assembled in a test and used on another group of students. This is the process used in the development of most standardized tests. It is much beyond the scope of most classroom teachers. The teacher who wants to find spelling words for a test to select students for the spelling bee competition will most likely find a list of words that have been used in the past for spelling bees. We will be most concerned with norm-referenced tests in Part IV of this textbook, but in this chapter it will be useful to refer to them occasionally to contrast the item analysis process for classroom tests.

Items on Criterion-Referenced Tests

There is no theory about the range of difficulty on criterion-referenced tests. Rather, items should accurately measure the instructional objectives. An item on which all students are correct is as useful as an item on which all students (or most students) are wrong. An item that all students pass means we have done a good job in teaching the objective and the students have done a good job in learning. There is no ideal percentage of students who will pass.

Items for a criterion-referenced test are developed through an analysis of the criterion. Let us say that a group of parents are interested in supporting a youth soccer program at your school and you are a kindergarten teacher. You know that while many of your children are ready to participate in such a program, many are not. In order to play soccer, children need to have a certain level of sensory-motor development and they also have to understand the idea of games with rules. You develop a two-phase criterion-referenced test:

1. Can a child kick a ball rolled toward him two out of four times?
2. Can a child play the game of "Chutes and Ladders" following the rules?

You administer this test to all students in your class. Those who can do both, you put into the youth soccer program in which they actually play games of soccer. Those who cannot do both you put into practice groups which develop their physical and/or game-playing skills, but they do not play actual games. Most of your children may pass this test, or perhaps none of them will pass. You have selected all you think can succeed at the task, while you have selected a more appropriate task for those who do not have the prerequisite skills.

In another situation, you have completed a unit on single-digit multiplication facts and you are now ready to go on to multiplication involving carrying. You administer a test of single multiplication mathematics facts. Students who earn a grade of 85 percent or above move on to the next step. Those who fall below this criterion go through two weeks of remedial work in multiplication facts. You are not selecting the best multipliers; you are selecting those who have the expertise to move on.

Are Classroom Tests Norm-Referenced or Criterion-Referenced?

Although teachers may occasionally use tests to select students for something like the spelling bee competition, most classroom tests are more like criterion-referenced tests than norm-referenced tests. Strictly speaking, criterion-referenced tests are like college pass/fail courses or decisions about whether to promote or retain students at the end of the school year. But in most classrooms we cluster students in terms of their relative mastery of the criterion. Using a test to determine to what degree students have mastered the objectives is the origin of grading.

Whether we are using an absolute criterion (pass/fail) or a relative one (A/B/C/D/F), setting the criterion always involves a strong subjective element. Whether we should demand a 90 percent grade to certify nurses on their board tests, or whether a score of 95 percent or 88 percent will do just as well is a judgment call. Rarely in the classroom do we have hard evidence on which to base these judgments. Often school districts set out percentage scores to represent different letter grades, and sometimes teachers are very proud of having higher percentage scores than other school districts. But those percentage scores are somewhat arbitrary, as we will see in Chapter 14 when we address the topic of grading.

▒ ITEM ANALYSIS OF CLASSROOM TESTS

What do we do when we give a test and our students do poorly? Some teachers throw out the test. Some retain the test scores and give the students a pep talk about doing better the next time. Others reteach the unit and give a second test.

When large numbers of students do poorly on a test, we must ask ourselves a series of questions:

1. Were the objectives above the level of the children's ability to understand them? For example, you may have assumed that your students knew basic information which was essential to understanding the material in the unit with which, in fact, they were unfamiliar. I remember watching a student teacher a few years ago trying to teach a unit on ancient Greece. Not going over a time line impaired her students understanding of much of what she was saying. The fact that 400 B.C. came before 300 B.C. utterly baffled the students. This simple omission completely undermined her teaching a sequence of events.

2. Did something disrupt the process of instruction? Events outside of a teacher's control can sometimes disrupt the most carefully laid plans. A fire drill may have meant switching lesson four with lesson five, but when five was taught before four, students' learning was affected.

If the answers to these first two questions are no, then the teacher may want to examine the test itself. Maybe there is something wrong with the items on the test. You can examine each item, wondering whether the items were confusing, or too hard, or did not quite measure the objective. Another procedure would be to analyze each item statistically. (Don't get alarmed, this isn't really difficult!) We use two simple statistics: **difficulty,** *the percentage of students getting the item correct*, and **discrimination,** *the difference between the percentage of the highest-scoring students and the percentage of the lowest-scoring students.*

Difficulty

Item difficulty is straightforward. Any item most students fail is one that needs attention. Consider a 10-item matching test for a class of 20 third-grade students in which we asked them to match the names of common geometric shapes with their written names. We thought we had done a good job in teaching these definitions, but only one student got 80 percent, two 70 percent, four 60 percent, six 50 percent, and seven 40%. Using our normal grading procedures, this means that 13 students failed, and the average grade was 52 percent. If we do an item analysis, we may discover whether there were technical problems with the test. Our first step is to add up the percentage of students getting each item correct. The results of this analysis are described in Table 11.2.

The first thing this suggests to us is that students have done rather well on five of the items (1, 3, 7, 8, and 10); the scores are not as bad as they seemed at first. Let us look at the questions most of the students got right and those that most got wrong. We notice that the ones they got right are the

TABLE 11.2   DIFFICULTY OF 10 MATCHING ITEMS

1	85%
2	15%
3	80%
4	10%
5	20%
6	40%
7	90%
8	85%
9	15%
10	80%

simpler figures (triangle, square, rectangle, circle, and oval). We might stop and say we need to reteach the newer shapes (rhombus, parallelogram, pentagon, hexagon, and octagon).

If that is not the case, and students actually missed some of the simpler figures, we may want to take the next step, which is to compute a discrimination index for the five items with low passing rates.

Discrimination

Some items on a test are going to be harder than others. Remember that we have no theory on criterion-referenced classroom tests about what percentage should pass an item. Maybe giving students an occasional low grade will motivate them to study harder. This is just a 10-point quiz.

Yet there may be something wrong with the assessment. In the next step we see whether the students who scored in the top of the test did better than those who scored in the bottom of the test. If the better students did worse on an item than those on the bottom, we should be very concerned.

Usually, we compare the percentage of students passing the item in the top third of the class with those passing the item in the bottom third of the class. In this case seven students scored at 60 percent or above, and seven students scored 40 percent. We compare them in Table 11.3. The scores in the first column are the percentage of students getting the item right among the highest scorers; the scores in the second column are the percentage getting the item correct among the lowest scorers; and the scores in the third column are the discrimination indices (high percentage minus the lowest percentages).

Positive discrimination indices mean that the better students do better than the poorer students. That is what we would expect, and therefore we are relatively happy with items 2 and 6. These are just hard items. When the poorer students do better than the better students we may question the item; therefore, we are very concerned with items 5 and 9. Item 4, whose discrimination index is 0, requires a judgment call on the part of the teacher.

TABLE 11.3 DISCRIMINATION INDICES FOR FIVE MATCHING ITEMS

Item	Highest	Lowest	Discrimination
2	43%	0%	+43
4	14%	14%	0
5	14%	28%	−14
6	71%	14%	+57
9	0%	43%	−43

As the teacher in this case looked at the items, she noticed that items 4, 5, and 9 were *quadrilateral, rhombus,* and *parallelogram.* Rhombi and parallelograms are also quadrilaterals, and she determined that her specific examples made these decisions very difficult for her students; she decided to throw out these three questions. She regraded the test on the remaining seven items. Now the average score was 68, and only four students had failed. She retaught the material for two days and then gave students another test. This time the scores were much more in her area of comfort.

⬚ ITEM ANALYSIS IS NOT JUST FOR OBJECTIVE ITEMS

Suppose in a 10-point essay question about Columbus on an eighth-grade social studies mid-term examination, the teacher had developed a grading rubric (see Chapter 16), which looked for five specific bits of information about Columbus and a general statement of the conditions that led to Columbus's voyage:

> Describe the conditions that led to Columbus's first journey. Include in your unified essay information about his national background, the country he sailed for, at least two important historical events of 1492, and the names of his sponsors.

She had decided in advance to award 1 point for mentioning the fact that Columbus was Italian. After grading 106 essays she noticed that only two students had mentioned he was Italian. She then looked at the textbook and saw that the only mention of Columbus's Italian heritage is the statement that he was born in Genoa. She realized that most eighth-grade students do not know where Genoa is, so she decided that this item was too hard.

In another very different situation a teacher decided to evaluate sixth-grade students' writing over a semester with a writing portfolio. This teacher decided to allow students to select the items to go into their portfolios. Each student was asked to select four to six examples of his or her

TABLE 11.4   ITEM ANALYSIS OF PORTFOLIO RATINGS IN A
WRITING CLASS

| OBJECTIVE | NUMBER AT EACH RATING | | | AVERAGE |
	0	1	2	
1	1	7	32	1.78
2	3	9	28	1.63
3	4	3	33	1.73
4	5	3	32	1.68
5	29	7	4	0.38

writing that showed five of the main thrusts of the semester's writing program, which focused on creative writing of narrative:

1. Who: A detailed description of the characters
2. What: A story that had a beginning, a middle, and an end
3. Where: A vivid description of the setting
4. When: A story with references to season or time
5. Why: An analysis of the characters' motives

The teacher developed a checklist of either 1 or 2 points for each of these objectives. She evaluated the 40 students in her two classes on these five objectives and got the results shown in Table 11.4.

This difficulty analysis shows that objective five was not met by most students. This suggests that either the objective was too difficult for students or that they did not understand the objective well enough to select the appropriate materials for their portfolios or that the grading criteria were inappropriate.

What to Do About a Defective Item

There are no hard-and-fast rules about what to do with a defective item. In one case above the teacher decided to regrade what was originally a 10-item test on the basis of the 7 items that seemed sound. If only 1 item on a 20-item test is found to be defective, the teacher may just decide to subtract 5 points for each wrong item and not count the defective item. This will give each student a 5-point bonus—not a serious problem. If as many as 25 percent of items are found to be defective, it may be better to write a new test. Will students go for another test? This will not be a problem when many students have done poorly, although you may consider allowing the students who did well on your first test to opt out of the new test.

You may want to consult Chapter 14 on grading for some other options. The important issue, however, is that if you have written a defective item, your students' grades should not be influenced by your mistake.

Questions for Reflection

1. Make a list of times when you think it is legitimate for a teacher to use norm-referenced grading; make another list of times when you think criterion-referenced grading is more appropriate. What basic ideas hold these two lists together?

2. Suppose you are the teacher who gave the quiz on geometric shapes described earlier. How would you explain to your students your decision to throw out some items and to give a second test? How would you explain it to parents? Write a note home to parents, describing your decision, that you would attach to the children's quiz.

CHAPTER

12

Subjective Items

I remember helping a friend on his dissertation. I administered standard Piagetian items to various groups of students. Perhaps you remember one of the most common of Piagetian questions, involving pouring water from a tall, thin beaker into a short, fat beaker. You begin with water in a tall, think beaker. You mark the beaker at the waterline. You make sure the child notices. Then you pour the water into the shorter, thicker beaker and notice how high it comes up (must less high than in the tall, thin beaker). Then you pour the water back, making sure the child notices that the water comes back to the same place it was before. Then you ask the question:

> Was there more water when it was in the tall, thin beaker, more when it was in the short, thick beaker, or were they the same?

We know the answer: They were the same. Matter is neither created nor destroyed by transformation. Around the age of seven, children get this right. Piaget said when they get this answer right, they are in the **concrete operational stage** of intellectual development, *a period when children can apply logical operations to solving problems about specific facts.* When children are five years old they will get this question wrong because they are in the **pre-operational stage** of intellectual development, *a period when children are thought not to be able to use logic to solve problems.* The water is higher in the tall beaker, and it looks like there is more of it, so pre-operational children usually say there is more water in the tall, thin beaker than in the shorter one.

I gave this problem to a gifted, eight-year-old child, and she told me there was more in the higher beaker. She was old enough to know better, and she was gifted. How could she have made such a mistake? When I asked her why she thought there was more water in the tall, thin beaker than in the shorter one, she said: "But you left a few drops in the tall thin beaker when you poured the water to the shorter beaker."

According to the way we score this item, she was wrong, but she was clearly right. In this case we need the intelligence of a professional to make a decision about a student's response. This is a subjective item.

In this chapter we discuss two types of subjective items, fill-in-the-blanks and short-answer items. A third kind of subjective item, essay questions, is discussed in the following chapter.

▨ FILL-IN-THE-BLANKS ITEMS

Teachers like fill-in-the-blanks items because they appear easy to create and relatively easy to grade. We can take a key passage from the material we have been teaching, omit the important word and there it is. For example, take the description of pre-operational and concrete operational intelligence given above.

We need to substitute something for "get this answer right" in Piaget's definition of the concrete-operational stage.

1. Piaget said that when children can conserve mass, they are in the _____ stage of intellectual development, a period when children can apply logical operations to solving problems about specific facts.

2. When children are five years old they cannot conserve mass because they are in the _____ stage of intellectual development, a period when children are thought not to be able to use logic to solve problems.

These seem to be two pretty good fill-in-the-blank items.

Before we congratulate ourselves too heartily, we need to ask a few questions. First, do we want students to be able to supply an answer, rather than to recognize the correct answer? I selected this particular content because this is material normally covered in a course in human development, not testing. In a human development class I would surely want students to be able to supply this information, but in a testing course, I'm not so sure. Perhaps a matching item would meet the objectives better:

_____ 3. Can conserve mass   **a.** Pre-operational
_____ 4. Cannot conserve mass   **b.** Concrete operational
_____ 5. Can use logical operations
_____ 6. Cannot use logical operations

The second question we need to ask is whether we have left out the right information. Question 1 could also leave out other parts of the statement:

1a. _____ said that when children can conserve mass, they are in the concrete operational stage of intellectual development, a period when children can apply logical operations to solve problems about specific facts.

1b. Piaget said that when children can _____ mass, they are in the concrete operational stage of intellectual development, a period when children can apply logical operations to solve problems about specific facts.

1c. Piaget said that when children can conserve mass, they are in the concrete operational stage of intellectual development, a period when children can apply _____ _____ to solve problems about specific facts.

1d. Piaget said that when children can conserve mass, they are in the concrete operational stage of intellectual development, a period when children can apply logical operations to solve problems about _____ _____.

Question 1a is appropriate if the instructional objective was to learn the names of theorists. Question 1b is much harder than either 1 or 1a. Question 1c is harder still and will probably require many judgment calls on the part of a teacher. Would *logic* be an acceptable answer? What about *conservation, reasoning, operations*? Question 1d has many options: *real-world problems* comes to mind. A fill-in-the-blank item works best if the blank is the central term in the question. Questions 1b, 1c, and 1d are less successful because they ask students to supply secondary information.

Swiss-cheese items

A Swiss-cheese item has many blanks in a single question:

1c. _____ said that when children can conserve mass, they are in the _____ stage of intellectual development, a period when children can apply _____ _____ to solve problems about _____ _____.

It is possible to solve this item if we remember that Piaget was the only person in the course who used the term *conserve mass*. Children who can conserve mass are concrete operational. Maybe some students will get logical operations, but I doubt that many would be able to fill in the final blanks.

I would never recommend using Swiss-cheese items. First of all, they are very time-consuming to take. Second, if a student begins with a wrong idea, she will get most of the other answers wrong, too. Consider the item on early exploration:

7. _____ sailed his ship, the *Half Moon*, for _____ to _____.

While we may want students to memorize the names of explorers' ships, if students fail to remember that Henry Hudson's ship was the *Half Moon*, they will also get the other two questions wrong. How should one grade this response?

> 7. ___*Columbus*___ sailed his ship, the *Half Moon*, for
>   ___*Spain*___ to ___*The Bahamas*___ .

A student (and perhaps a parent) will correctly note that although Columbus did not sail the *Half Moon*, Columbus did sail for Spain and went to the Bahamas. Should the student not get at least some credit for this answer? The answer to this is probably so, although in this case the student has supplied very basic information. Swiss-cheese items set up many such problems, which can be avoided by not using them.

There can be, however, more than one blank in a fill-in-the-blank question. Question 8 is perfectly acceptable if our objective is for students to memorize Piaget's stages of intellectual development in order:

> **8a.** The four stages in Piaget's theory are the _____
> stage, from birth to 18 months; the _____ stage,
> from 18 months to about 7 years; the _____ stage,
> from 7 to 13, and the _____ stage, following age 13.

or

> **8b.** The four stages in Piaget's theory are:
> 1. _____ (birth to 18 months)
> 2. _____ (18 months to 7 years)
> 3. _____ (7 to 13 years)
> 4. _____ (after 13 years)

The difference is that a Swiss-cheese item just makes a blank of all of the important information, and here we are asking for the same kinds of information (names of the stages) in each of the blanks.

Teachers often give students context cues to help them with fill-in-the-blank items. The most common of these is to cue students whether the response is one, two, or three words:

> **9.** Piaget's second stage is called the _____, while
> the third is called the _____ _____ stage.
> (Answers: pre-operational; concrete operational)

Is this a good idea? There are two answers to this question. First, for students who are beginning to learn how to take fill-in-the-blanks tests, such cues are helpful, but the teacher should be careful to be consistent:

> **10.** The original name for New York City was _____
> _____.
>
> **11.** Columbus's main ship was called the _____.

These two consecutive questions may cause problems for
two blanks in question 10 help the student remember New Amst
student may think *Santa Maria* cannot be right because there is c

The second problem here is that in a subjective item ther
than one correct answer. In question 1c, I put two blanks bec....
ticipating the response *logical operations*, but the answer *logic* is also correct.
The context cue designed to help students in this case may actually hinder.
My suggestion would be *not* to provide context cues: If you feel that such
cues are necessary, consider using a response bank with more options than
blanks.

▨ SHORT-ANSWER ITEMS

Because there is no formal definition of a **short-answer item,** we may say it
is *a supply item that does not require organization.* When we turn to essay items
in the next chapter, we will expect some formal organization of the response.
Giving definitions, listing information, and describing something in a single
sentence are examples of short-answer items. Usually fill-in-the-blanks
items assess Knowledge and Comprehension objectives, but short-answer
items can assess learning at any level of the cognitive domain taxonomy.

A fill-in-the-blank item may require some judgment on the part of the
teacher because there may be more than one possible answer; short-answer
items require preparation: The teacher will need to know what he is looking
for before grading the response. This preparation can be in the form of a
rubric, which is discussed in detail in Chapter 16. For the time being we can
define a **rubric** as a *scoring key.* For example, if a question counts 2 points,
the rubric will tell us what constitutes a 2-point answer, what constitutes a
1-point answer, and what responses get no points.

Definitions

Let us begin with a definition item:

12.   What is a norm-referenced test? _____
_____

We need to decide what should be included in a response to this question before we begin to look at any student responses. We began in Chapter
1 with a definition of a test as a sample of behavior taken under standard
conditions. Do we expect that the three components, *sample, behavior,* and
standard conditions, will be included here, or should we allow the student to
use the word *test* in her response? If I were to give this question on a quiz at
this point in a course in assessment, I would not expect students to define a
test this way. I would want answers to focus on the fact that a norm-referenced test compares students' performances or rank-orders students.

Here are four responses to this question from students in a graduate course I taught several years ago:

a. A standardized test

b. A test where the scores are reported in standard scores such as percentiles, not percent of information learned

c. A test that is designed to rank-order students

d. A test administered under standard conditions

Now we see why these questions are called subjective items. For example, most but not all standardized tests are norm-referenced, so response (a) shows some learning, but not complete learning. (Likewise, some classroom tests can be norm-referenced.) This is a 1-point answer. Response (b) was not the response I expected, but the answer is very good. Actually, this student had higher understanding than I expected. A norm-referenced test reports scores of a student's standing in the group of test takers (standard/percentile scores) rather than percent correct. This would be a 2-point answer. Response (c) was the answer I had expected: 2 points. Response (d) shows that the student does not understand the difference between standard administration conditions, a quality of all tests, and a test that is designed to rank-order students. This answer is wrong: 0 points.

Now that I have graded a few responses, I can create my rubric:

2 points   Student indicates the idea of comparison or rank ordering

1 point   Student gives an example

0 points   Wrong answer or missing answer

Lists

Another kind of short-answer question is a list question. We have two preliminary decisions to make here: (1) Do we want the student to remember the whole list or just some of the items; and (2) is it an ordered list?

I remember in the ninth grade having to learn the five components of Calvinism when we were reading the novel *The Scarlett Letter*. In this case the teacher wanted us to remember the whole list, and she gave us a **mnemonic,** a *memorization key,* TULIP:

Total Depravity

Unconditional Election

Limited Atonement

Irresistible Grace

Perseverance of the Saints

This teacher wanted us to remember all five of these ideas. In other situations we may want students to remember just some of the items in a list:

13. Name three of the pieces of evidence that Darwin used to develop his Theory of Evolution: _____

Most biologists will list six or seven pieces of evidence that Darwin wove together to create his theory. Perhaps in a college course, we would want students to know them all, but in a middle school science class, we may settle for three.

Now, we want students to list Piaget's four stages in order. What do we do if the student writes the list this way?

Sensori-motor, pre-operational, formal operational, concrete operational

First, we note that the student got them all, but the last two are in reverse order. If this was a 5-point question, the student should certainly not get the full 5 points. Yet this response is better than if the student wrote:

> pre-operational, formal operational, concrete operational, and sensori-motor

A more complex rubric comes in handy here:

5 points	All four stages, in correct order
4 points	All four stages, two in wrong order
3 points	All four stages, three in wrong order; or three in right order
2 points	All four stages, all in wrong order; three stages, two in wrong order
1 point	Three stages, all in wrong order
0 points	Listed only one or two stages; left item blank

This rubric emphasizes getting the stage names correct and in the right order. Listing only one or two stages gets no credit. It is also possible to use a simpler grading key:

1 point for every stage listed   +1 point for all in right order

−1 point for two out of order

−2 points for three out of order

−3 points for all four out of order.

If a student wrote

> pre-operational, formal operational, concrete operational,

he or she would get 2 points (three items, two out of order). Ordered lists are hard to grade. I would recommend using fill-in-the-blanks items like 8a or 8b on page 120 rather than an open-ended, order lists in most situations, if for no other reason than that you will have fewer arguments from students wanting to squeeze an extra point out of their responses. Or you could simplify it even further:

1 point for every stage listed   +1 point for all four in right order

Single-Sentence Responses

A final short-answer item that we might consider is a single-sentence answer to a question, such as

14. How do you know that the SATs are a norm-referenced test?

    1. *Scores on the SATs are reported in terms of relative performance, in z-scores, and in percentiles.*

    2. *They rank-order students.*

    3. *They are carefully administered and graded by computers.*

These three possible answers show us that when we ask such open-ended questions, we are going to get a wide range of responses. While answer 1 has more information than 2, both show the student knows the answer. If this were a 2-point question, I would give both answers a 2. Response 3 is true, but it does not tell us why the SATs are norm-referenced. Some norm-referenced tests are graded by computers (all of my classroom tests, for example), and most tests are carefully administered. Here, we are looking for a single quality that defines norm-referenced. If that quality is there the response gets 2 points.

15. Why did Columbus sail west and not east?

This question asks for two bits of information: why west? why not east?

    1. Columbus sailed west and not east because he knew the world was round.

This answer only gives us part of what we are looking for, so if we are awarding 2 points for this answer, we would give it only 1 point. Answer 2 contains both bits of information.

    2. Trying to get to China by sailing around Africa was expensive and dangerous; knowing the world was round, Columbus sailed west.

Finally, what does a teacher do about an answer like this:

west—world round   east—too hard

We may have asked students to write their answers in complete sentences, and this is clearly not a complete sentence. I recommend this decision be based on the ability of the individual student. Perhaps a young student who is struggling with writing should not be penalized; she got the content correct. There are other ways of remediating this situation, such as having the student rewrite the answer at home in a complete sentence. Likewise, a student with a learning disability may need to revise this answer into a complete sentence when he goes to the resource room. An older student with high ability may be penalized for such sloppy answering. Like so many other things in this chapter, this requires a judgment call on the part of a teacher.

Questions for Reflection

1. Find a three- to four-page section of a textbook for the grade level you intend to teach and write a 10-item fill-in-the-blanks test to cover its content. Give the material to a fellow classmate and have him or her read the material and answer the quiz. See if there are any items where you have to make subjective judgments.
2. Construct a five-item short-answer test on the same material. Create a scoring rubric. Have your colleague complete this test, too. See whether you were able to anticipate possible different responses. Check to see if your colleague agrees with your scoring.

13

Essay Items

*W*riting has recently become central to the curriculum in a way that it has not been previously. The emphasis on writing probably is one of the most important legacies of the education reforms in the last 20 years. Unfortunately, we know very little about how to teach students to be better writers. We can summarize what we know in three general principles:

- Give students many opportunities to write and to write different kinds of writing.
- Encourage students' writing; make writing an overall positive experience.
- Provide specific positive and negative feedback to students about their writing.

As primarily a teacher of college students, I would have to commend the writing programs in elementary and secondary schools on the first two of these principles and fault them on the third. Public and private elementary and secondary schools are providing students with many more opportunities to write, and they are making writing a more positive experience. Many teachers seem to feel, however, that if they criticize student writing, they will make writing unpleasant. Yet without positive and negative feedback, student writing is not likely to get better. Teachers are caught in a real dilemma.

In my discussions with classroom teachers about how they teach writing, many teachers who would never provide negative feedback to a journal or a creative writing story are ruthless when they grade essay items on tests! When a teacher decides to put an essay item on a test, two real probabilities exist:

1. The student's ability at writing will be diminished because of the stress of the testing situation and the timed nature of most tests, and

2. The teacher will probably give some negative feedback to the student in terms of writing mechanics (grammar, spelling, etc.), organization, and factual content.

All the care that the teacher may take in other writing situations to make writing a positive experience sometimes goes out the window on a test. Perhaps the real problem is that teachers are too positive in nontest situations and too negative in test situations. The contrast between the very pleasant experience of writing in some situations and writing on tests leads some students to hate and fear tests. If certain mistakes were corrected outside of the testing situation, students would be less likely to make those mistakes on a test.

What I have said could be construed as an argument against essay items on tests. Yet learning to write essay exam answers is an important skill for students to learn. Most states now have writing competency exams, and students who are college bound will not only have to take high-stress, high-stakes exams such as the SAT-IIs, but once they get to college, many courses will have essay tests. Teachers need to help students learn to be better essay-writers in test situations, while balancing their goals to make writing a positive experience for students.

There are also real-world situations in which students need to learn to write carefully, accurately, and correctly: letters of application for school and employment; licensure examinations; professional correspondence; and record keeping.

I worked with a sixth-grade teacher a few years ago who wanted to address this dilemma. Her students were preparing to take the state competency exam, which had an essay component. Before her project she gave students time to write in their journals every day, but she never provided any feedback on their writing. She came up with a useful approach to the problem. She had students write an essay every day for 20 minutes on an assigned topic. Students were allowed to return to their essays at different times during the day. At the end of each week, students selected their two favorite essays, and she took them home to comment on. We developed a procedure for providing students feedback on their essays.

1. If there were mechanical problems, the teacher corrected one such problem on the student's essay in red ink. If she made such a correction, she also singled out one thing she liked about the essay and wrote a note praising the student for a good choice of words or including an interesting detail.

2. For each essay she filled out a form which included:
   a. The best thing about your essay is _____.
   b. One thing you might work on is _____.

She tried to be very specific in this feedback. Here is an example of a student essay and the feedback she provided, both on the essay and on the form.

Compare and Contrast a Pine and a Maple Tree
Good topic sentence!

Maple and pine trees are very different. A pine tree is an ever-green. It has prickly leafs called needles and it stays green all year round. All at once it dropps its leafs but then there are new ones to take there place, so it still is green. The maple trees sometimes have green leaves which look like my hand opened wide but then they turn red or yellow and all fall off the tree and then there are

Don't tell me what you

no leaves for the whole winter. ~~I forget what kind of a tree is a~~

don't know: deciduous

~~maple tree but it is not a evergreen.~~ You get sirup from maple trees and turkentin from the pine trees. Both of them grow here in my backyard.

Feedback Form

The best thing about your essay is: *the interesting detail that maple leaves look like your hand opened wide. This is very good writing. You contrast this with the needles on the pine tree. Needles and an open hand look very different, don't they?*

One thing you might work on is: *You end your essay by telling me that both maples and pines grow in your backyard, but your topic sentence says that maples and pines are very different. It might be better to end with a statement about how they are different. Maybe you could say, Although both maples and pines grow in my backyard, we get different products from them. We get syrup from the maple tree and turpentine from pines.*

You may also note that on the feedback form to the student, the teacher uses correct form of several spelling mistakes, and she provided a model sentence for the student to follow. All but two of the students passed the writing competency test on their first try, and writing in student journals during free time actually increased after she began providing both positive and negative feedback to the students.

CREATING ESSAY QUESTIONS THAT PROMOTE SUCCESS

Often teachers write essay exams for their students that are very similar to those they had as college students:

Compare and contrast	How are the Constitution and the Bill of Rights the same and how are they different?
Analyze a list in paragraph form	Describe the four steps in the scientific method.
Narratives	Describe the events that led up to the Boston Tea Party.
Summaries	What are the characteristics of the noble gasses?

Each of these is a different type of writing. I cannot remember a single instance in my 12 years of elementary and secondary school where a teacher ever helped me learn how to answer an essay test question. Few of the teachers I surveyed before writing this book indicated that they provided any instruction to their students about how to take tests. That would be the second step in promoting successful student essay item writing. Before this step, however, the teacher should

1. **Determine if the students can write different types of essays before placing those items on a test.**

If students cannot write a narrative or a compare-and-contrast essay outside of the stress of a testing situation with its time-constraints, then it is highly unlikely they will be able to write those types of essay items in a test situation.

2. **Teach students your expectations for essay tests and give them approaches on how to answer them.**

For example, summaries and reporting lists in paragraph form usually require one paragraph with a topic sentence, evidence, and a conclusion. Compare-and-contrast and narrative answers have different structures. It is useful to tell students there is a system for answering a compare-and-contrast question:

   a. Describe the first item.
   b. Describe the second item.
   c. Tell how they are alike.
   d. Tell how they are different.
   e. Write a concluding statement.

For simple concepts, like contrasting an evergreen with a deciduous tree, each part of the outline might be one sentence. For more complex ideas, such as comparing and contrasting the Constitution with the Bill of Rights, each component may be a paragraph.

After giving students practice on one kind of item (e.g., compare and contrast), the teacher can move on to other items. She can teach her students how to look for cues in the question for required responses. Teaching students to pause for a few minutes and construct a simple outline of what they want to say may be the best advice you give them.

3. Give students practice in test-like situations on answering essay questions.

The example I gave above of the teacher preparing her students for the state writing competency exam had aspects of the test situation: She assigned the topics (which were similar to previous writing exam questions) and she had students write for 20 minutes. Because this was a high-stakes test (they could not enter senior high school before passing the test), she gave them many weeks of practice. For preparation for a classroom test, much less preparation may be warranted.

4. Give students cues in the question about what is expected of them.

You will get better questions if you begin with a question like this:

> **1.** Compare and contrast the Constitution and the Bill of Rights. Describe the Constitution and the Bill of Rights, then tell me how they are alike and then how they are different.

Over time, you can give fewer and fewer cues. These four steps will likely lead to higher rates of success on essay test items than if you approach the process with a sink-or-swim mentality.

▓ GRADING ESSAY ITEMS

Unlike the short-answer items discussed in the previous chapter, an essay item on a test has both content and structure. When we develop the grading rubric, we need to determine how much will be devoted to content and how much to structure. We also need to determine whether we will consider mechanics (spelling and grammar).

I believe that an essay on a test should be graded primarily on content, particularly during the elementary and middle school years, but I believe some attention should be given to organization. I would probably not give essay items before middle school, although I would have students practice writing on tests with short-answer items in a sentence. Essay items can be introduced in middle school with some success if the teacher will devote time to helping students learn how to answer them. At the senior high school level, essay writing on tests might be very common and more attention could be paid to structure and mechanics.

As for mechanics, middle school teachers have three options, based on the ability of their students: (1) ignore it; (2) correct mistakes without having mistakes affect students' grades; or (3) count mechanics as part of the grade. The normal procedure for attending to mechanics is to deduct points for grammar and spelling mistakes. I do not recommend that procedure. I have received examples of graded tests where a 10-point item with good content and good structure was given 4 points because the student misspelled half a dozen words.

Teachers may be cautious about the first option, ignoring mechanics altogether, if they are sending tests home to parents who have high expectations for their children. Parents may wonder why their child received a grade of A on an essay that was riddled with technical errors that were not noted. In advising student teachers I have suggested that when they begin to teach students how to answer essay items, they may not want to pay attention to spelling and grammatical errors. I have also suggested they send a letter home to parents well in advance of the first test, explaining their point of view:

> We are just taking up writing essay items on tests. This is an important skill for students to learn, and it involves many different components. First, the student must get the facts right and down on paper. Then the essay must be organized. Finally, I will expect the answer to be correct in terms of writing and spelling.
>
> I think it is important for students to learn not to be anxious about taking tests. So at first, I am going to give students some leeway in terms of organization, writing, and spelling. When you receive the student's tests, there will be some things you may notice that you consider wrong. You may bring these to your child's attention if you want, but for the time being I will be interested in getting the facts down on paper. Later in the year, we will begin to work on structure, grammar, and spelling. Even then, I may not mark every mistake. I think it is discouraging for students to receive a paper that looks like I have bled on it with red ink! Please realize that in other kinds of activities we are working diligently on spelling and grammar.
>
> I would greatly appreciate your feedback on this important area of your child's education.

Particularly with middle school students learning to take essay tests, I would create a rubric that awards points for good organization and good mechanics, and I would share the rubric with the students. I would never create a situation in which multiple mechanical errors could completely eradicate the points earned for content. Let's reexamine the essay quoted above about maple and pine trees:

> **2.** Compare and contrast maple and pine trees. Describe the maple and the pine, and tell me what kinds of tree they are. Then tell me how they are alike and how they are different in terms of the shape of the leaves, when they have leaves, and what kinds of products we get from them.
>
> Maple and pine trees are very different. A pine tree is an evergreen. It has pricly leafs called needles and it stays green all year round. All at once it dropps its leafs but then there are new ones to take there place, so it still is green. The maple trees sometimes have green leaves which look like my hand opened wide but then they

turn red or yellow and all fall off the tree and then there are no leaves for the whole winter. I forget what kind of a tree is a maple tree but it is not a evergreen. You get sirup from maple trees and turkentin from the pine trees. Both of them grow here in my backyard.

I am going to assume that this is going to be about a 20-point item on a test, which will include attention to writing structure and mechanics. The question clearly defines what I want the student to tell me:

1. the kinds of trees maples and pines are
2. the shape of the leaves
3. when the leaves are on the trees
4. products from the trees.

I can then construct a rubric:

Essay Grade Sheet

Content (2 pts for each; 16 pts possible)   Total Points _____

    kind of tree   _____ pine   _____ maple

    shape of leaves   _____ pine   _____ maple

    time for leaves   _____ pine   _____ maple

    products   _____ pine   _____ maple

    Comments: _____

Structure (1 pt each; 2 pts possible)   Total Points _____

_____ Topic sentence   _____ Conclusion

    Comments: _____

Mechanics (1 pt each; 2 pts possible)   Total Points _____

_____ Grammar   _____ Spelling

    Comments: _____

Final grade _____ points   Letter grade _____

The student did a good job on content. He did not remember the term *deciduous*, so he earned 14 of the 16 points on content. On organization there was a good topic sentence, but as we noted above, the concluding sentence left something to be desired. There were no grammatical errors; there were seven spelling errors, so I might award one point for grammar, but not for spelling. I would return the Grade Sheet like this:

Essay Grade Sheet

Content (2 pts for each; 16 pts possible)   Total Points __14__

kind of tree	_C_ pine	_X_ maple
shape of leaves	_C_ pine	_C_ maple
time for leaves	_C_ pine	_C_ maple
products	_C_ pine	_C_ maple

Comments: _Very good writing; you forgot the term deciduous for maples_

Structure (1 pt each; 2 pts possible)   Total Points __1__

__C__ Topic sentence   __?__ Conclusion

Comments: _Good topic sentence, but your conclusion that they both_
grow in your backyard does not go with your topic sentence that they
are different.

Mechanics (1 pt each; 2 pts possible)   Total Points __1__

__C__ Grammar   __X__ Spelling

Comments: _Work on spelling these words: leaves, turpentine, and prickly._

Final grade _____16_____ points   Letter grade _B+_

I am not proposing that students receive this level of feedback on every essay they write for all teachers. Completing this form would take two or three minutes, which for a class of 24 would be an extra hour's work for a teacher. Yet, periodically giving this level of detail to students will be useful to them, particularly if they are just learning how to take essay tests. This level of feedback on one item on a three-item test may be useful to students.

The relative weight given to content versus structure and mechanics is also not a hard-and-fast rule. I assumed this was for a sixth-grade student. The weight given to structure and mechanics for students more familiar with essay tests may be higher.

This chapter has sketched out some basic ideas about essay items on tests. We can expect less from writing on tests than we can from other, less stressful and less time-constrained situations. More information about assessing student writing is contained in Chapters 17 and 18.

Questions for Reflection

1. You may not agree with the way I graded the essays on trees. Or you may think that the feedback form was too detailed. Define a group of students, create your own feedback sheet, and then score the essay.

2. Here is an essay by a fifth-grade student in response to the question: Explain why smoking is dangerous to your health. You had expected the student to mention smoking's effects on lungs, heart, and stamina. How would you score the essay?

> Smoking is a very nasty habit, and it's against the law to smoke in many buildings today. Smoking makes people cough and it turns your teeth yellow and they get decaid and they fall out. Smoking causes some kinds of cancer to.

CHAPTER

14
Grading

*A*s I was writing this chapter, a student came by my office to discuss his grade. He had received a B+ in the course. The cut-off point between an A and a B was 90 percent. He had a test average of 88. He had a final exam grade of 89. He made a 92 on his term paper, and he had a daily quiz grade average of 90. According to my grading formula, he received an 89.2 in the course.

The student wanted very much to get into law school, and he felt that if I had given him a 95 on his term paper, which he considered an A paper, rather than an A− paper, he would have earned an A in the course, which would help him out considerably toward meeting his professional goals. Not only did he suggest that his paper was better than I had graded it, he asked me to notice that he had attended class every day, participated in class discussions, and had volunteered for a research study I was conducting (although I had not suggested extra credit for such participation).

I have very specific criteria for my term paper, and as I discussed this with the student, he had to admit that his paper was an A−. I had to admit that I had listed as an objective students' class attendance and participation and that I failed to consider outstanding attendance and participation in my grading formula. If I had given even one point for outstanding participation, this student would deserve an A in my course. I was willing to admit that I had an unassessed objective, and I gave him an A.

The point here is that no matter how objective a grading scheme is, there is a measure of subjectivity to it. I think we should try to be as objective as possible because testing and the grades we base on testing have important consequences for students.

In this chapter we discuss several issues on the process of assigning grades. We first look at qualitative versus quantitative grading. Then we turn our attention to grading practices based on norm-referenced or criterion-referenced assumptions. Then we discuss the topic of grade inflation and the so-called Lake Wobegon Effect. We turn our attention to some miscellaneous grading practices before concluding with some guidelines for discussing grades with students and parents.

▓ QUALITATIVE VS. QUANTITATIVE GRADING

Qualitative grading is *a practice of providing verbal rather than numerical evaluations of student work and progress.* On the other hand **quantitative grading** is *the practice of providing numerical or alphanumeric evaluations of student work and progress.* We will consider alphanumeric grades (A, B, C, D, F) as quantitative grading because almost invariably such letter grades are tied to numbers. Letter-grading schemes such as E, S, N (Excellent, Satisfactory, Needs Improvement) are qualitative grades, because rarely are such grades tied to a numerical scheme. In these opening sections I will be using information I developed from interviews with experienced teachers, which I conducted before beginning this book.

Qualitative Grading: Free Narratives and Standardized Narratives

About a third of the elementary teachers I surveyed provided narratives rather than grades for their students; about a third used narratives and grades (usually not A's, B's, C's, etc.); about a third used grades only. Narratives were much less common in middle schools. Although some secondary schools used narratives, all also required number or alphanumeric letter grades. In most cases this was not a teacher decision; it was a school or school district policy. Many of the teachers who used grades were uncomfortable with the grading system at their school; likewise, many teachers who used narratives were dissatisfied with some aspects of narratives, most notably the heavy time demands that narratives imposed on them.

The idea behind a narrative is that a teacher's description of student work is more valuable to the student, parents, and next year's teachers than a composite letter or number. Ideally, a narrative should include (1) a statement of the child's achievement, including strengths and weaknesses; (2) a statement of the child's approach to the material (does the child seem to like the work? what are his usual methods of work? how does his approach affect his performance?); and (3) guidance for continued achievement or improvement. Let me give you an excellent example of a teacher's narrative for a fourth-grade student in spelling:

> Allison's spelling is much improved. She is now nearly at grade level according to a spelling inventory given three weeks ago. She studies hard for spelling tests, but she still uses invented spelling when writing at the computer. She is just beginning to transfer what

> she learns in spelling lessons to her writing. She has recently begun
> using the spell checker on the computer. Allison makes fewer mis-
> takes with consonant sounds than vowel sounds. Particularly, she
> needs to practice the i before e rule and work with silent e's.

Allison's parents should be pleased with this evaluation, and Allison knows what she needs to work on. If this were the year-end evaluation, her new teacher would have a good idea of where she might begin with Allison. I have four cautions about such narratives:

1. They are very time-consuming to write. This example is 89 words long. The teacher in this class wrote narratives for reading, writing, spelling, social studies, science, art, arithmetic, and physical education. That comes to over 700 words for each of 24 students, six times a year. That's over 100,000 words a year, or the equivalent of a 250-page novel!

2. Whatever the reasons for narratives, most of the examples I have examined emphasize student effort rather than student achievement. Here is an example I consider typical of those I have read:

> James is making progress in writing, although he still seems to
> view it as a chore. He does not use the spell checker without
> prompting and rarely revises his work. He will need to work
> harder if he plans to pass the state writing competency test.

This narrative leaves much to be desired. Although James is making progress, we do not have a gauge of his achievement standing. We know he is less than enthusiastic about writing and his prescription is only to work harder: We do not know on what skills he should work.

3. Many teachers have three or four basic messages, which they repeat with minor variations: High-achieving students are described as working hard, doing well, and being pleasures to work with. Average students are described as working satisfactorily, keeping up, and needing some extra effort. Somewhat below-average students who work hard are described as hard workers who need extra support at home; below-average students with motivation problems are described as poorly disciplined. After reading several hundred similar narratives, I realized teachers would save much time by providing a rubric to the parents. One teacher in a school district that required narratives developed such a form, which is reproduced as Table 14.1.

This teacher took the position that he needed to provide more specific feedback to students who were experiencing difficulty than to students who were doing excellent or satisfactory work. The general evaluation comments are routine, allowing the teacher to concentrate on making suggestions to parents about what could be done to improve their children's performance. The teacher said that before he invented the form, he had spent a great deal of time writing statements about student achievement, but most fell into these four categories. Eventually, all third-grade teachers in this school adopted this narrative form.

TABLE 14.1 PARENT FEEDBACK FORM USED IN THIRD GRADE

Student Name ___*George*___   Subject Area: ___*Math*___

_____ **Doing Above Expectations.** Your child is always prepared and interested in class. His/her work is above average. Keep up the good work.

__✓__ **Doing Expected Work.** Your child is usually prepared and interested in class. His/her work is at a level of average or (somewhat above average third-grade) student. One thing I would work on is: *recalling subtraction facts.* *I'll send some suggestions.*

_____ **Needs a Little Exra Work.** Your child is doing less than expected in this subject. With some extra work I am sure s/he will catch up. Here are some suggestions for doing this. _____

_____

_____

_____ **Needs Serious Assistance.** Your child is experiencing significant difficulty in this subject, and I would appreciate an opportunity to discuss this issue with you. In the meantime, here are three things we might want to work on:

1. _____

2. _____

3. _____

4. Be accurate. Teachers who send ungrammatical or poorly spelled communications home will sometimes find those communications resurfacing to haunt them.

Qualitative Grading: Checklists

Some school districts have simplified the process by providing a checklist of descriptors gleaned from observing teachers' writings. In a school where I supervised student teachers, the principal who liked to use computers compiled statements about language arts and developed a 32-item checklist. Teachers checked those appropriate items for each student and on another form wrote a one-sentence, individualized statement. The principal had a printout of the items checked sent to each parent. The principal developed this checklist so the individual sentences were combined to produce a report. The checklist appears as Table 14.2.

TABLE 14.2   FOURTH-GRADE CHECKLIST FOR LANGUAGE ARTS

_____ Homework is always done on time.	_____ Much missing homework.
_X_ Homework is sometimes late.	_____ Needs work on group work.
_____ Homework is often late.	_____ Reads above average.
_X_ Works diligently in groups.	_____ Needs help in reading.
_____ Has difficulty with group work.	_X_ Makes some mistakes in writing.
_X_ Reads well.	
_____ Writes correctly.	_____ Writes interesting compositions.
_____ Makes too many writing mistakes.	_____ Does not take writing seriously.
_____ Takes writing seriously.	_____ Gets distracted.
_X_ Approaches work seriously.	_____ Cuts up in class.
_____ Is a discipline problem.	_X_ Makes some spelling mistakes.
_____ Is an excellent speller.	
_____ Needs help with spelling.	_X_ Review spelling words each week.
_____ Should read more at home.	
_X_ Keep up the excellent work!.	_____ Encourage writing at home.
_X_ Please check that his homework is done.	_____ A little help at home will do wonders!
_X_ Does excellent homework.	_____ Please call for a conference.
_____ Homework needs more care.	

Checklists make the teacher's job much easier and provide rich information about student performance. By also providing a short, specific comment about each student's work, the teacher makes the process more personal.

The computer program printed out the following narrative based on the items the teacher checked:

> Andy does excellent homework, although his homework is sometimes late. Andy works diligently in groups. Andy reads well. He makes some mistakes in writing. He approaches his work seriously. He makes some spelling mistakes. It would be useful if you review his spelling words each week and please check that his homework is done. Keep up the excellent work!

To which the teacher added, "Andy needs to work on the difference between plurals, singular possessives, and plural possessives. I will send home a worksheet on this."

Qualitative Grading: Descriptive Categories and Letter Grades

Many school districts use descriptive grades during the early grades. Sometimes these descriptions are left up to teachers and sometimes they are provided by the school district. They may include such terms as *excellent, superior, outstanding, satisfactory, competent, needs improvement*, and *unsatisfactory*. These adjectives convey useful messages to parents.

The problem with such classifications is that their actual meaning is difficult to tie down. Does an *outstanding* rating of a kindergarten student's language arts mean she is above national norms in achievement, high in the class in achievement, or very enthusiastic? Perhaps at the kindergarten level we are less concerned about this than we are by third grade. Eventually, we need to use grades that convey to the students' future teachers, parents, and the students themselves interpretable information.

Letter grades in the early grades are rarely alphanumeric. Most often grades fall into categories that are above average, average, below average, and unsatisfactory. Many different schemes are used, and these are rarely tied down to differentiate achievement from motivation. Narratives supply that interpretation, but single adjective descriptors or categorical letter grades do not.

There are many reasons why grades should not be tied too closely to achievement in the primary grades. Some children enter kindergarten after being cared for by a grandmother while mother and dad work. Grandma loves her grandchild and takes care of her social and health needs, but she does not concentrate on writing letters, counting, learning color names, or learning geometric shapes. This child may know how to bake a cake, find her way home, and play an elementary game of gin rummy, which will eventually help her arithmetic. Other children are put in academic preschools where they are drilled on skills that will make them shine in kindergarten: They can count to 100, say the alphabet in order, and know the difference between a rectangle and a rhombus. After five months in a kindergarten, the first child is at a disadvantage compared to the graduate of the academic preschool. We really do not want to grade the first child as a C− student, while the second is given an A+. If both try hard we might want to give them both excellent evaluations. Eventually, perhaps as early as second grade, we need to begin to provide meaningful information about the academic achievement of students. In most school districts I have examined, grades based solely on achievement begin by third grade. We may want to supplement qualitative information about effort and enthusiasm with achievement marks. Some form of quantitative grading usually appears at this point.

Quantitative Grading: Tough Graders vs. Kind Graders

What does an A really mean? If you were to look in the college catalog of a college where I used to teach, you would find a very confusing message, although at first glance it does not seem so. Here are grade descriptions:

A	Outstanding	90–100
B	Above Average	80–89
C	Average	70–79
D	Below Average	60–69
F	Failing	59 and below

If you notice that the definitions in the second column (outstanding, above average, etc.) were norm-referenced, and the numerical guides in column three are criterion-referenced, then you understand one of the root problems of grading. Does a grade tell us where the student falls in relation to his peers, or does it tell us how much material he has mastered?

Once you have decided whether you are a norm-referenced grader or a criterion-referenced grader, then you need to decide whether you want to be a tough grader. If you are a tough grader and a norm-referenced one, then you may define A as the top student in your class: only one A. But you could equally well decide, if you want to be a kind grader, that the top 25 percent of your students should get A's.

If you go for the criterion-referenced approach, you could decide (if your school district will allow you to do this) that 95–100 is an A (tough grader), or 88–100 is an A (kind grader).

You can write tests that include items where your expectation is every child should get the answer to every question; you may throw in a few challenging questions; or you can write killer tests. I remember sitting in a teacher's lounge as a beginning teacher and listening to a colleague chuckle to himself as he went through the textbook, muttering under his breath, "I bet nobody gets this one!"

Probably the most common way of making up tests is to blend a criterion-referenced and a norm-referenced approach: to use a numerical system (criterion-referenced) but adjust it if the grades are too high or too low. If these adjustments are made rationally, using item analysis, this is a reasonable solution. Most teachers I know write tests composed of items they expect everyone to know and put in a few challenging items.

Your philosophy of grading is your own; these are decisions you will have to make as you teach, based on your experience with students and teachers, and in response to your school's guidelines. There are no right or wrong answers.

Quantitative Grading: Numbers vs. Letters

As a college adviser, I have access to a large number of my students' high school transcripts. Some high schools record grades by letters, some have pluses and minuses attached, some give numerical averages, some are carried out to decimal points. Some schools are very proud of using one system rather than the other.

My personal position is that teacher-made tests and other classroom assessments are not reliable enough (see Chapter 4) to warrant the precision implied by numerical grades, particularly those carried out to decimal points. Using numbers leads one to believe the grading process is very precise. The example at the beginning of this chapter is telling: Can I really be sure what a 89.2 means? Have I included every objective and was each measure reliable and valid?

Often the number we put on a student's report card is not indicative of her performance at all. For example, if Mary's six-weeks spelling grade is made up of six quizzes, and Mary earned 100, 100, 90, 40, 100, and 100, Mary's average is 88.3. Only one of her quiz scores was in the area of the mark we have given to represent her spelling performance. Of the 60 spelling words, she got 53 correct, but this is only an estimate of the 120 total spelling words Mary should have learned.

I am not a fan of pluses and minuses. Unless every test used in computing a grade is developed with a table of specifications (Chapter 9) and scrutinized by an item analysis (Chapter 11), all we can do is classify students into three to five groups (E, S, N or A, B, C, D, F). If we use pluses and minuses we begin to classify grades into 10 to 13 categories, and I feel that such a process is overclassification.

Quantitative Grading Schemes: Point Systems vs. Averages

Once we have resolved personally whether we are criterion-referenced or norm-referenced, tough or kind, we still have to combine quiz, test, and examination scores (as well as other projects and papers) into a system that will produce either a number or a letter. There are two procedures for doing this: point systems and averages.

Point systems have the advantage of making the math simple for both the teacher and the student. Suppose you need to put together grades of five quizzes, two tests, an exam, and a book report. You have decided the exam will count 25 percent, the quizzes will count a total of 25 percent, each test will count 15 percent, and the book report will count 20 percent. If your quizzes each had 10 items on them, then each quiz could count 10 points. Following this system you would have:

SOURCE	NUMBER	POINTS EACH	TOTAL
Quizzes	5	10	50
Tests	2	30	60
Exam	1	50	50
Book report	1	40	40
Total			200

If Gregory got 9, 7, 5, 4, and 8 on his quizzes (total = 33); 27 and 23 on his tests (total = 50); a 44 on his exam, and a 38 on his book report, then we could combine these numbers (total = 165). If we want a percentage grade, we can divide by the total number of points: 82.5 percent. We could also have a grading scale such as A = 180–200; B = 160–179; C = 140–159, and so on, which would indicate that Gregory earned a B.

This example uses a scheme based on 200, but any number is possible. Suppose you got sick and only gave four of the quizzes. You could quickly convert this scheme into:

SOURCE	NUMBER	POINTS EACH	TOTAL
Quizzes	4	10	40
Tests	2	30	60
Exam	1	50	50
Book report	1	40	40
Total			190

If Gregory now got 25 on his quizzes, 50 on his tests, 44 on the exam, and 38 on the book report, you could divide the total of 157 by 190 (percentage = 82.6), which also works out to be a B.

If you use a weighted mean, the math is much more complicated. In this case you will

1. convert all scores into percentages;
2. find the quiz and test averages;
3. multiply each source of data (quizzes, test, exams, book reports) by the weight (percentage of total given to each source);
4. add up your weighted percentages. (See the section in Chapter 6 on the weighted mean.)

Point systems are recommended, unless you have a grading program on your classroom computer that will compute the weighted mean for you effortlessly. Point systems have the added advantage of allowing students to compute how well they are doing at any time. Suppose after Gregory has gotten a 9, 7, and a 5 on his first three quizzes, a 27 on his first test, and a 38 on his book report, he wanted to know his status. He could add the points together (86) and divide by the possible points earned (30 for quizzes, 30 for the first test, and 40 for the book report = 100); at that point he had an 86 percent.

▓ NORM-REFERENCED VS. CRITERION-REFERENCED GRADING

As we discussed above, teachers should always be aware that it is possible to write hard tests or easy tests or anything in the middle. As much as we would like every test to be exact and fair, developing a table of specifications and conducting an item analysis is not always possible because there are not enough hours in a teacher's day and there is always an element of subjectivity in grading.

If we want to measure an art history student's understanding of the facts of the Renaissance, we could ask many different questions. I have made up three five-item quizzes (Table 14.3), which you might want to take. These quizzes are based on the general goals for a 10th-grade art history unit on the Renaissance and include major Renaissance artists and their major works. The first quiz is easy. You should get them all correct even if you have never studied the Renaissance. All of the items are based on familiar works of art. Maybe you don't know who painted the Cowper Madonna, but you should know most of the rest and, by elimination, you should get them all right. The second quiz is much tougher, and only students who have studied the Renaissance would get them all correct. Quiz 3 would even be tough for college art history majors.

TABLE 14.3 THREE PARALLEL QUIZZES ON ART HISTORY

Quiz 1. Easy Items

Match the Renaissance figure with his major work:

_____ **1.** Michelangelo	**a.** Mona Lisa
_____ **2.** Leonardo da Vinci	**b.** The Cowper Madonna
_____ **3.** Botticelli	**c.** The Birth of Venus
_____ **4.** Donatello	**d.** The Sistine Chapel Ceiling
_____ **5.** Raphael	**e.** Mary Magdalene

Quiz 2. Moderate Items

Match the Renaissance figure with his major work:

_____ **1.** Michelangelo	**a.** *La Giaconda*
_____ **2.** Leonardo da Vinci	**b.** Obadiah
_____ **3.** Botticelli	**c.** Spring
_____ **4.** Donatello	**d.** The Creation of Adam
_____ **5.** Raphael	**e.** The Cowper Madonna

Quiz 3. Hard Items

Match the Renaissance figure with his major work:

_____ **1.** Michelangelo	**a.** The Uffizi Annunciation
_____ **2.** Leonardo da Vinci	**b.** The Santa Croce Annunciation
_____ **3.** Botticelli	**c.** The Kresge Nativity
_____ **4.** Donatello	**d.** The Madonna of the Stairs
_____ **5.** Raphael	**e.** Le Stanze della Signoria

An experienced teacher can make up items which are relatively easy and relatively difficult. If you give a really hard test, you may want to enhance your students' grades. You can do this by curving and scaling.

Curving is *a procedure based on norm-referenced testing. The teacher rank-orders students' grades and decides what percentage of grades should receive A's, B's, C's, and D's (or any other grading system).* In Table 14.4 a teacher curved the grades of 15 seventh-grade students. The teacher decided that there should be about 20 percent A's, 30 percent B's, 30 percent C's, and 20 percent D's. **Scaling** is *a technique derived from criterion-referenced testing. In its simplest form the teacher adds on a set number of points to each student's grade.* Also in Table 14.4 is an example of scaling. In the third column the teacher added 9 points to each student's grade (because he assumed that at least one student should make an A). Scaling can involve other techniques, such as adding on a percentage of a score, which would give more additional points to higher scoring students.

As you look at Table 14.4 you see that the raw scores produced two B's, three C's, seven D's, and three F's; the curving procedure changed this to three A's, five B's, four C's, and three D's; the scaling procedure resulted in one A, four B's, six C's, three D's, and one F. Certainly students would be happier with the curved or scaled grades, but should the teacher do it? (It is also possible to curve a very high set of grades down.) The teacher could have decided on 50 percent A's and 50 percent B's, or he could have added

TABLE 14.4 EXAMPLES OF CURVING AND SCALING

RAW SCORES		CURVED GRADES	SCALED SCORES	SCALED GRADES
81	B	A	90	A
80	B	A	89	B
78	C	A	87	B
77	C	B	86	B
76	C	B	85	B
69	D	B	78	C
68	D	B	77	C
68	D	B	77	C
67	D	C	76	C
63	D	C	72	C
62	D	C	71	C
60	D	C	69	D
57	F	D	66	D
54	F	D	63	D
49	F	D	58	F

19 points to each score. When one curves or scales grades, adjusting the raw score is very subjective.

I do not necessarily recommend scaling or curving. I particularly do not recommend the idea of developing killer tests and then raising the grades through one of these techniques. Sometimes college professors do this, but the main result is that students learn that they do not know much and they are not good test takers.

▓ GRADE INFLATION

One current criticism of American education is grade inflation. If we compare grades now to the grades given 30 years ago, students today get higher grades, on average. There are many accounts of grade inflation. More college students today want to go to graduate school, and grades of B or better are necessary to get into graduate school. More high school students today want to go to college, and grades of B or better are necessary to get into good colleges. The whole process keeps filtering down the grades, and we now find reasons to have a higher curve than we used to.

A generation ago most teachers were influenced by norm-referenced test theory. In its strictest form in a class there should be 2 percent A's and 14 percent B's (based on the properties of the normal curve. My college in the 1960s was very much in this mode. Many of my teachers never gave A's, while others gave one A in all of their classes each semester. Now we are more influenced by criterion-referenced theory, which suggests that everyone who meets the criterion for an A (maybe an average of 90 percent) should get an A.

The Lake Wobegon Effect

Garrison Keillor's book, *Lake Wobegon Days*, has a phrase that has been used to describe one approach to evaluation: in Lake Wobegon all the students are "above average." By definition, however, half of children will be below the median, which is one kind of average. When we evaluate students not all will be in the upper half of the group.

American teachers are kind by nature. They want their students to succeed. To apply the term *average* to a student seems to be a devastating indictment. Parents, too, do not want to hear this evaluation of their children.

Although critics of education think that grade inflation is a huge problem, it really is not. People who use grades are aware of the issue: They know that a B today is not what it was a generation ago. This is not a reason to give out high grades because it will make students and parents happy. Grades should be meaningful, but they do not need to mean the same thing they meant 20 or 30 years ago.

▨ MISCELLANEOUS GRADING PRACTICES

American teachers want their students to do well. We believe that doing well in classes (making good grades) will enhance students' self-esteem. Besides scaling and curving grades, many teachers have developed other means of increasing students' test scores or test averages. Practices which merely inflate students' grades are to be avoided, but sometimes these practices can be used prudently in grading.

Extra Credit

Extra credit seems to be universal in American education. From elementary school to graduate school, students want to know how they can earn extra credit after they do less well on an assessment than they had hoped. It seems almost heretical to suggest that extra credit should be eliminated.

Extra credit that is directly tied to the objectives is warranted; extra credit that makes students happier is probably not. Getting extra credit for revising a paper makes sense. Likewise, doing an extra report on the content of a unit would make sense. Getting extra credit for staying after school and helping the teacher with janitorial activities might be suspect.

Dropping the Lowest Grade

Teachers dropping students' lowest test scores to increase students' grades is a wide-spread custom in education, but it will disconnect the assessment process from the objectives. In a high school American history course, we may have nine tests during an 18-week semester. If we drop the lowest of these tests, we are basically saying that some objectives need not be met. We may end up saying that Bill does not need to know about the Civil War and Jane does not need to know about the Constitutional Convention. It would seem to make more sense to allow students to take a make-up test on the material.

Separation

I have known a number of teachers who look for gaps in class score distributions. A biology teacher friend of mine showed me his class grades. At the top of the class were the following averages:

99	92	85
98	91	<u>84</u>
<u>98</u>	90	
	<u>90</u>	

He gave the top grades an A+, the next group A's, the next group B+, etc. The only justification for this process is eliminating arguments. The student who got a 92 was 6 points away from the lowest student who got an A+. This will eliminate a problem like my student who missed the cut-off point by 0.8 of a point.

▨ TALKING ABOUT GRADES WITH STUDENTS AND PARENTS

One of the most unpleasant tasks of being a teacher is conveying bad news to students and parents about performance on tests or other assessments. After 25 years of being a teacher, this task is still difficult for me, as you can see by my opening example. Here are a few simple guidelines that may make the process easier.

Guidelines

Getting Students Used to Your Grading Techniques and Policies   At the beginning of a school year, take a few minutes of your time to explain to students, even kindergarten students, what your grades mean. If you explain that an A is a special grade, they may come to view a B as very positive feedback.

If you are new to a school, find out what kind of grading policies the teachers who taught your students last year used. I saw an example of this when a student teacher graded quizzes using a point system rather than a percentage system. She handed back her first set of quizzes with grades of mostly 8's, 9's, and 10's, when students were used to 80's, 90's, and 100's. Some students thought they had failed miserably because they were expecting percentages rather than points!

Being Positive   Emphasize what students get right, not what they get wrong. A grade of +8/10 is better than −2/10.

Respecting Privacy When Returning Tests to Students   Students now have legal rights to expect their grades will be confidential. When I was in elementary school, teachers commonly returned tests in the order of the grades, from highest to lowest. Such a procedure could get you in legal trouble now. Even large grades that can be seen by other students could be considered a violation of students' rights to privacy. Having students fold papers in half and write their names on the outside is a good idea, so that when you return tests, students' grades cannot be seen by others. Students naturally seem to want to know how they compared to classmates and friends, but discourage such behavior in your classroom: Students who do well may put pressure on their peers to reveal less than satisfactory grades.

Acknowledging excellence is still permitted in the classroom. If students give you permission to post their tests, essays, or drawings so that other students can learn what an excellent piece of work looks like, you can put up exemplary work publicly. Even in this case I would cover myself by having parents give me permission to do so in a blanket form early in the year.

Returning Failing Work   Even at the college level I do not return failing work without giving students an opportunity to discuss their work with me. At my university, tests are graded by computer and the results are immediately e-mailed to students with an answer key. For students who get D's or F's, I send another e-mail immediately; I remind them of my office hours and suggest they come by to discuss the test with me.

Things are different in the elementary and secondary classroom. You cannot give back all passing students' work and then have a conference with those who failed. Quickly, all the students in the class will learn what this means. If you are going to give back failing work to students, it is a good idea to discuss the student's work with him privately before you give back the tests to everyone else. (Give the actual test back to the failing students at the same time, so other students do not notice that the students with failing work did not get their tests back with the rest.) Show the failing students their papers and talk to them about what they could do better. Confer with a few other students at the same time about other issues, so that you do not single these students out.

Dealing with Angry Parents   Very little good can come out of a conference with a parent who is angry about the grades his or her child has received. Extending such a conference by arguing your side may have the effect of escalating the confrontation. I would suggest the following strategy.

Listen to the parent's position. If there is some validity to it, do not make a hasty decision. Tell the parent you will get back to her in a day or two. If you do not think the parent's position has merit, state your reasons for the grade. In both cases try to end the conversation at this point. Here are some specific suggestions.

If the parent talks about the child's ability ("I don't know how you can give Alice a C. She's never made below an A− on any written homework before."), you can agree with the parent about Alice's ability, but you need to return the conversation to the test or other assessment at hand. Maybe Alice did not understand the assignment or maybe this time she did not try very hard. Past performance is really an irrelevant issue, and most often when I have been involved in such situations, the parent's assertions turn out to be much exaggerated.

If the parents use loaded terms like *unfair*, ask them to specify how the test was unfair. Try not to get angry, or at least do not show that you are.

If you decide the parent's position has no merit, you may want to briefly turn the conversation to how assessments can be improved in the future. ("Well, I asked for a full-page essay with attention to spelling and punctuation, and the answer Fred turned in was just five lines long and had many mistakes in it. Maybe this would have been acceptable for third grade, but now I have a higher standard. If you would like, I could give you some practice questions he can do at home, and you can help him with it.") But do not get into an argument with the parent.

If the parent is still angry, offer to schedule a meeting with your school administrator to discuss the problem. A third party will likely help calm the situation.

Try to avoid blaming the student. Do not spring new problems you are having with the child on the parent at this time. ("Bill's been something of a discipline problem over the past few weeks. Is there anything going on at home I should know about?") If you suggest a problem at home, an angry parent may take out his or her anger on the child after the conference is over.

Questions for Reflection

1. Many teachers today establish a classroom newsletter as a way of keeping up good communications between the teacher and parents. For the grade level you expect to teach, write a statement of your grading philosophy that you might include in a first issue of your newsletter. Try to avoid using technical terms like *norm-referenced* or *alphanumeric*. If possible, have someone critique your statement, but not a fellow education student; a teacher or a parent would be better.

2. Three students, Abby, Betty, and Cindy are doing poorly in your reading group. They are a year behind grade level. They are not doing well in spelling or punctuation, either. Abby does all of her work, and you can see that she is making progress. Betty only occasionally does her homework and seems not to be trying very hard. Another teacher suggested that her parents are separating. Cindy is the class clown, and she seems to get a lot of attention by her misbehavior and her poor work. Write descriptive comments home to parents reflecting each child's achievement, attitude, and a plan of action. Be brief—you have 21 more comments to write later.

3. You have just received a note from Bill's parents. He is making mostly A's in your class, but he got a B+ in geography and a B− in spelling. He works very hard. Bill's parents indicated that they hope that he will be accepted into a very good prep school in two years, and eventually get into an Ivy League college. They are disappointed by his B+ and B− and want to have a conference. You review your grades, and you are quite convinced these are the grades he deserves. As you prepare for this conference, what three or four points would you like to stress with Bill's parents?

15

Accommodations for Exceptional Individuals

$\mathcal{M}$y first teaching job was eighth-grade biology. My students were very attentive, and I hope only a few of them noticed I was just a day or two ahead of them. I had one boy who troubled me. Nicky always came to class, always answered questions, and always turned in his tests completely blank. In the teachers' lounge I found he did the same thing in all of his other classes. After the second or third test, I began asking him to come to my classroom during his free period. I asked him the test questions orally, and usually he made an A or B. When I asked him why he did not take the test, he simply said, "I can't read it."

At that time the idea of a learning disability was just becoming known in schools. I asked the school psychologist to test him. After interviewing him the psychologist concluded he was a bright young man, but he seemed unable to read at all.

One day in class I was writing a formula on the board in scientific notation, and I asked the students what a Σ meant. Nicky raised his hand and told me its name in Greek. None of the other students knew the answer, and I asked him how he knew that.

"I'm Greek," he said. "That's my alphabet."

Nicky was the son of an American serviceman and a Greek mother. He had grown up in Athens and gone to Greek-language schools. He also spoke English with a perfect American accent. But he had never been taught to read English. After three months of tutoring, he was reading almost as well as any other student in the class.

✻ ACCOMMODATING STUDENTS' NEEDS

More than one in twenty students nationwide has been identified by schools as having a learning difficulty. We will discuss the classifications of these difficulties in a later Chapter and how certain standardized tests are used in diagnosing these problems. The most common difficulties regular classroom teachers will encounter are learning disabilities. A **learning disability** is *a serious lag in one or more verbal skills in a student of normal overall ability.* Other students in regular classrooms may have learning problems brought about by their home environment. Other children will have serious attention problems.

Federal and state laws require that many of these children be given accommodations in assessment procedures. On an individual basis you may be required to test these children somewhat differently than you test the other children in your class.

Sometimes teachers are upset by having to accommodate these students. They think it isn't fair to treat some children differently from others. When this issue comes up in my assessment classes, I give four reasons for this treatment:

1. Isn't allowing children with visual problems to wear glasses during a test giving them an unfair advantage? Glasses, hearing aids, and crutches are examples of accommodations for children's disabilities that we never question.

2. Maybe what you accommodate is an unnecessary part of testing. Why are most classroom tests timed when we do not include speed in our objectives? I have never had a student write an objective like, "Students will be able to compute two-digit by two-digit multiplication problems really fast." Most school tests are timed, and allowing children with learning disabilities extra time because of their slow reading ability is the most common accommodation.

3. I tell the story about Nicky and try to explain that he could take the tests orally and let me know what he knew about biology: It was his lack of ability to read the Roman alphabet that prevented him from taking written tests. Nicky had a cultural disability, and by accommodating him through an oral test, I could determine what he knew about biology while he was working to catch up on his ability to read English.

4. When these three appeals to reason and compassion fail, I remind my students that it is the law.

Each child who has been identified with a learning problem will be assigned to a special education teacher as well as a regular education teacher. The special education teacher and the regular classroom teacher are a team that will ideally work together to the advantage of the student. The special education teacher will be able to assist the regular classroom teacher in making accommodations and will likely be available to administer tests if the accommodation would be disruptive to the regular classroom.

On the other hand, it is probably a bad idea for the regular classroom teacher to send the student to the special education classroom for every assessment activity. The goal of special education is to keep students in their regular classrooms doing regular work to the greatest extent possible. Students who may need a few extra minutes to complete a test may do just as well if they stay in the classroom with their peers than if they are dismissed to go to the resource room.

▩ THE INDIVIDUAL EDUCATIONAL PLAN

Each child who has gone through the identification process for special education will have an **individual educational plan (I.E.P.),** *an individualized document that contains a year-long educational program, including a diagnosis, a set of educational objectives, a statement of the extent of special educational services, and a list of accommodations.* The I.E.P. is written by the special education teacher and the regular classroom teacher with input from the school psychologist, other professionals, and the child's parents. When the student becomes 18, he or she will participate in the writing of the I.E.P. We will now briefly examine the parts of the I.E.P. before turning to assessment accommodations.

The Diagnosis

The diagnosis will specify the skills the child is having trouble with and the extent of that trouble. If the child's problem is in the area of reading, there will usually be a detailed description of what the child can and cannot do. A fifth-grade child may have an overall reading level of a third-grade student, but his recognition vocabulary is low, and his reading speed is therefore compromised. His independent reading level may be on a second-grade level. Another child may have an auditory processing problem resulting in frequent errors in translating what he hears into correct spelling. That child may read only a year behind grade level, but his spelling may be four years behind grade level and his writing skills likewise impaired. A fifth-grade student with a mathematics disability may still be working on addition and subtraction and even there have difficulty translating word problems into correct solutions. The diagnosis is based on the results of standardized tests and the careful descriptions of his strengths and weaknesses by his teachers.

Learning Objectives

A major portion of an I.E.P. will be a statement of the educational expectations for the child for a year. In areas where the child can work, the objective may be that he or she will do the same work as other children with some instructional accommodations. A child with a mathematics disability may be able to do social studies and language arts with the rest of the class without accommodation and science with minor accommodations, but not be able to do the same mathematics curriculum as the other children in her class.

In the area of disability the objectives are more detailed. They are rarely at the level of daily instructional objectives, but they are measurable objectives not general goals. They may specify a dozen or so outcomes, even including the instructional materials. Table 15.1 contains some of the objectives from an I.E.P. of a sixth-grade student with a reading disability.

TABLE 15.1 READING OBJECTIVES FROM THE I.E.P. OF A
SIXTH-GRADE STUDENT WITH A READING DISABILITY

1. Will use level 3A SRA materials to develop word recognition, with special attention to consonant blends.

2. Will use a third-grade basal reading series to develop oral reading skills; will spend 180 minutes per week in a resource room.

3. Will develop writing skills using a word processor and spell checker. All writing will be done on the computer.

The teacher of the classroom to which this student is assigned will need to accommodate these instructional activities. Even if the teacher has a different philosophy of education (for example, if she is opposed to the use of basal readers or she usually has students write on paper), her philosophy for this student is superseded by the I.E.P.

Level of Services

In this section of the I.E.P., the amount of time the child will spend in the special education classroom and the regular classroom will be specified, as well as areas he will cover in each venue. In some school districts, children will spend part of the day in regular classrooms and part of the day in a special education classroom. Most often, the child will go to the special education classroom for remedial education in skill areas such as reading, writing, and mathematics. The child will remain in a regular education classroom for content classes such as social studies, science, health, literature, music, etc. In this model, **mainstreaming,** *the child spends as much time in the regular classroom as possible but goes to a special education classroom for skill training.* A more recent practice, **inclusion,** has *the child remain in the regular classroom and when skills are being developed, the special education teacher comes to his classroom.* Whichever approach is used there will be some accommodations listed in the I.E.P. Some accommodations will deal with the way the child is taught; others will deal with the way he or she is assessed.

Children with more serious disabilities, such as emotional disturbance and mental retardation, may spend most of their time in a special education classroom and also be assigned to time in regular classrooms for the so-called minor subjects, such as art, music, and physical education.

The accommodations listed in an I.E.P. will include accommodations in instruction, as well as assessment. Some of these accommodations are obvious: A child with a hearing or vision problem may need to be seated near the front of the room or near the teacher, and the teacher may need to adjust his or her teaching style. A teacher who wanders around the classroom may have to spend more time in the front of the class if she has a hearing impaired child in her class. Many teachers today group children in clusters where children face each other in small groups, rather than use rows of desks. Problems can occur for children with hearing, vision, or attention problems, and the physical arrangement of the classroom may be affected.

Some accommodations are more profound. A deaf child may have a signer assigned to her classroom. A child with a life-threatening health condition may be assigned a nurse. Some children with very serious learning disabilities may have an aide assigned to them. Sometimes teachers must find, with the help of the special education teacher, materials on the same subject matter that is being studied by other children, but written at a simpler reading level.

⌗ ASSESSMENT ACCOMMODATIONS

There are many ways in which assessment may be accommodated for children with learning problems. The most common types of accommodation are timing, location, oral administration, item types, and content. Below we discuss the nationwide and practice of such accommodations.

Timing

As just mentioned, the most common accommodation is time. A basic idea behind the laws on special education is that you cannot discriminate against a child on the basis of her disability. A child who has a disability that causes him to read slowly will need more time to take a test. If you do not give him that time, you are discriminating against him on the basis of his disability.

Usually we set a time limit on a test because of our schedule and not for an educational purpose. Particularly with test items that assess Application, Analysis, Synthesis, and Evaluation, timed assessments may not be good for all students. For students with learning disabilities, even tests primarily devoted to Knowledge and Comprehension objects will also need to be given in an untimed format.

Location

Occasionally I have seen I.E.P.s that specify children will take tests in the resource room, sometimes because the classroom is too distracting, sometimes because the test in the classroom is too stressful. Regular classroom teachers need to discuss the parameters of tests with their special education counterparts to insure that the same objectives are being measured in the resource room as they are in the regular classroom.

Oral Administration

Children whose reading or writing level is well below the demands of a test are often allowed to take a test orally. These are not tests of reading or writing, but tests where reading and writing are used to assess a student's content knowledge. Sometimes teachers resist such practices, but we must return again to the objectives. If I am trying to decide whether students know the events leading up to the Second Continental Congress, the rules of soccer, or what time is expressed by different configurations of big and small hands on an analog clock, written responses to written questions or oral responses to oral questions will do equally well. We normally assess these competencies by written tests because they are convenient: We can test a whole class in one short time period. An oral test will do just as well.

Some types of traditional tests, like a 10-item matching test, do not translate well into oral administration. How would one translate the test in Table 15.2 into an oral examination?

For a student with a learning disability, beginning with Mercury and then asking each of the 10 possibilities would overtax his memory, even if, after the first question was asked, the options were eliminated. The regular classroom teacher and the special education teacher should meet and try to transform this written test into an oral test. (See Table 15.3.) Classroom teachers often give their classroom tests to the special education teacher and then complain that the special education teacher made the test too easy. The relation between the regular classroom teacher and the special education teacher is supposed to be one of collaboration. If regular classroom teachers treat special education teachers as aides rather than as colleagues, they should not complain if the special education teacher acts independently.

Item Types

Sometimes, specific disabilities make particular kinds of items difficult. For example, students who have reading disabilities in which they make

TABLE 15.2 A MATCHING EXAM IN ASTRONOMY

_____ 1. Mercury	**a.** the famous ringed planet	
_____ 2. Venus	**b.** one of many small objects in a belt	
_____ 3. Earth	**c.** half of this planet is the hottest in the solar system	
_____ 4. Neptune	**d.** about the same size as the Earth, but hotter	
_____ 5. Pluto	**e.** has a moon named Miranda	
_____ 6. Mars	**f.** the red planet	
_____ 7. Asteroids	**g.** the "third rock from the sun"	
_____ 8. Jupiter	**h.** named after the Roman god of the ocean	
_____ 9. Saturn	**i.** the biggest planet	
_____ 10. Uranus	**j.** the coldest planet	

Answers: c, d, g, h, j, f, b, i, a, e

TABLE 15.3   EXAMPLES OF ORAL QUESTIONS ON A PLANET QUIZ

1. Is Mercury the _____ hottest planet, _____ the largest planet, or _____ the red planet?

2. Two of these are correct. Jupiter is the _____ largest planet, _____ the hottest planet, _____ has a rotational day of about 10 hours, _____ has a moon named Cupid.

3. Which is the planet that is farthest from the sun which we can see with the naked eye? _____ .

---

frequent letter reversals (e.g., reading the word dog as god) have difficulty with multiple-choice items. These students' I.E.P.s may specifically preclude the use of multiple-choice tests. Other students who are slow readers because of memory problems may have problems with multi-fact true-false questions, such as "The Colonists in Massachusetts reacted against the Intolerable Acts by disguising themselves as Indians and throwing tea into Boston Harbor in 1774." Most of this statement is correct, except it was the Tea Tax, not the Intolerable Acts.

Content

Finally, a student's disability may make it impossible for him or her to answer questions on tests or other kinds of assessments. A student with a mathematics disability may not be able to use higher math in answering a question. If a fifth-grade student is still working on addition and subtraction in a unit on weather, you may not be able to ask, "What percentage of the days during the last two months has it rained?" That question requires division skills. The student may be required only to list the number of days on which it rained and the number on which it did not. Collaboration between the regular classroom teacher and the special education teacher will help to resolve these issues.

▨ ACCOMMODATIONS IN PERFORMANCE-BASED ASSESSMENTS

In the next section of this book we discuss authentic or performance-based assessment. Many students with disabilities will also have difficulties with these assessments. Students with certain emotional problems or speech problems may have profound difficulty making oral reports. Children who have difficulty with sequencing will have difficulty producing books or series of drawings, and students with writing disabilities will have difficulty keeping journals. All of the considerations mentioned in this chapter apply to nontraditional forms of assessment as well.

Questions for Reflection

1. Suppose after a test, one of your students raises his hand and says, "I don't think it's fair. Why can't we have extra time on the test like the mental kids?" Your two students with learning disabilities are in the classroom and hear this. How would you respond to (a) his criticism and (b) his language? Write notes home to both the parents of the children with learning disabilities and the child who asked the question.
2. Take one of the quizzes you prepared for an earlier chapter and accommodate it for oral administration.

PART III

■

Performance-Based Assessment

$\mathcal{I}$n the following nine chapters we consider performance-based assessment. I have deliberately used the term *performance-based*, rather than *authentic* or *nontraditional* for a number of reasons. Although I described the last section as traditional teacher-made tests because it conveyed the meaning of paper-and-pencil assessments made by teachers over the past 100 years, the assessment techniques described in this section are not nontraditional. Portfolios are the traditional method of assessing art, writing, and music students. Oral reports are the traditional method of assessing students in speech classes. Projects have been a component of education since the Progressive Era; cooperative group work was the hallmark of the 19th-century one-room schoolhouse.

I would like to reserve the term **authentic** to mean *a process by which we measure the objectives in a way that matches the objectives*. If we want students to be able to make oral reports, we should let the students make oral reports, not take a multiple-choice test about the components of a speech. If we want students to conduct and write up a science experiment, the authentic way of assessing the goal is to evaluate their lab techniques and their abilities to write a scientific report. If we want students to demonstrate their grasp of content through any media, we can assess drawings, performances, or essays. Yet, some objectives can be authentically assessed by a paper-and-pencil test. If we want students to learn the periodic chart, solve simultaneous algebraic equations, or learn a set of spelling words, the traditional classroom test is perhaps still the best way of assessing these objectives.

The various activities in this section are based on students' performances: writing essays and other written products, keeping journals of various types, undertaking projects, participating in group work, producing art, and so on. It is therefore best to call this section performance-based assessment.

We begin this section with an overview of the rubric, which is a scheme for assessing all performances (including traditional tests). We develop short examples of how we might use different rubrics to measure different performances. Then in two chapters, one on assessing content and one on assessing writing skills, we examine more closely various aspects of evaluating writing. Chapter 19 is devoted to journals; Chapter 20 looks at the assessment of projects. Chapter 21 focuses on oral reports. Chapter 22 examines the complex issues involved in assessing products produced by group effort and the evaluation of group process. Chapter 23 examines an assessment approach—the portfolio as a way of combining a variety of performances and assessing them. Chapter 24 combines the ideas in this section with the ideas developed in the previous sections to develop a comprehensive, integrated approach to classroom assessment.

CHAPTER

16
Rubrics

*I*f you pick up the recent literature on assessment, one word you will encounter again and again is **rubric,** *a system for assessing a complex response by a student.* Rubrics may be checklists or descriptions of behavior. They may translate into points or letter grades or other categories—or they may not. As you read about them rubrics may seem to be new and fairly mysterious. They are neither. What is new is that teachers are expected to know how to develop them and use them.

Part of the recent emphasis on rubrics comes from the renewed emphasis on complex instructional and assessment tasks. As we described in Chapter 2, during the 1920s and 1930s there was an emphasis on projects and research in education, but during that time there was very little emphasis on assessment. From the 1940s into the 1970s, education seemed primarily interested in factual assessment. But for the last 20 years we have become interested again in complex tasks, such as research, speeches, and projects, and there has been a strong emphasis on assessing these tasks. During this time we have also become focused on group work and writing. These tasks are not easily measured by objective test items; rubrics assess these skills directly.

▓ RUBRICS IN TRADITIONAL TESTING

Rubrics are used in traditional testing, although they are only rarely specified. A teacher might give a short test, which consists of 10 matching items, 10 fill-in-the blanks items, 10 true-false items, and two essay questions, to a middle school class. In a basic rubric the teacher may decide the matching and fill-in-the-blanks items count 3 points each, the true-false items count 2 points each, and the essay questions count 10 points each. If students answer objective items correctly, they get the full number of points.

As the teacher grades the test, she may encounter items she considers partially correct in the fill-in-the-blanks section of the test. She may give one point for the answer "Honest Abe" on the question, "Who was the president of the United States during the Civil War?" Teachers may also decide to subtract a point for misspelled answers.

Honest Abe	1 point
Linken	2 points
Lincoln	3 points

This is an elementary rubric. She will need to develop a more complex rubric for the essay items.

Essay Test Items

Most teachers grade short-answer and essay items on tests without a formal rubric. Although this may be acceptable for experienced teachers, particularly on small tests or formative evaluations, new teachers should use formal rubrics. It is highly recommended that all teachers do so on important, summative tests. The use of rubrics makes the scoring of essay items more reliable. (The teacher is more likely to give the same scores to similar answers from different students.) Developing a rubric helps the teacher decide what to look for in an essay item, and by using a rubric, the teacher is better able to explain a grade to a student or parent.

Suppose that a fifth-grade teacher gave the following question on a test: "In an organized paragraph, describe the causes of the American Civil War. Include specific details. Use good spelling, punctuation, and grammar." She expected students to mention three things emphasized in the unit: slavery, states' rights, and the election of Abraham Lincoln. She conveyed her expectation that the essay would be grammatical and follow paragraph form, and be spelled and punctuated correctly. Suppose a student turned in the following essay:

> After the elecshun of 1860, the southern state were fraid that Linken was going to polish slavery. The sourthern state believed in states rights including the rite to on slaves. So they seeded the union.

This essay has all of the content the teacher was looking for, but it is full of spelling mistakes. In fact, there are six spelling mistakes and two wrong words. It also ends with a sentence fragment. Often teachers who do not use rubrics use **negative scoring,** *a procedure that begins with the assumption that everything is okay, but when mistakes are encountered, points are deducted.* If the teacher began with the idea there would be one point off for each misspelling and grammatical mistake, then this 10-point essay would receive a 1.

This essay, however, deserves a higher grade because it contains all of the content. There is reasonable elaboration in details. (The student mentions the year of Lincoln's election, connects the issues of states' rights and slavery, and gets in the details about the Union and the South.) This response has good paragraph organization for an essay test written by a fifth-grade student.

The teacher may want to use **positive scoring** in which *points are added up as elements occur in the response.* Here the teacher may develop a rubric that looks like this:

Mention Lincoln's election	2 points
Mention states' rights	2 points
Mention slavery	2 points
Extra details	1 point each (up to 2)
Good paragraph organization	1 point
Excellent spelling	1 point

In this case the student would receive all points, except for spelling, 9. Let's apply this rubric to the following answer:

> The causes of the American Civil War were the election of Abraham Lincoln, slavery, and states' rights.

	POSSIBLE POINTS	EARNED POINTS
Mention Lincoln's election	2 points	2
Mention states' rights	2 points	2
Mention slavery	2 points	2
Extra details	1 point each (up to 2)	—
Paragraph organization	1 point	—
Spelling	1 point	1

Here the student would receive a 7. Each of the major ideas are mentioned, the spelling is good, but there are no details, and because the answer is one sentence, there is no paragraph organization.

This is not the correct rubric, but only one of a huge number of possibilities. Some teachers would want to score the essay separately for content and writing. Some would want to leave writing mechanics out of the rubric altogether. Some may want to have 1- and 2-point answers for the three major content areas, so that naming the cause warrants 1 point; explaining what it means warrants 2 points.

Often after grading a few student responses, the teacher will become dissatisfied with the initial rubric. Sometimes the rubric, in practice, is too demanding; other times the teacher may discover it is not picking up on important issues. Scoring a few student products first and then revising the rubric is a good practice, particularly for teachers who are new users of rubrics.

▥ TWO BASIC RUBRICS

There are two basic forms of rubrics, item-based rubrics and descriptive rubrics. An **item-based rubric** *often resembles a checklist, where you are looking for the presence or absence of certain elements,* as in the preceding examples. Let us imagine we are grading a written paragraph on baseball and we are looking primarily at paragraph organization. We have told students to use a thesis statement, at least three supporting statements, and a conclusion. We have told students to use vivid writing and to be careful about grammar. On an item-based rubric we would list each of those details:

0 1	A thesis sentence
0 1 2 3	Supporting evidence (up to three sentences)
0 1	Vivid writing
0 1	A concluding sentence
0 1	Conclusion and thesis are related
0 1	Correct grammar (no more than two errors)

Let us examine a slightly edited eighth-grade student's paragraph on baseball with respect to this rubric.

America's Game

> Baseball is called the American pasttime. Although based on the English game of cricket, the game of baseball is American in origin. It was developed in Cooperstown, New York during the middle of the 19th century. Baseball is one of the three most watched sports in the United States, but it is not as popular in any other country. The poet Walt Whitman said that if you want to understand the American character you need to understand baseball. I think he meant that baseball reflects the American character, which is for people to be individuals, but work together for a common goal.

I would rate the student high on each of the elements of the rubric. The paragraph is about why baseball is peculiarly American. The thesis sentence announces the theme immediately. There is ample supporting evidence. The writing is fairly vivid and grammatical. The conclusion is directly related to the thesis. The rubric produces scores from 0 to 8, and I think this response deserves an 8:

0①	A thesis sentence
0 1 2③	Supporting evidence (up to three sentences)

0①	Vivid writing
0①	A concluding sentence
0①	Conclusion and thesis are related
0①	Correct grammar

The second approach, the **descriptive rubric,** *clusters descriptions of different responses at several evaluative levels.* We might rate students' essays on baseball on the following rubric:

_____ Excellent	Clear thesis and conclusion statements which are related. Evidence provided that supports the thesis. The writing is vivid and grammatical.
_____ Good	The thesis is clearly stated and supported by evidence, but the logic wanders. Writing is fundamentally correct and interesting.
_____ Needs Work	No thesis, which leads to a disorganized paragraph. Some errors in grammar. Writing could be improved.

The essay above fits neatly into the Excellent category, but let's examine another essay from a classmate of the first writer.

why I like baseball

> I like baseball because I'm good at it. my teem usually wins. my batting average is .308 and I've stolen second base five times this year. I need to work on my throwing accuracy and I've had three errors charged to me this year, although one time it wasn't my fault. Baseball is fun.

This paragraph is clearly not up to the same standards as the first one. The student has capitalization problems and makes one spelling error. There is a thesis statement of sorts, but the writer only tells us that he is good at it, then he wanders off to assess his weaknesses. The final statement is not really a conclusion—it moves from his personal interest to a general statement about fun.

If we were to apply the first rubric, we could provide the student with very good feedback: Giving him the benefit of the doubt, we could say there is a thesis statement, and there are three bits of information (his team wins; he has a good batting average; and he can steal second base), although they are not separate sentences. There is no real concluding statement, so there is no relation between the thesis and conclusion. There are too many grammatical errors and little vivid writing. I'd probably give him a 4:

0①	A thesis sentence
0 1 2③	Supporting evidence (up to three sentences)

⓪1   Vivid writing
⓪1   A concluding sentence
⓪1   Conclusion and thesis are related
⓪1   Correct grammar

This student is not excellent, and because his thesis statement is weak, he might be given a Needs Work. Others might give this response a Good, if we accept "I like baseball because I'm good at it," as a thesis statement.

I prefer the item-based rubric format in this situation, and I generally favor it for written work. For oral reports, assessment of group participation, projects, and the evaluation of a group of a student's work in a portfolio, I favor the descriptive approach. This is a personal opinion, and others will disagree with it.

Translating Rubrics into Grades

There is one important thing to note: When we use rubrics like this, we should not necessarily think in terms of percentages. A student who gets 4 out of a possible 8 points on a rubric does not get 50 percent. We will translate points into grades or categories through a different process than dividing earned points by possible points using a rational process. We are interested here in the basic structure of a paragraph. What constitutes a minimum basic structure? I think if a student has a thesis and a conclusion, the thesis and the conclusion are related; and if there are at least two supporting statements, then she should get a good rating. Therefore 5 = Good or maybe even 5 = B, if we are giving letter grades. We also want to think about what is an unacceptable score. These were paragraphs written by eighth-grade students, and a score of 2 or less may be unacceptable because a score of 2 or less implies very little in the way of organization, which is what the exercise was designed to show.

A rubric can translate directly into a point system. For example, the points on an essay question on a test should produce a set of numbers that can be directly combined with multiple-choice and short-answer questions to produce a final grade.

Table 16.1 shows possible ways we may translate these scores on the rubric into categories, grades, and actions. Some teachers will like letter grades at this grade level; others will prefer to assign evaluative categories. The actions deal with public recognition of excellence by posting grades on the class bulletin board, or allowing, suggesting, or requiring rewriting. An item-based rubric provides students with specific feedback about rewriting their paragraph, which a descriptive rubric does not. When revision is not possible (students may not be able to redo projects, give oral presentations again, or work in groups on the same material again), descriptive feedback works as well.

TABLE 16.1   POSSIBLE TRANSLATION OF SCORES ON A PARAGRAPH
RUBRIC INTO GRADES, CATEGORIES, AND ACTIONS

SCORE	GRADE	CATEGORY	ACTION
8	A+	Excellent	Post the essay on the bulletin board.
7	A	Excellent	Post the essay on the bulletin board.
6	B+	Good	Allow the student to rewrite (optional).
5	B	Good	Suggest the student rewrite (optional).
4	C+	Fair	Require a rewrite.
3	C	Fair	Require a rewrite.
2	U	Needs improvement	Require a rewrite.
1	U	Needs improvement	Require a rewrite.
0	U	Needs improvement	Require a rewrite.

▦ RUBRICS AND PERFORMANCE ASSESSMENT

I hope I have suggested that there is a rubric behind traditional paper-and-pencil tests, and a teacher's assessment techniques can be made clearer if he or she uses a rubric when assessing written work. This section deals with performance assessment, which in addition to writing includes journals, oral reports, drawings, assessment of how well a student works in a group, projects, science experiments, student-authored plays, and composition of songs. Until very recently many teachers either evaluated these activities very subjectively or tended to ignore them in the assessment process. I have observed many teachers who included interesting culminating activities at the end of a unit but gave grades based entirely on traditional tests. In the chapters that follow we expand on the specifics of different performance assessments. The following examples are used to give you an overall feel for the process.

Journals

Journals are used for various purposes in the classroom. When I asked teachers how they assessed the journals, I received answers from "Not at all; they are the student's private business" to "The usual spelling, grammar, content" to "I develop a rubric and assess student learning."

Our assessment of journal entries depends on our objectives for them. The teachers who said they did not assess journals were mostly unable to tell me why they included them in their daily routine; they had no real objective for them. Other teachers said they read them over to see what the students were thinking. Others, whose middle school students' journal entries were made outside of class, said they just assessed whether the students did them or not.

It is probably a good idea for students to engage in writing on a daily basis. In many of the cases described above, the journals were an instructional activity, not an assessment. These teachers genuinely believed it was important for students to write without the fear of getting negative feedback. Research consistently favors practice in writing with specific feedback as the best way of improving student writing. So, if the purpose of keeping a journal is to improve writing, teachers will need to give students feedback. I also agree that if teachers encourage students to express private thoughts in their journals, the teachers must respect the students' privacy. Teachers can accomplish both objectives by occasionally asking students to share with them one or two entries from their journal, and the teacher can provide students feedback on writing style and mechanics without invading their privacy.

Sometimes journals can be part of the assessment process, as part of a long-term science project, for example. In a first-grade class I observed a few years ago, children kept a record of the weather every day for three weeks, writing complete sentences using three weather words dealing with temperature (hot, warm, cool, cold), clouds (cloudy or sunny), and precipitation (raining, snowing, sleeting, or fair). Each day the students wrote a sentence such as, "Today it is cold, cloudy, and snowing." The objectives were to learn these words and to make accurate observations. At the end of 15 days of observation, students tallied the number of each condition and drew three bar graphs. The teacher evaluated the journals by observing the spelling of the weather words during the third week, by noting if the student had made all 15 observations, and by inspecting the graphs. The rubric looked like this:

_____ Spelling	2 = all correct,	1 = 1–2 mistakes,
	0 = 3 or more mistakes	
_____ Observations	3 = all 15 days,	2 = 13–14 days,
	1 = 11–12 days,	0 = fewer than 11
_____ Graph	5 = completed (with help)	

Oral Reports

An important life-skill is to be able to stand up in front of a group of people and give a presentation. Several years ago I saw an excellent exercise for teaching sixth-grade students to make a presentation.

Each student had to present their hobby. One of the children I observed collected coins. The teacher's goal for the presentation was to have the students explain their hobbies clearly. Each child had to make a presentation of about three minutes and emphasize three facts or ideas. After each presentation the rest of the class was given a matching quiz on the three facts. The student's grade on the presentation was the average score of their classmates' grades on the three-fact quizzes, an unusual but effective approach to assessing an oral report.

The teacher also videotaped each child's presentation and reviewed the presentation with the student after looking at which facts their classmates knew and which ones they did not. The coin collector had presented the old British monetary system of pence, shillings, crowns, pounds, and guineas, and few students recalled the information. When they looked at the videotape, the student presenting said, "If I want the students to remember this, I need to say it more than once."

Group Process

We now are very committed to group work in elementary and secondary education, and if we use this in our classrooms, we need to assess how well individual students do as members of cooperative learning groups. On a basic level, we want students working in groups to show leadership, do their work on time, and be helpful to other members of the group. One way of assessing these objectives is to ask the other members of the group to rate how well their colleagues met the objectives. Table 16.2 is an example of an assessment device given to peers for such ratings. This form is a kind of rubric itself.

Now you have three ratings for each student by the other three students in their group. You can turn these into points. Your assessment rubric might look like this:

1. number of leader nominations × 2 points ——
2. number of on time ratings × 3 points ——
3. number of help ratings (a lot = 2; a little = 1) ——

Ben received three nominations as a leader (6 points), three "on-time" ratings (9 points), two "a lot" ratings (4 points), and 1 "a little" rating (1 point), for a total of 20. Clearly Ben is a leader and deserves credit as a good group leader.

TABLE 16.2 A MIDDLE SCHOOL PEER EVALUATION INSTRUMENT

1. Who was the leader of your group? _____ *Ben* _____

2. Check which people did their part of the project on time. (Put a check on the small line and the students' names on the longer line.)

√ ___ *Ben* ___	___ *Latonda* ___	√ ___ *Susan* ___

3. How much did each person help you on this project?

Ben	*Latonda*	*Susan*
√ a lot	___ a lot	___ a lot
___ a little	___ a little	√ a little
___ none	√ none	___ none

Susan received no nominations as a leader (0 points), three "on-time" ratings (9 points), and three "a little" ratings (3 points), for a total of 12. Again, don't think of this as 12 points of our 21 or 57 percent. Think about what the total means in terms of behavior: Susan gets her work in on time and she is somewhat helpful to everyone; she is a good group member but not a leader. Maybe on another task she would be a leader.

Alex got no nominations as a leader (0 points), only one of his three colleagues rated him as getting his work in on time (1 point), one student rated him as being helpful "a lot" (2 points), and two rated him as "not helpful" (0 points). A total of only 3 points is a cause for concern. Maybe he lacks group skills, which you can teach him. Maybe he is shy. Maybe he is rejected for some reason. This is useful information for a teacher to have, but including these ratings as part of a grade is a judgment call on the part of the teacher. Chapter 22 discusses such issues in greater detail.

Drawings for Content

The psychologist Howard Gardner's (1982) theory, Multiple Intelligences, is very popular with teachers now. Gardner argues that children have different strengths in their modes of thinking: Some students think verbally, the measurement of achievement on traditional tests. But Gardner suggests that other children think better through other modalities, such as drawing, music, or dance, and we should let students use those modalities to tell us what they know.

I have some misgivings about the implementation of this suggestion in some classrooms, although it is an intriguing idea. My misgivings fall into three categories. First, if we are trying to teach students to write, then we have to have students write. Learning to write well takes many hundreds of hours of practice. Excusing poor writers from writing experiences will make them fall further behind. This criticism means that we have to be sure of our objectives. If we are assessing for content, then alternative means of assessment are warranted. When we are primarily teaching and assessing writing skills, allowing students to use nonwritten media seems to miss the point.

Second, many teachers think Gardner is suggesting using other modalities for all students; but just as some students are weak in writing and reading, some are weak in dance, music, and drawing. Requiring different modalities is sure to give all students a failure experience. Gardner's idea is choice, not requiring different modalities. Third, I have some reservations about grading activities such as drawing for academic content.

Given these reservations, let us think briefly about how a drawing might be used to demonstrate student learning. We have just completed a unit on banking in which we want students to understand the following: (1) Banks get their money from depositors to whom they pay low interest; (2) banks get their money from investors with whom they share their profits or losses; (3) banks earn money by lending money to creditors who pay them a higher interest rate; and (4) banks have expenses like rent, employee salaries, and advertising. At the end of the unit you ask students for an essay, an illustrated essay, or an annotated picture showing these four facts. One talented seventh-grade student draws a response to this question. At the far left of his drawing is a depositor entering the bank beneath the sign that indicates the current interest rate on pass-book savings is 2.99 percent. Beneath the teller is a picture of her current salary check. In the back of the bank is a loan officer lending money beneath a sign that gives the current home loan rate of 8.50 percent. Beneath the officer is his salary check. Outside are two people: the landlord of the building, who holds his rent check, and an investor, who gets his dividend check. The student had drawn the savings rate, the employee's checks, and the rent check in red, and the person getting the home loan in black, indicating credits and debits. This picture is literally worth a thousand words.

Many pictures will not demonstrate content this accurately, and if you allow students to use art to convey content, you may have to award less than excellent evaluations of them. Talk to your school's art teacher before you begin this kind of activity and ask his or her advice. In my experience art teachers are wary of using art in this way.

Portfolios

A **portfolio** is a *collection of student products used for summative evaluation.* Portfolios are a central part of the authentic assessment movement, and they are discussed in detail in Chapter 23. The portfolio is the performance assessment equivalent of the gradebook. A gradebook contains evaluations (often in numbers) or ratings on essays, tests, quizzes, projects, and so forth. The portfolio is a collection of a student's representative work. If you sit down with a student, a parent, or a committee that is thinking about putting a child into the gifted class, a series of numbers is less impressive than a set of the actual work the child has produced.

Imagine that you have decided to use a portfolio to evaluate students' performances in science. You have five overarching goals for your fourth-grade students:

1. Make careful numerical observations.
2. Describe verbally the observations you have made numerically.
3. Use different kinds of graphs (histogram, bar graphs, and pie charts) to represent data.
4. Understand electrical circuits.
5. Understand magnets.

Throughout the year you put tests, journal entries, diagrams, drawings, records of oral presentations, and worksheets relevant to these goals into folders for each child. Toward the end of the school year, you translate these goals into specific objectives. For example, Goal 3 can be specified by the three kinds of graphs you want your students to know how to produce and interpret. You now go through the portfolios looking for examples of each graph. You discover which children demonstrated which kind of graphic performance. Alternatively, you can determine your rubric beforehand, put your checklist on the outside of the portfolio, and as you put in each kind of graph, you can check it off.

▓ RUBRICS AND TEACHER EVALUATION

Here is one final thought on rubrics: How will you be evaluated as a student teacher or as a faculty member?

When I was student teaching several decades ago, my college supervisor came in three times, sat in the back of the room, and watched me teach. After she observed me we had a conference, and she shared her observations with me. After each of these conferences I decided a different career would be in order. At the end of the semester, I got an A. I had no idea where this grade came from, because all I had received from her was negative criticism.

Today, when I observe student teachers, I also observe them three times, but each time I ask them to prepare a specific lesson. I want them to give a factual lesson; I want to see them lead a class discussion; and I want them to engage students in a hands-on, group activity, such as making a book or constructing a model. I give my students the rubric I will use to evaluate them in each of these observations.

Before your college supervisor or your principal comes to observe you, it is a good idea to ask what kind of activity he or she would like to observe and what is being looked for. Here is the rubric I use in observing the class discussion:

_____ States that students should ask questions and make comments (encourages discussion).

_____ Asks questions at the appropriate developmental level.

_____ Takes opportunity to restate previous learning.

_____ Is aware of all student behavior (are all on task?).

_____ Asks questions of all students.

_____ Asks questions of both boys and girls.

_____ Includes students with special needs.

_____ Summarizes student ideas at strategic moments.

_____ Asks questions beyond the factual level.

_____ Asks students to make predictions.

_____ Shows good rapport with students.

_____ Maintains a lively pace.

_____ Shows a knowledge of the idea being discussed.

_____ Maintains discipline.

_____ Shows enthusiasm for the topic.

Questions for Reflection

1. Take a small bit of content in a class you may someday teach. For example, have students recall the plot of a short picture book, learn about an historical event, or learn about a scientific theory. Write a set of objectives for student learning and translate those objectives into a grading rubric. Now write directions for at least three different ways in which students could demonstrate their mastering the content of your assignment (writing, making a project, oral presentation, etc.).

2. Imagine you are the instructor in your assessment class. Devise a set of objectives for question number one; develop a rubric to measure those objectives; and then evaluate your answer to question number one by that rubric.

CHAPTER

17
Assessing Writing for Content

$\mathcal{I}$ have stressed the importance of separating process skills and content skills when assessing complex behaviors. Nowhere is this more important than in assessing writing. We use writing to assess higher-order understandings, and we want to teach students to become better writers. Trying to do both at the same time, particularly in the elementary and middle school years, is likely to overtax many students. The teacher and her students should know which one is the focus of any particular activity. Ideally, the two processes will come together, but they do not have to come together in a single act. We can encourage our students to get the information down first and then work on writing in a revision process. Even professional writers often separate the two processes.

The skills in early writing fall into three categories: mechanics (spelling, grammar, punctuation), organization (paragraph and larger), and expression (using vivid words, imagery, varying sentence structure, etc.). Later, we will include a fourth process skill, documentation, which includes compiling bibliographies and citing work from library research. Assessing these skills is the topic of the next chapter.

In this chapter we focus on assessing writing for content. Content need not just be facts (Knowledge and Comprehension objectives), but can include Applications and the higher cognitive domain objectives of Analysis, Synthesis, and Evaluation. We could also use writing to assess objectives from the Affective Domain. It might be useful to think of this chapter as using writing to assess a student's knowledge, and the next chapter as assessing writing itself. A good deal of what is in this chapter and the next has been covered in a somewhat different form in Chapter 13 on assessing essay items on tests. In that chapter we had to take into account that we were assessing products written in a stressful, timed situation, and we had to have rather modest expectations for writing skills. In this chapter and the next, we talk about formal writing not produced on tests. In the chapter that follows these, we discuss writing journals, although journals need not be about writing, as art and science teachers know.

▓ ASSESSING YOUNG STUDENTS' WRITING FOR FACTS

I hope I do not sound like a CD caught in a feedback loop, but it is worth saying again that if we know ahead of time what we will be looking for and make the assignment clear to students, it will be much easier to assess the writing than if we make a writing assignment without much care to our objectives or how we will assess it.

Consider the following essay written by a second-semester second-grade student, beginning with his summary report of his research on the countries of origin of his family.

My FeLeo is Fom. a marke I am fom. a marke .to Bot my. teh FeeLo is Fom OWeoy. I Bed ter 2es testwek. and Im geo t go ter. Bot I Get We to tor Go tere a geh I here. I got a oeoy seko. teo ise a waae to. Pelay steot tero. My DaDe was fom jeheod. I wet to I got to see a cobra saek ti was renL.

My setre get a foeier coet it is a pere Bare ti is BoLe Bet my mom weto it got oidL Be Coes ti wet to Be in the werehe I heve a fed in grateod Bet hetre 18 he L eve nen mexo bof ec isgo to vet me teos yer Botie ket wot he is my veo Bte fed. Weo het Gew to scoells to gehtr I wetd for a waeo Bot I mes my Gelle feed.

A rough translation of this essay is:

> My family is from America. I am from America, too, but my other brother is from Okinawa. My bigger sister is Taiwanese, and I'm going to go there. But I guess we took tour go there again, I hear. I got a real Seiko. There is a Walkman, too. Play stereo there. My Daddy was from Japan. I went, too. I got to see a cobra snake. It was real.
>
> My sister got a fur coat. It is a pure bear. It is beautiful. But my mom wore it got old because it went to be in the winter. I have a friend in Great Britain who's 18. He lived in Mexico before. He is going to invite to their boat 'cause which he is my very best friend. When we go to school together I went for awhile, but I miss my girlfriend.

According to some theories of language arts instruction, the teacher's main response to such writing is to accept what the student has written and encourage the open expression of ideas through the written word. In the case of this sample, there are a few problems with following this prescription, not the least of which is that the student did not answer the question he was given. The boy is the son of two American parents of German ancestry. His father was in the military, one of his brothers was born while the family was stationed in Okinawa, and his sister was born while they were stationed in Taiwan.

Should we deal with this writing as a writing exercise or the final report of a lengthy research process? This boy's writing sample suggests the assignment was far above his writing, organizational, and content abilities. The student teacher who assigned the topic had many such failures, although well over half of the class came up with papers that showed they understood the assignment. The student teacher had not thought carefully about her objectives in terms of the students' ability to meet them. She had noticed that most of the students spent time daily on computers writing journal entries, and she assumed they could produce a final report. Parents were interviewed as part of this assignment, and I suspect many of the students who produced nice, organized reports had substantial input from their parents.

The unit on family origins was embedded in two second-grade goals: to learn about differences in families and to learn to read maps. Children were asked to interview their fathers and mothers about their own families. One of the main objectives was to determine what the nationality of the father's surname and the mother's maiden name was. They were to find out whether their grandparents were all born in the United States, and if not, in what country they had been born. No questions about brothers and sisters were included in the assignment. After the papers were turned in, the teacher had wanted to put the various family names on a world map and later to show where the students' grandparents had been born. The teacher knew that she should not put this boy's family in Japan. There is no information about his grandparents.

While this was the summative activity in the unit, I encouraged the student not to grade this piece of writing. If we were to grade it by a content rubric, the boy would get a zero:

Country of father's family name   0

Country of mother's family name   0

Country of birth of four grandparents   0

We can use this rubric to grade another student's essay. This was the most successful student essay in the class. (I've changed the names.)

> My familie name is Morris. My father said that this name is english. His familie is been in America a long time. Both his mother and father were bor in America. My mothers familie name is Monteleone. Monteleone means mountain lion. It is a italian name. My mothers parents were born in America to. All for of my grandparents were born in Virginia like me. We must not like inegrating.

Country of father's family name	1
Country of mother's family name	1
Country of birth of four grandparents	4

There are some mistakes (capitalization, punctuation, spelling, grammar), but this is a very good essay for a second-grade student, and it contains all of the content we wanted. The question that comes to mind is how can we get the first student's essay to more closely resemble the second's?

The teacher's solution was to develop more structured interview forms for the boy. They were written in very simple English. The mother's interview form looked like this:

Mother

Mother's family name is _____.

That name is _____.

Where was her mother born? _____.

Where was her father born? _____.

One thing about her family _____.

Before the boy went to interview his parents a second time, the teacher gave him all the words on the list as spelling words and gave him a spelling test on them. This included 14 words (mother, father, family, name, is, that, where, was, her, his, born, one, thing, about). Although her cooperating teacher was very committed to whole language and invented spelling, she agreed that these were fourteen words that would be useful to the student and necessary to complete the assignment.

She also sent a note home to the parents, describing the purpose of the assignment and what they should do in the interview:

> Kevin is finishing up a project on families. He will need to ask you about your family name, what nationality that name is, and in what country his grandparents were born.
>
> Please make sure that he spells your family names correctly. Then tell him something interesting about your family. This information should be very simple.

When Kevin returned with the two questionnaires filled out, the student teacher sat down with him and helped him write the first paragraph about his father, following the form exactly (the form was specifically designed to produce a well-organized paragraph if the information was turned into successive sentences):

My fathers family name is Becker. That name is german. My fathers mother was born in a Merica. Meo father father was born in a Merica. His father sel shoe.

She then let him write the second paragraph on his own:

My MaMe family is Layman. Tet name is grman. My MaMe MaMe was bah in a Merke. My MaMe DaDe was bah in a Merica. MaMe MaMe med bred aVr tesTe.

(My mother's family is Layman. That name is German. My mother's mother was born in America. My mother's father was born in America. Mother's mother made bread every Tuesday.)

Now we can assess this essay for content, and it meets our criteria:

Country of father's family name	1
Country of mother's family name	1
Country of birth of four grandparents	4

To get to this point required more structure on the part of the teacher, but the student was able to learn how to collect data and report it. Kevin also seems to have picked up a little spelling, but, when given free reign, he reverted back to invented spelling in many instances.

This example, I hope, underscores the necessity of separating writing skills from content, and it presents cautions about using writing to assess content in the very early grades. The most important caution is that writing assignments assessed for content in the earliest grades need to be very structured. Through second grade, most students are struggling with sentence organization. It is only in late second grade and early third grade that students will begin to put two and three sentences together in a logical fashion. Early writing tends to spring from one idea to the next, as in Kevin's original essay: My Daddy lived in Japan. I went there, too. I got to see a cobra snake there. It was real. My sister got a fur coat while she was in Japan. It was made of bear skin. It is beautiful. But my mom wore it, and it got old because it became winter.

Children begin to organize their writing through narrative rather than the formal logic of the essay (Bereiter, 1980; Perera, 1984). First-, second-, and third-grade writing would be better served by teaching students to write narratives and descriptions rather than didactic paragraphs.

▦ BOOK PUBLISHING

Making books is a useful way of helping students understand narrative and learn about books. Student-made books are a staple of language arts classrooms that use the whole language approach to reading and writing. The orthodox whole language approach is less concerned with children's learning specific skills than it is with their learning to appreciate the written word.

Many classrooms now use many of the techniques of the whole language approach without adopting the entire philosophy. When children publish a book and read it to their classmates, or put it in the book corner for others to read, many teachers will have specific cognitive goals they can assess through the student's book. One such cognitive goal is coherent narrative. Many teachers would not want to put a book in the book corner that did not exhibit most of the characteristics of coherent narrative during a unit on narrative. Students may use invented spelling in creating their books, but the teacher may gently guide students through correcting spelling before the book is published.

One teacher, working in a modified whole language classroom, introduced such a unit by reading many picture books to her fourth-grade students. While discussing these books with her students, she guided them to understand a basic structure of most books:

- Beginning

    1. The setting is described.
    2. The characters are described.
    3. A problem is introduced.

- Middle

    1. The characters try to resolve the problem.
    2. Usually the first attempt does not work.

- End

    1. A solution to the problem is found.
    2. The solution is explained or a moral is stated.

Students fabricated books with a cover and 8 or 12 pages. Students drew pictures, wrote text on computers, and then assembled their books. One child's text read as follows:

Off Limits to Suzie

1. In my house, we have a living room. We can play in every room in the house, but the living room is off limits, because there are many expensive things there.

2. My mother has her friends over to play cards in the living room. They admire all of her expensive things.
3. My father sometimes has his friends from work over for a party in the living room. They admire all of his expensive things.
4. My big sister has her boyfriend over. He admired all of my parent's expensive things, but my big sister says, "Let's go to the den."
5. The problem is my baby sister Suzie. She's only two years old. She loves all the expensive things in the living room.
6. She thinks they are her toys.
7. At first my mother said, "No, Suzie, don't play with those things. They are expensive." She said this a million times.
8. Suzie doesn't understand what expensive means.
9. Suzie thinks that "no" means, don't go in there while mother is watching.
10. Suzie sneaked in there all the time.
11. Finally mother said, "I guess we will have to put all our pretty, expensive things away until Suzie can learn not to play with them."
12. Now when mother's friends and daddy's friends come over, all they can admire is Suzie.

This is, of course, excellent work for a fourth-grade student. Particularly I like the repetitive rhythm and the humor. When we look to see which elements of narrative are there, we find that they all are. The teacher used a six-item rubric and gave 0, 1, or 2 points for each element. This story got all 12 points.

_____ The setting is described.

_____ The characters are described.

_____ A problem is introduced.

_____ The characters try to resolve the problem: usually the first attempt does not work.

_____ A solution to the problem is found.

_____ The solution is explained or a moral is stated.

Another member of the class had a less successful book (although not a failure). In fact, the teacher suspected that the second student adapted the first story.

1. Once upon a time there was a big old dog.
2. He liked to go into the living room and roll on the rug.
3. His owner told him not to go in there.
4. The dog didn't understand.
5. Sometimes they spanked him with a newspaper.
6. But when they weren't looking, he went in anyway.
7. What will we do? asked the owner.
8. They took up the rug, and then the dog didn't go in there.

The teacher provided this student with the rubric with additional comments on how he might make the book better:

_1._   The setting is described (Tell me more about what is in the living room. All I know is that there is a carpet in it. Is it an expensive rug or an old rug?)

_1._   The characters are described. (I like it when you call him a "big old dog," but you don't describe the owner at all.)

_2._   A problem is introduced. (I understand the problem, but you could make it stronger if you let me know exactly why the owner didn't want the dog to roll on the rug.)

_2._   The characters try to resolve the problem; usually the first attempt does not work. (What was the dog thinking when he was spanked with the newspaper?)

_2._   A solution to the problem is found

_0._   The solution is explained or a moral is stated. (What happened after they took up the rug? How did everyone feel, including the big old dog?)

This student received 8 out of 12 points, which might be a C or satisfactory. The narrative makes sense, but it is lacking in details about setting and characters, and it had no real ending. This rubric evaluates the narrative meaningfully to the child, and the comments give him specific direction for improving the story.

▦ ASSESSING CONTENT WITH MIDDLE SCHOOL CHILDREN

By middle school children should be able to organize paragraphs. It is one of the tasks of the middle school to help students organize longer pieces of writing. In order to do this we often break down the task into ordered components for our students. For example, in a middle school science report, we may expect organized paragraphs that (1) state the hypothesis, (2) describe the methods, (3) state the results, and (4) relate the results to the conclusion.

We are not directly considering organization in this chapter, but this scheme, if we look at it component by component, will let us focus on content. I would like to consider two student reports of a science observation write-up in fifth grade. This is not an appropriate experiment for students to do by themselves because it involves boiling water and an imploding drink can.

We know that as gasses are heated, they expand. If we filled a space with heated air and then suddenly reduced the temperature of the air, the air would contract. If we did this inside a flimsy aluminum can, we might expect the can to crumple up. We expect that, but it will come as something of a surprise to most fifth-grade students.

There are a couple of ways of introducing the idea of heated air expanding and cooled air contracting. One would be to watch demonstrations on a video tape. Another would be to use balloons. If you blow up balloons and let the air inside cool to room temperature, the circumference will get smaller (although some students will think air has escaped). Put the balloons in a refrigerator and they will get smaller still; put them in a warm oven (no more than 130 degrees) and they will get bigger.

The procedure with the aluminum can is simple: Boil water; invert an aluminum can over the boiling water to collect the steam (without scalding your hand); after two minutes plunge the can down in about two inches of iced water. (It's best if you hold the can throughout the experiment with something like canning tongs.) The can will usually crumple up. If you want to do this demonstration, I'd recommend trying both the balloon and the can demonstrations several times ahead of class. Some cans collapse better than others.

Have students write a laboratory report you have structured around four sets of questions:

1. What happens to air when it is warmed? When it is cooled? What would you expect to happen if you suddenly cooled hot air inside of an aluminum can?
2. Describe the steps involved in the demonstration.
3. Describe what happened when you put the can in the iced water.
4. Why did the can collapse?

The first question was asked before the demonstration and students were given ample time to answer the questions. The rubric that a teacher might employ is:

The student states that warmed air expands.	0	1	
The student states that cooled air contracts.	0	1	
The student makes a hypothesis (using the constructs).	0	1	2
The student explains his or her reasoning	0	1	

The first two content elements (expanding and contracting) are straightforward: The student either writes the content or does not. For the third content element we have included the possibility of 1- and 2-point answers. We want students to make a prediction, and we want that prediction to be based on the ideas we are examining. If a hypothesis is not related to the ideas of expansion and contraction, we give 1 point; if it is related to the ideas, we give it 2 points. The hypothesis is real and we do not care if the hypothesis is correct: It should merely be logically related to the first two statements. We want a statement tying the student's hypothesis to the ideas. Here are two students' responses:

Sarah: When air is heated it gets bigger, and when it gets cooled it shrinks up. If we put hot air inside a can and then cool it down, I think that the can will sweat like cool drinks do on hot days.

Jeff: Hot air expands while cool air contracts. When we cool hot air in a can nothing will happen, like when you put warm cokes into the refrigerator.

These are pretty good answers. Sarah does not use the terms *expand* and *contract*, but she gets the idea: 1 point for both parts one and two. The teacher and I gave Sarah a 1 for her hypothesis because she gets the process backward: She is describing warming, not cooling (but she's in the ballpark). We also gave her 1 point for her evidence: She's been thoughtful, just not logical. The total is a 4.

The teacher and I gave Jeff a 5. We were both a little concerned that Jeff says *hot air* expands, rather than *warming air*, but he is a fifth-grade student, and we can ignore some rough edges. We would make a correction on his paper, just as we might change Sarah's *gets bigger*, to *expands*, but he gets full credit. His hypothesis is wrong, but he used good logic: Cans do not collapse when we put them in the refrigerator. Of course, he is talking about liquids, not gasses, but this is excellent fifth-grade logic.

Now we perform the two-step demonstration: filling the can with hot air and cooling the air by putting it in the iced water. We want each of the procedures to be accompanied by a statement of what happens to the air inside. Here is our rubric, followed by the two students' responses:

Fill the can with steam.	0	1
Air is heated.	0	1
Put the can in iced water.	0	1
Air is cooled.	0	1

Sarah: First Ms. Taylor boiled some water and then turned the coke can upsidown so that the hot steam filled the can. She used a thing to hold the can so that she didn't burn herself. Then she put the can down in a pan of cold water.

Jeff: First, the can was held over boiling water to heat up the air inside the can. Mrs. Taylor held the can with a holder so that she didn't hurt herself. Then the air was colled down by putting it into a pan of water with ices in it.

Both of these descriptions are good. Both students included step one and a mention of the fact that the air was warmed. Both included putting the can in the water. Jeff included cooling, although Sarah omitted this detail. Four points for Jeff and 3 for Sarah. Both students have writing errors, but we are just considering content here. In a fifth-grade science lab report, we might correct spelling, punctuation, and grammar, but not reduce the grade for such mistakes.*

For the results we require only a statement that the can collapsed (1 point) after some time passed (1 point). Both students got 2 points here.

> *Sarah*: When Mrs. Taylor put the can in the water, it made a creaking and cracking sound, and then after about a minute, it began to crumble up.

> *Jeff*: After two minutes the can began to make a crunching noise and then it exploded back.

We would certainly want to comment on these students' word choice. Sarah needs to learn the difference between *crumble* and *crumple*, and this would be an excellent time to teach Jeff the word *implode*, although *explode back* is a good approximation.

The final and most difficult part of this report is answering the question, "Why did the can collapse?" We want the student to say that when the air was cooled, it contracted. The teacher decided this was the only content she required, but she would give an extra point if the student included additional information. Sarah wrote a minimal response:

> *Sarah:* When the can was put into the water, the air inside got colder and that made the can crumble up.

Jeff seemed to understand several other dimensions of the demonstration:

> *Jeff:* When you put the can in the water, the air inside the can cooled down and took up less space. Because the can was in the water, no air could come in to fill up the space, so that pulled on the can. The can isn't very strong, so it fell in.

The teacher on this exercise gave A's for grades of 10 or better, B+ for a 9, B for an 8, and so on. Here is the tally for these two students:

---

* I do not want to give the impression that I advocate that spelling, grammar, punctuation, organization, good choice of words, and so on only count in language arts/English classes. I believe all of these issues should be of concern in every class involving writing. I'll return to the idea of what is our primary goal of a particular exercise. Fifth-grade students in a science class should be relatively free to devote their cognitive resources to thinking about the demonstration and not worrying too much about mechanics. If students make a few errors, simply noting them may well be enough. Students with a large number of errors might be required to correct their papers in order to achieve the grade. Students should learn that writing is not a one-step process. (Too many of my college students think they can write a paper in one sitting.) Teachers might approach such a lab report as a first draft. They would provide suggestions for making the content better and make corrections about mechanics, then give a final grade on a revision.

	SARAH	JEFF
Warmed air expands.	1	1
Cooled air contracts.	1	1
Made a hypothesis.	1	2
Explained their reasoning.	1	1
Fill the can with steam.	1	1
Air is heated.	1	1
Put the can in iced water.	1	1
Air is cooled.	–	1
Crumples up.	1	1
After time passes.	1	1
Cooled air contracts.	1	1
Extra point		1
Total	10	13

Maybe Jeff deserves an A+.

Questions for Reflection

1. Here is an example from the first grade. Using the rubric above, provide the student feedback. Now create another rubric with another set of content objectives and provide the student feedback.

> All I can remember about the first grade is that I was running around the playground. I attended Preston Elementary and I had Mrs. Smith. I can remember the first day. My mom dropped me off and she paid my book fee and left. She picked me up and took me home. My days at Preston were swell. The ladies was my territory. I chased the ladies all around the playground. Micheal Jackson was the thing then. He was the man in charge. Everyone wanted to be like Mike, Not Jorndan. In the first grade I through it was going to be forever before I got out of school but now its almost here it wasn't that long of a wait after all.

2. Have the students in your class find writing samples from their school years, collect samples from younger brothers and sisters, or collect samples from classrooms in which you are observing. Comment on the writing and the age of students. (Many beginning teachers are quite unprepared for how students write at the ages they are planning to teach. If you familiarize yourselves with their general abilities, you will have better first-time experiences than the teacher of the genealogy project.)

CHAPTER

18

Assessing Writing for Writing Skills

*W*hile I was writing this chapter I was enrolled in a college-level course in Italian composition. In the two years I took Italian we translated isolated sentences, conjugated verbs, and took vocabulary tests. Suddenly, I was asked to write coherent essays on topics such as "The Pros and Cons of International Study" and "Why I Prefer the Films of Fellini to Those of Visconti." In some respects, I was facing the same problems as a middle school student summarizing his research on the French and Indian War.

I write a good deal in my professional life, and writing comes relatively easily for me. But when I tried to express myself in Italian, my train of thought was constantly interrupted by concerns about vocabulary, spelling, grammar, and correct usage of words. As I tried to avoid an unfamiliar grammatical construction or work my way around difficult vocabulary, the whole logic of my essays would collapse. I truly empathized with those teachers who advocate a whole language approach to writing. At times I closed my dictionary and just plowed through what I wanted to say, and I was more satisfied with the writing. Eventually I had to go back and make the writing accurate: One sentence I wrote roughly translated as "I needed two woods and a loaf of bread," which would be difficult for an Italian hotelier to recognize as a request for a room with two beds and a bath. Our students, too, will need to be accurate writers.

As we teach students to write, it is probably a good idea to help them separate two processes: (1) **drafting,** or **composing,** *the process of putting down a first version of a piece of writing*, and (2) **revision,** or **editing,** *the process of making corrections and improving the original draft.* During the drafting phase of writing, students should be relatively free of concerns about mechanics and organization; during the revision process students should attend to those processes particularly. Helping students separate these two

---

186

processes will eventually improve their writing ability. Helping students learn that writing is a multistep process is also important.

We have used the term *formative assessment* to mean assessments teachers use to gauge whether instruction is proceeding as planned. Halfway through a unit on long division, we may give a test to see who is getting it and who is not. There is a parallel process in writing: providing students feedback in the process of writing that will help them produce a better product. Providing students feedback on a draft is an instructional process, even though it will resemble the assessment process of evaluating a final product after revision.

▓ EXERCISES ABOUT WRITING

Perhaps during the earliest years of writing instruction, we do not want to cause students to get tripped up by worrying about spelling and grammar. We want them to learn to enjoy writing, and we want them to have the experience of putting down their words on paper in a flow of ideas. As early as third grade, we will want to encourage our students to write within the bounds of correct usage. The following material is specific to writing exercises about writing, not content.

Spelling

Whether we want a specific group of students to be accurate spellers depends a great deal on our philosophy of language arts instruction. I think spelling should not be much of a concern in the process of drafting a piece of writing for students at any age. Spelling is something that can be gone over later in editing. I have a hard time remembering how to spell words like *bureaucracy, bourgeoisie,* and *foray.* (When I spell checked each of these words, I had misspelled them! Apparently, I cannot spell words of French origin.)

When we are ready to require students to spell accurately, I like the idea of circling a misspelled word and letting students find the correct spelling on their own.

I also like the idea that if we use negative scoring (taking off points for errors in spelling, grammar, and the like) students have the opportunity to revise their writing to remove the lost points. In elementary and middle school it may be appropriate for students to be able to earn back all lost points. By high school it may be more appropriate for students to earn back only half of the points lost, to encourage them to be accurate in the first place.

Children with certain kinds of learning disabilities will have enormous problems with spelling, and classroom teachers should consult with the child's special education teacher about appropriate methods of assessing and remediating such problems.

Grammar

Teachers have the tendency to copyedit grammar problems. Just as for spelling, I think it is better for the teacher to underline the whole sentence or phrase in which the grammar problem occurs and note *gram* above it.

Grammatical errors, however, are a different sort of problem than spelling. Grammatical errors often reflect the grammar the child has learned in his home and community; spelling errors usually reflect simple mistakes related to the quirky nature of English spelling. In my community many children from lower socioeconomic families routinely use the constructions "he don't know" or "I ain't going." Teachers are caught in a bind about what to do about such usages. If we tell students they are wrong, they will be put in a conflict between school and their family. If we do not correct them, students will be penalized later in life when they apply for jobs or write college admissions essays. One helpful way out of this situation is to distinguish between written English and spoken English.

Organization

In teaching writing we devote a great deal of time to the basic structure of the expository paragraph (topic sentence, evidence, conclusion). Yet there are other kinds of writing and organization concerns that go beyond the paragraph. Students need to write in many forms and we need to tell them what those structures are.

Vivid Writing

A student in my assessment class a few years ago undertook a project on vivid writing with fifth-grade students. She wanted to develop a system that would provide students with feedback on their writing and help them write well enough to pass the state writing competency exam. I want to give you five examples of the first writing assignment: "What do you remember about your first grade?" The teacher chose this topic because she believed it would not put students at a disadvantage because they did not know the content of the essay.

> 1. My 1st grade teacher had big bean bags in the back of the room. They were fun to sit in an read all the wonderful books around the room. I also remember we had centers to do. My favorite ones were the ones with the huge headphones. We used to listen to people read their SRA books on the tapes. We had map time for $^1/_2$ of the year which made me very angry.

> 2. 1st grade was really fun and I really liked it. Mrs. Lamb was really friendly and really nice.

> 3. The first day of first grade was an exhilarating event. I was ecstatic that I was no longer in kindergarten. I was above that—I was big stuff. I felt confident about being in first grade, and staying at

school all day long. I came to my classroom and was overwhelmed with excitement. I sat down next to my best friend and we began to talk about our summer. Our teacher told us to quite down, and she introduced us to the first grade, our room, and each other. She decided we needed to sit next to a person that we didn't know. Mrs. Godwin, our teacher, split me and my best friend up. I was heartbroken when I had to sit beside a boy. I hated boys. I sat down in my chair, and looked straight ahead. The boy turned to me and said he liked my lunchbox. I told him I liked his. Then we began to talk. We were best of friends by lunch time.

4. I remember I had a mean teacher. She used to leave a kid in charge when she'd leave the room to write down names of students who were talking and it was always me. I really don't remember anything else.

5. I Don't leMmer No'thing.

Examples 1 and 4 are responses one wants in terms of vivid detail, yet they both have a wandering structure. Example 2 is an example of a student product which could be much improved by specific feedback. We all know that using the word *really* four times in one sentence does not contribute to good writing. Example 3 has both vivid detail and structure.

Example 5 provides us with a real dilemma: This was the first essay written by Evan, a student with a learning disability who was mainstreamed into the classroom during this exercise. The student's I.E.P. indicated he had short-term and long-term memory problems, so it is possible he did not remember much about his first-grade experience. The four words in his essay indicate he has significant writing problems.

It is also possible that this student has learned a strategy for getting out of difficult academic activities. Here is another situation where the teacher needs to consult with the special education teacher to develop alternative tasks and assessment methods. I want to describe in some detail what the teacher did to help this student become more comfortable with writing assignments.

The special education teacher wanted Evan to be excused from writing assignments and sent to her resource room to work on other language arts objectives. The teacher observed that one of the goals for Evan was to develop basic writing skills. Although identified as having a learning disability, Evan would have to take and pass the writing competency exam like all students. The teacher and the special education teacher eventually set the following sequence of goals for Evan:

1. Evan will write 100 words related to a topic using a computer and the word count function.
2. Evan will learn to write 100 words specifically on a topic.
3. Evan will learn to use a spell check when writing on a computer.
4. Evan will learn to spell five words on each weekly writing assignment.

5. Evan will learn to write topic sentences.
6. Evan will lean to write one simile in each writing assignment.

The first objective was written with the understanding that Evan needed to produce writing. At this stage, any 100 words would do. Here is Evan's third essay:

> THE MOON. SOMETIMES IS RED. SOMETIMES IS ROUND. SOMETIMES UP IN THE SKY SOMETIMES DON IN THE SKY. SOMETIMES WIT. SOMETIME OUTSIDE MY WINNO. SOME-TIMES BIG SOMETIMES SKNNI SOMETIMES IT NOT THER I WONER WER IT GO TO THEN MOON IN THE DARK IS SHINNY MOON IN DATIME IS NOT BRIT BUT STILL I CAN SEE IT WHEN THERS NO MOON AT NITE IT IS REAL DARK OUT AND I CANT SEE MUCH OF ANYTHING. MY DAD AND ME WENT HUNTN LAST WEEK AND WE STAYD IN MY UNCLES CABIN ALL NITE LONG AND I GOT UP IN THE MIDL OF THE NIGHT AND IT WAS PIT BLAK OUT (109 WORDS EXTRA CREDIT)

How do we assess such a response? Because our objective was only for him to write 100 words, he met the objective. And it can be noticed that he also learned to use the word count function on the computer, as he demands extra credit for his nine additional words. The use of all capital letters was a decision to eliminate one problem that Evan seemed unable to deal with also.

Evan quickly moved on to being able to write 100 words focused on the topic, but the spell check proved to be a complication, as it is for many learning disabled students who do not make the usual mistakes. For example, in the essay above the words winno (window), wer (where), and huntn (hunting), do not produce the correct word. Even as spelling was implemented Evan remained overwhelmed by spelling errors. He was beginning to work on topic sentences when the semester came to an end. The goal of writing a simile was never reached. To get a feel for how much Evan had learned during these 12 weeks, the teacher asked him to write another essay on his first-grade recollections:

> IN THE 1 GRAD WE WERE SUPPOS TO LERN TO READ BUT I DIDNT. MY TECHER WAS KIND BUT TRY AS SHE MAY AND TRY AS I MAY I COUNDLN MAKE NO SENS OF THE LETTERS. I LIKED ADDING AND MATH AND ART AND I HAD LOTS OF FRENS. I LIKED LUNCH AND AFTER LUNCH. I HATED MORNINGS WHEN WE HAD READING.

(There's a topic sentence here, which is a victory of sorts.)

Documentation

At the high school level, teachers will want to introduce the procedures of referring to research material through appropriately documented citations. Documentation is a highly complex process. (The American Psychological

Association guidelines fill a book of over 300 pages.) When introducing this component of writing, teachers should introduce a few issues at a time and realize that students will make many mistakes. Probably the best starting points are citations for direct quotations and the compilations of bibliographies. Even most high school students will have difficulty with the idea that ideas suggested by reading sources need to be documented.

▨ POETRY

Throughout the curriculum students are exposed to poetry, and many teachers will ask students to write poetry. We normally think of poetry as individualistic, creative expression, and many teachers will simply want their students to give it a shot.

English poetry attends to meter, rhyme, and imagery. Not all poetry attends to meter and rhyme. In middle and high schools teachers may want students to write metered and rhymed poetry. Most often, teachers will attend to imagery.

Here is a situation where I think the rubric should be inflated. Do we have the goals or objectives that our students will become proficient poets? Probably not. Everyone who gives it a shot should get a B. If they try rhyme or meter, they should get a B+. If they accomplish a real poem, they should get an A and get to read it to their classmates.

▨ RUBRICS INTEGRATING CONTENT AND WRITING SKILLS

Sometime during middle school—certainly by high school—we will want our students to be able to write for content and to show writing skills. Our main concern here may be to continue to separate content and writing mechanics in our assessment process. In the past teachers have practiced negative scoring, which, unless contained, allows a good content answer to be overwhelmed by technical mistakes. When I took freshman composition in the 1960s, there was a common grading policy, called a fatal error. The idea was that if certain grammatical errors occurred (for example, the split infinitive, such as "to really understand"), the faculty member stopped grading and gave the essay an F. Three spelling errors were also considered a fatal error. Many students in my class never got the ideas in their essays addressed because of these problems.

If we can keep content and skills separate we will serve our students better. Creating a rubric where writing skills do not overwhelm content is useful. If we assign a term paper to our eleventh-grade English class, we might want 20 percent of the final grade to be mechanics and 80 percent to be content. Grading procedures that allow content to be erased by mistakes, although easy to grade, do not help our students learn to think.

192 PART III Performance-Based Assessment

Questions for Reflection

1. Go back to the examples in the previous chapter and develop a second rubric to provide feedback and grades for the essays in terms of writing mechanics and structure. Compare your rubrics and grades with those of another student in your class.

2. In the grade you aim to teach assume you have students who experience many mechanical and organizational problems. Develop a time-line to remediate these problems. (Which get attention first? When do problems get noted? When do problems get graded?)

19

Journals

*C*atherine Matthews and Helen Cook (1996) describe an intriguing science activity for elementary school children on the topic of child development. Once a month a first-grade teacher had her daughter and infant granddaughter visit the classroom. The child was only 12 days old before the first visit. Before each visit the children predicted what the baby would look like, what he could do (and not do), and how much he had grown. As a class, the children made measurements that were recorded in their science journals, and then the children made individual notations (usually by pictures) of their own observations of the infant. Children also asked questions of the mother about what he ate, his clothes, trips to the doctor, and so on. Journals are an ideal tool for a science activity that spans a long period of time. At the end of the project, students can refer to their journals to find data and other entries that will help them with their final project or report.

Twenty years ago, the custom of journaling was almost unknown in elementary and secondary school classrooms. Now it is everywhere. Of the 100 teachers I interviewed before writing this text, 83 used journals regularly or daily. When I asked teachers to tell me why they had students keep journals and in which subject areas, the responses were quite varied. About half of the teachers used journals in language arts and half used them in science. Fewer than half used journals as part of assessment, and 16 teachers said they never looked at them. A dozen teachers were unable to tell me why they included them in their daily routine, except they thought it was a good idea. Some teachers thought journals were good transition activities: When students finished an assignment early, they could take out their journals and be occupied while other students completed the previous work.

Journals can be an instructional activity or a behavior management technique. Often they are touted as a way of having students become reflective learners, although that does not automatically happen. We are concerned in this chapter primarily with the use of journals as a component of assessment.

▦ WRITING JOURNALS

One of the reasons that educators have pursued the idea of journals is because many successful people report that as young people they kept diaries. Writing every day in a diary helped these people become proficient writers and reflective thinkers. When one looks at a document such as Anne Frank's diary, we can see a young person becoming a stronger and more vivid writer and a person struggling to make sense of the world around her. Although we would not expect our students to create such a moving document, we can expect our students to learn from the process of writing and reflecting.

Writing about events helps us remember those events, even if we rarely revisit our writings. The act of writing is a powerful cognitive activity that helps us remember through the act of making sense of our experiences. One sometimes wonders, however, whether a journal kept as a class requirement will have the same impact as a journal kept because one had chosen to recall and think about events.

Activity vs. Feedback vs. Assessment as Goals for Writing Journals

Although this book stresses the integration of instruction and assessment, as we think about the use of journals in the language arts classroom, we need to think about whether our primary reason for including them is one of learning, instruction, or assessment. By this I mean (1) do we believe that the act of writing will naturally create learning in our students, or (2) do we want to take the opportunity of student journal writing as raw material with which to teach students about the process of writing, or (3) are we looking for evidence of learning in a journal for assessment purposes?

Writing Journals as Activity   It is legitimate to believe writing every day is good for students. Recently I spent several years trying to become reasonably proficient in the Japanese and Italian languages. I find that keeping daily journals strengthens my ability to communicate in these languages. By writing about the events in my own life and trying to express ideas, I learn the vocabulary and grammar necessary to say the things I am likely to want to say. This is a useful supplement to learning to write about topics I am not interested in. (For example, "I am very honored to meet the vice president of your company," a sentence I cannot imagine ever using.) Sometimes I am merely working through some mechanical issue, and sometimes I am reflecting over my struggle with the language. Likewise, many young writers of English will find the act of writing useful.

It is clear that such an orientation to journals excludes them from assessment. A student may ask the teacher how to express a particular thought, but, in this case, the journal is a relatively private activity. Teachers who suggest such activities hope the process helps their students' self-expression, helps them build confidence in writing, and requires them to be reflective over their learning and their life. Just doing it is enough. Students can write about what they want, and they may even be encouraged to put things other than writing in their journals. Visual students may draw instead of write. When I was in middle school, I liked to make up and solve word problems and systems of simultaneous algebraic equations. Students interested in architecture may design houses and buildings. Others might develop football playbooks, write poetry, or create geometric designs.

Journals as Raw Material for Instruction (Feedback)   In a more proactive writing program, the teacher would like to see students' writing from time to time in order to give them feedback to improve their writing ability. Often these journals are more structured. I have given a number of cases in which teachers gave daily writing topics for students to write about in their journals. At times the teacher will collect journals or ask students to submit samples. The teacher will then provide feedback to the student, sometimes in terms of content, more often in terms of writing. Consider the following journal entry by a twelfth-grade student:

> I just completed reading *Paradise Lost* and I'm confused about who
> I am supposed to like. Adam and Eve seem so boring but Lucifer
> is such an intriguing person.

The teacher could respond on many levels to this entry. Milton makes Lucifer the most interesting character in the poem. The teacher could explain why that is so. The teacher could also comment on the student's problems with commas in separating independent clauses.

Journals as Pure Assessment   Other approaches use the journal as one method of assessment or even the principal assessment technique. In this case students know the whole journal will be read by the teacher. The journals are not student focused, but teacher focused. For example, if a tenth-grade literature class is reading a short story every day, some teachers may require students to make a entry about each story, and the journal will substitute for tests or essays about the material.

When Should Journals Not Be Assessed?

I think it is very important for teachers to think through the instructional and assessment uses of journals before they make journal assignments. If a journal assignment is described as private, the teacher must respect that privacy. I am not sure why a teacher would do this, however.

A few years ago a student in my student teaching seminar was working with fourth-grade students on a unit about social customs. She gave students time every day in class to write about their families. After a few weeks she collected the journals. Among the entries she found:

> Last night Uncle Benny came over to the house and he and daddy
> smoked pot and watched a video they wouldn't let me watch.

This kind of revelation by a student is extremely serious. In the state in which this was collected, the teacher was required to report such information. On reflection, the student teacher realized she had not made it clear she would be looking at the journals, a mistake she will not make again.

▦ JOURNAL RUBRICS

There is little guidance in the professional literature about assessing journals. Journaling is often seen as an activity that will automatically have a pay-off for students. In a discussion I had a few years ago with teachers who used journals, we decided there were three levels of assessment that we could apply to journals: (1) did'em assessments (did the student make entries?), (2) raw journal assessments (what can we see that students learned by looking at the journals themselves?), and (3) refined journal assessments (assessments of selected, revised journal entries).

Did'em Journal Rubrics

The rubric here is very straightforward. Did the student make all the entries? If these are in-class journal entries, you can observe whether students are working in their journals. You do not need to look at the journals if privacy is an issue. If students write journals on computers, you can look at the word counts to see whether students are adding to journals.

Raw Journal Rubrics

If you are using the journal as a way of giving feedback to students, all you really need to do is assess whether they were done. Here the main issue is for the student to produce writing on which you can comment.

Refined Journal Rubrics

If you have students select some parts of their journals for you to assess, then the usual methods of assessing writing pertain. Usually, teachers will tell the students what they are looking for, and students will select a part of their journals that closely meets those requirements and refine it to meet those objectives.

▦ MATHEMATICS JOURNALS

Always on the look out for making math more interesting and meaningful, some intrepid math educators have developed ideas for mathematics journals. Two innovative ideas involve math problem journals and math use journals.

Math Problem Journals

Math problem journals are an adjunct to the practice of giving students, usually at the middle and high school level, daily multistep/practical problems.

When we study division we usually give children problems that can be solved using division; when we study square roots, we give children problems that can be solved using the square root. Often, when children encounter real-world math problems, they don't know how to solve them. Many math educators recommend solving problems every day that require various operations, not just the ones the students are working on at that time. For example, while working on square roots, you might give students a multistep problem involving percentages and proportions such as:

> Mrs. Smith bought a new sofa for $300. It was on sale when she bought it. The price had been reduced by 25 percent. Your mother went to buy the same sofa. Now the price has been reduced by 35 percent. How much will it cost your mother?

Clearly, this problem has nothing to do with square roots. You have decided to give out these kinds of problems every day, but you do not necessarily expect students to solve them the day you give them out. If students think they have a solution, they will turn them in, but they keep a record of their attempts to solve the problem in their math problem journal. They can return to old problems or work on the day's problem. After time has passed you might collect journals and look at them to see why the students got stuck.

This journal is best managed with a looseleaf notebook where you provide pages with the problems on them on a daily basis. The front part of the journal has active problems—those the child has not yet solved; the back part of the journal has the problems the child has solved. This kind of organization allows you to do both summative assessment and diagnostic assessment conveniently. At the end of a grading period, when you collect the journals, you can see how many problems are still active. If you have given 20 problems and five are still active, the child has completed 75 percent of the problems. You can then evaluate how many of the active problems are close to a solution. This information should be useful for summative evaluation and grading. Because you know the operations required for each problem, knowing which problems are still active will tell you which kinds of problems each child has difficulty with. If you have given three problems involving division of fractions, and Brett has all three still in her active file, then you know Brett needs work on recognizing this kind of problem.

Math Use Journals

Students use math use journals to make entries about their observations of the use of mathematics in their everyday life. The primary purpose of such a journal is to sensitize children to the utility of mathematics. A student may observe that computing sales tax requires the use of decimals or that ordering carpet requires finding areas. By observing their lives and the important people around them, children can see where mathematics is useful. Such journals are also useful to teachers who want to construct real-world problems for children—you can steal their ideas. The amount of mathematics children encounter in their daily lives varies. Some children can find examples every day, but others will have difficulty.

▨ TEACHER JOURNALS

If keeping journals is good for kids, shouldn't we do it too?

I heartily recommend all teachers keep a teaching journal. I was required to keep one during my student teaching days, and I have continued the practice ever since. (Otherwise, I would not be able to remember many of the examples I have used in this book.) There are at least three reasons for keeping such journals.

1. *Keeping a record of daily activites can be useful later in understanding developing situations.* I'm going to tell you a story that came from my first year of teaching kindergarten. There was a boy in the class who was run over by an older child on a bicycle. The accident broke a dozen bones in my student, and he missed school from late September to the middle of December. When he came back to school, most of the other children had formed friendship groups, and the boy was an outsider. I made careful notes of his behavior every day after his return. One day, something happened that seemed trivial at the time but which would later develop into a serious problem. Here are my notes:

> Ricky hasn't found anyone to play with yet. Today he spent a long time in the play area. He took a purple dress out of the dress-up chest and put it on. He went to the mirror and looked at himself. He laughed for a long time. He then went and got another dress and wrapped it around his head. He went back to the mirror and laughed again.

Sometime during each of the next four days he repeated the same behavior exactly: the same two dresses and looking at himself and laughing in front of the mirror. Then his behavior got more complex:

> Today after putting on the purple dress and wrapping the white one around his head and laughing in front of the mirror, Ricky got a half dozen of the other kids to go along with his idea. They all got down on their hands and knees in a line and he stood behind them. After a few minutes they all got up and had a good laugh. Whatever this means, Ricky has figured out a way of getting into the group. The other kids now seem to accept him.

Two days later this activity took a bizarre twist, (described on page 199).

2. *Keeping a record helps you see what is going on.* In that kindergarten class, I forced myself to write about what each child did every day, just a sentence or two. I had 26 students, so it usually took 15 minutes to make my journal entries. This process led me to notice at the end of two weeks that one of the other children seemed not to talk. At the end of four weeks, I had carefully observed that she had never spoken to me, and I had never seen her talk to another child. When I asked her questions she responded by shrugging her shoulders or nodding her head. Had I not been keeping a journal, I might not have noticed this problem as quickly. In fact, I was in a team-teaching situation, and when I brought my observations to the attention of the other teacher, she was sure that Rose talked. As it turned out, she didn't. Both of her parents were deaf, and she required the services of the speech and hearing teacher to help her catch up.

3. *Records can be useful in your professional evaluation.* In the middle of Ricky's odd behavior, my supervisor made a surprise visit. After observing me teach a music lesson, the students had a free play time. Ricky immediately went over and put on the two dresses. My supervisor noticed him, and asked me whether I thought cross-dressing was a good thing to allow a boy to do. I showed her my notes and explained that somehow this had gotten him into the play group. She nodded a reluctant assent. At this point Ricky was standing behind the other children, but this time, before he had put on the dresses, he had taken off his belt. With the other children in a line in front of him, he snapped his belt over their heads. My supervisor looked at this scene in horror. After two more snaps she began to give me a stern lecture. "But the other children seem to be going along with this," I said.

She continued the lecture about gender identity and aggression, when Ricky shouted: "On, Dasher; on, Dancer; on, Prancer and Vixen. . . ."

The purple dress was as close to a Santa-red outfit as any in the dress up chest. The white dress was a beard, and the laughter in front of the mirror was practicing Santa behavior. The other children were reindeer. Without my notes, I am convinced my career as an educator would have ended that day.

Questions for Reflection

1. Write a statement showing how you might use journals in your teaching. Include attention to the objectives you have for journal use; how often you would look at them, if at all; and how you would assess them. Write this in the form of an item in your class newsletter describing journals to parents.
2. Find someone you know who keeps a journal and ask them what benefits they derive from the process.
3. Begin to keep a teaching journal today, if you have not already begun to do so. Even if you are only a sophomore or junior in a teacher education program, these notes will become valuable to you when you begin to write applications for student teaching or write essays for employment. After a week, review your journal as though you were your assessment teacher.

20

Projects

A third-grade teacher and friend of mine who knew I taught a course in assessment brought me four photographs of projects her students had made and told me the projects should spark an interesting class discussion. The projects were done at home by students as part of a required unit on Egypt under the following state standard of learning:

> Students will learn about the customs of Ancient Egypt in order to develop an understanding of cultures different from their own.

The teacher sent a note home with students giving parents the following instructions:

> I want every student to make something representing his or her knowledge of Ancient Egyptian civilization. They should make a model representing something very different in Ancient Egypt from what it is now. I want this project to be the student's idea, although you may help.

The photographs were of:

1. A Barbie doll with a hole drilled in her head, covered with Vaseline, wrapped in toilet paper, covered with tin foil, and put in a shoebox with some Egyptian symbols in crayon on the top.
2. A "pyramid" made out of balsa wood placed in a desert of salt and starch. Unfortunately, instead of a pyramid (four isosceles triangles on a square base) the student had made a tetrahedron (three equilateral triangles on a triangular base).
3. A richly detailed model of the Temple of Aswan made out of fired clay. The level of skill involved clearly indicated someone other than a nine-year-old had significantly participated in the making of the model.

4. Using a book about the Egyptian writing system, a student drew cartouches (ovals with hieroglyphs on the inside, used for writing proper names) of all the names of her fellow students.

I gave the students in my class the standards of learning and the letter from the teacher and I asked them to assess each project as outstanding, satisfactory, or unsatisfactory. Table 20.1 shows the ratings the students gave.

Interestingly, there was little agreement among the students in the class. No students rated the Barbie excellent, and no students rated the cartouche project unsatisfactory. The other two projects received at least one excellent, satisfactory, and unsatisfactory rating.

The students who rated the Barbie project unsatisfactory all indicated it looked quickly done. All of the students who gave excellent ratings to a project indicated they thought a lot of work had gone into the project. The students who gave the tetrahedron poor grades mentioned it was wrong; those who gave the temple project an unsatisfactory rating said it was clear the parent had done the project.

Then we created an assessment rubric as a class. The goal of the project was to create a model of something different in Ancient Egyptian culture from our own culture and to represent the student's knowledge of Egyptian culture. The project only had to be the student's idea, and parental help was possible. The assessment rubric was:

Did the student represent something different?

Did the student represent something from Egypt?

We decided excellent would satisfy both criteria; satisfactory would satisfy only one, and satisfying neither would be unsatisfactory. Table 20.2 shows the new ratings. No student's project was rated as unsatisfactory, and there was general agreement about the ratings: the Barbie, temple, and cartouches projects were rated outstanding; the tetrahedron was rated satisfactory. The students agreed the rubric made the ratings more consistent, but some felt the results did not measure what the project was intended to measure.

TABLE 20.1 GRADUATE STUDENT RATINGS OF FOUR THIRD-GRADE PROJECTS ON EGYPT WITHOUT A RUBRIC

	EXCELLENT	SATISFACTORY	UNSATISFACTORY
Barbie	0	3	7
Tetrahedron	1	5	4
Temple	4	2	4
Cartouches	5	5	0

TABLE 20.2 GRADUATE STUDENT RATINGS OF FOUR THIRD-GRADE PROJECTS ON EGYPT WITH A RUBRIC

	EXCELLENT	**SATISFACTORY**	**UNSATISFACTORY**
Barbie	9	1	0
Tetrahedron	2	8	0
Temple	9	1	0
Cartouches	10	0	0

I told the students the teacher evaluated the Barbie, temple, and cartouches outstanding, and the tetrahedron project satisfactory. I had made the same evaluation. One student raised her hand and said: "I guess if we wanted to give points for hard work, that should have been included in the directions, and if we wanted to take away points for too much parent involvement, that should have been part of the instructions?"

▣ GOALS OF PROJECTS

I conducted interviews with teachers before I wrote this book. The majority felt projects were part of the curriculum, in part, for students to have fun and to express their creativity. Teachers were often at a loss assessing them. The teachers who felt comfortable with assessing projects had very clear goals in mind and could translate those goals into objectives and grading rubrics before the students began work on the projects.

In the terminology of instruction **projects** are *culminating experiences, activities designed to bring together a number of strands in a unit.* As culminating activities, projects often consist of higher-order objectives, which are integrative in nature.

In a language arts unit on a writing genre, we may ask students to produce their own example of the genre in which they demonstrate their understanding of the different aspects of the form. If we have been studying fables, we might ask students to create their own fable. One teacher, after reading a number of fables by Aesop, Native Americans, and African Americans, produced the following set of objectives for grading fables in such a unit:

> The student will demonstrate her knowledge of fables by writing a story of at least one page that
> > has a title
> > has a specific setting
> > involves characters who are animals who talk
> > includes humor
> > relates the action to a moral
> > states the moral clearly

Additionally, the teacher indicated the story should be written carefully, correctly, and contain an illustration.

She translated these goals into the following 10-item assessment rubric (checklist type):

_____ It has a title.

_____ It is at least one page long.

_____ It has a setting.

_____ It has animal characters.

_____ It has dialogue.

_____ It has humor.

_____ It has a moral related to the action.

_____ It states the moral clearly.

_____ It uses correct spelling.

_____ It has an illustration.

Here is a story written by a student in her class:

Mr. Fox Picks His Battle

One day Mr. Fox was walking down a road near his home in the woods. He happened to meet his arch enemy, Mr. Bear. Mr. Bear said to him, "Get out of my way, Fox. This is my road."

Mr. Fox looked around and saw that the road was wide enougf for both of them, so he moved over and let the Bear walk straight down the road.

Mr. Fox thought that today it wasnt important for him to walk down the middle of the road and it wasn't worth a fight. His mother had taut him to pick his battles. And thats the moral of this story.

The teacher assessed the student's story this way:

_X_ It has a title.

_X_ It is at least one page long.

_X_ It has a setting.

_X_ It has animal characters.

_X_ It has dialogue.

_____ It has humor. (Make Mr. Bear funny.)

_X_ It has a moral related to the action.

_X_ The moral is stated clearly.

_____ The spelling is correct. (Four errors: Find them and correct for point.)

_X_ It has an illustration.

Although this story is not going to be anthologized, the student demonstrates a basic understanding of the fable form. Humor is lacking, and the teacher decided the four spelling errors (taut, enougf, wasnt, and thats) did not merit the correct spelling point, but she gave the student the opportunity to make these corrections. (There was an illustration not reproduced here.)

The teacher also developed an evaluation criteria for this project:

9 to 10—outstanding

8 to 9—good

6 to 7—satisfactory

<6—unsatisfactory

This student received a *good* rating on the story, and the teacher gave the student options he could use to make the story excellent.

▓ CONVEYING GOALS TO STUDENTS AND PARENTS

The teacher who shared the Egyptian project with me was the first to acknowledge she had failed to think through the purpose thoroughly before initiating the project. (This was the first time she had taught the unit.) She reflected on the projects she received and felt she could have gotten more satisfactory projects had she conveyed the projects better to the students and their parents.

In revising her goals for the project, she decided the students needed to be given more specific guidance, and the object itself could not be the entire project. The next year, she began a brainstorming session with students in which she presented the projects:

> I want you to make an object that represents some aspect of Egyptian society that is different from the same object in today's society. I want you to make a model of the object and then be able to tell the class about the object and what the object is like today. I want you to be able to tell how the object is the same as it is today, and how it is different.

She then showed the students a picture of a pyramid. "This is a pyramid. This is where the Egyptians buried their kings." She showed the students a picture of John F. Kennedy's grave in Arlington and asked the students to tell what was the same and what was different from the way Egyptians buried their pharaohs and the way we bury presidents. She did the same thing with an Egyptian comb and an everyday comb.

She sent the following note home to parents:

> We will be doing a three-week unit on Egypt. At the end of this project, each student should make a model of some Egyptian object that interests them. Students will bring that object to class and tell us about it, and tell us how it is the same and how it is different from the same object in today's society. The idea should come from the student, but you may help them in making it. The

goal of this project is to learn about the object, not to spend a great deal of time making a complicated display. In class we discussed pyramids and combs, so students should not make models of these objects.

This project will be graded primarily on what the student can tell us about the object—how it is similar and how it is different from the same object today. They should know how it was made and what it was made of. In Egypt, combs were made of animal bone. Today, most combs are made of plastic. In Egypt, only rich people could have combs. Today, everyone has combs.

The teacher gave the students the following rubric:

_____ Is the model accurate?

_____ Can the student tell what it was originally made of?

_____ How is it different from today's object?

_____ How is it the same as today's object?

The project then changed focus, from an object-making one to a research project and oral report. She felt these objectives more closely matched the state standard of learning.

▨ CREATIVITY

Although teachers are interested in projects being creative, creativity is an elusive aspect of any academic work to assess. Experts in the area of creativity recognize two fundamental features of creativity:

1. The student's ideas are relatively rare. (The ideas are different from everyone else's.)
2. The student can produce many ideas.

The first quality of creativity is called **frequency**—*a creative project would be one that is relatively infrequent.* The second quality is called **fluency**—*a creative person can come up with many different ideas.*

If a teacher gave an assignment to make a model of an Egyptian object, she might, over several years, find the following table of objects:

Pyramids	34
Mummies	22
Sphinxes	12
Crowns	11
Hieroglyphs	10
Combs	1

Selecting a comb is a much more infrequent response and, therefore, a much more creative one. (On a single project, it is impossible to determine the fluency, because we don't know whether a student had many ideas or just one. It would be far easier to assess fluency in the brainstorming sessions before the project.)

If teachers want to give credit for creativity, they must be cautious. Consider the following fable written by a fifth grader:

The Lazy Cat

One day a hungry cat was prowling around her back yeard looking for something to eat. She saw a gray mouse eating berries, and she decided to catch him and eat him for dinner.

Slowly the cat krept up on the mouse. But the mouse saw the cat coming, and he ran up a tree. The cat decided to follow him, thinking, "That mouse is fat and delicious."

The mouse ran out onto a a branch. The cat said, "Miss Mouse, you can't ecscape. I am a good tree climber."

Then the mouse ran out onto a little limb and said, "You can't come out and catch me here. You are too fat. If you come out, the branch will break."

The cat thought about what the mouse had said and then she said to herself,"That mouse is probably not good to eat, because he is so smart, he is probably old and toug."

In some respects, this is a creative fable. It has many of the elements we are looking for in demonstrating a student's understanding of fable elements. It is also a retelling of the story of "The Fox and the Grapes," but because the grapes are replaced by a mouse, the moral becomes fuzzy. Perhaps the best situation is to assess the fable for its components and to leave creativity alone.

SCIENCE FAIR PROJECTS: INSTRUCTIONAL OBJECTIVES AND BEYOND

For many years I have been a judge at regional and state science fairs. I think science fairs are great opportunities for students to learn about the scientific method, data collection, and making presentations. Select students have an opportunity to have their science talent and their creativity recognized.

Classroom teachers should realize that if they have their students compete in science fairs, the criteria will be different for an excellent science project in the classroom and a winner beyond the classroom. Part of the difference is creativity, particularly frequency. Last year, at the regional science fair I judged, there were 31 social science entries. Eight of these were about gender and memory, and six were about the Mozart effect. The gender and memory studies asked students to remember a large number of pictures on a poster; some were boys' items, such as footballs and rifles, and some were girls' items, such as dolls and dresses. Usually boys remember more boys' items, and girls remember more girls' items. The Mozart effect has students listen to different kinds of music and take a cognitive test. (Sometimes people who listen to calm music do better than those who listen to rock music or no music.)

Every one of the projects I reviewed was excellent. They showed what the teacher wants in her classroom: an understanding of the scientific method. But the projects on gender and memory and the Mozart effect were less likely to win because they were less infrequent.

The project I liked the best came from a student who was concerned about professional prediction of professional football game outcomes. He noticed the experts predicted the outcomes of NFL games at about a rate of 59 percent. He got his dog to make predictions by placing his dog between his collection of miniature helmets of NFL football teams. He put a treat under each helmet. His dog predicted the outcomes of games at a rate of 53 percent.

THE PROBLEM OF AUTHORSHIP

We use the technical term **authorship** to refer to *the problem of who did the work.* The Egyptian temple project was evidently the work of a parent. Any time students do work outside of the classroom, authorship becomes an issue. Authorship becomes an issue in group projects, as well. (See Chapter 22.)

Authorship is primarily a problem when we assess student effort and creativity. In the grading rubric we developed about the Egyptian project, we did not take into consideration the amount of work. Had we done so, then authorship would have become an issue. We may want to relax our concerns about who did the work and accept the benefit of projects in involving parents in the school lives of their children.

We also need to assess whether the idea was the student's own. If we conduct brainstorming sessions before students begin their projects, then we can know whether the projects were their ideas or their parents'.

Questions for Reflection
1. Briefly describe a unit you may teach in which you would use a project. Write a set of objectives for the project; write a set of directions; and develop an assessment rubric. Give your set of objectives to a colleague and ask him to describe a possible student project he thinks may challenge your ability to assess it (like the Barbie with the hole in her head!).
2. Suppose you assigned a project, and when the projects came in, you had one you were convinced was done almost entirely by a parent. How would you deal with this situation with the student? How would you deal with this situation with a parent? How would you deal with another student who said that his deserved C+ on his project was because his parents had not done his project like the student above?
3. Recall a project you completed in elementary school. What do you recall most about that project? Indicate whether you found the project pleasant or unpleasant. What significant learning outcomes were associated with the project, if any?

21

Oral Reports

$\mathcal{T}$he first time I remember standing up in front of a class was to give an oral book report in the seventh grade. I had struggled through Jean Valjean's bone-crunching, depressing life for weeks in *Les Misérables*, probably the first grown-up book I ever read. I had few resources to help me understand the book, let alone present it to my classmates. All I knew were the events in the novel, but I also had a kind of juvenile outrage that a man's life would be so completely undone because he had stolen a loaf of bread to feed his starving family.

I think I summarized the book, episode by episode; it was not a very good report. I remember being nervous, with a dry mouth and rubber legs. After a day or two passed, I received a B from my teacher. I suspect I got that grade because I had slogged through such a complex work, but I am convinced my report had been boring. Probably my teacher had tried oral book reports as an experiment. As I cannot remember any further oral reports until years later, I suspect the teacher decided it was a failed experiment and went back to written reports. The grade was probably a fair evaluation, but I learned nothing from it about analyzing a complex work of fiction or about making an interesting oral report.

As a college teacher I observe many of my students are poised in front of a class. Many of these students give highly organized reports full of pertinent information. Others, though comfortable, seem to be mostly free associating and not to have given much thought to their presentations. A smaller group of students read prepared papers word for word. There are some students who are noticeably uncomfortable in making reports, clutching the podium or their stack of note cards with bloodlessly white fingers. Occasionally I have students who cannot bring themselves to make the report. We need to do a better job in preparing students to make public presentations.

▨ CLASS PARTICIPATION

Before turning to the primary topic of this chapter, I want to make a few comments about class participation. This issue is a little off the topic, but it fits in this chapter better than it does elsewhere in the book, and it is an important issue.

Many school districts have evaluations of student class participation on report cards. Many secondary teachers will include class participation as part of their grading formula. What is class participation, and how do we assess it?

American education sets a high priority on student classroom participation. We want students, from kindergarten through graduate school, to answer questions posed by their teachers, to ask questions of fact, application, and higher meaning, and to make comments on the educational process. We think of education as a collaboration between teachers and learners. This is quite different from education in most other countries. In Japan, for example, beginning in middle school, students are rarely asked questions by their teachers, and never encouraged to ask questions or make comments. In Italy and Bulgaria students are asked many questions by their teachers, but are not encouraged to ask their own questions. In almost every country but the United States, teachers lecture. In the United States teachers are encouraged to discuss ideas with their students, not lecture. We describe teachers as facilitators and partners rather than authorities or presenters. We normally think teachers build on the knowledge and interests of students; in order to know what students know, think, or value, we must ask them questions. We believe learning is an active process, rather than a receptive one. We want students to participate.

We put a high value on students' participation, and sometimes we want to assess that participation, if for no other reason than we want to give students feedback about their own contribution to their educations and how they might improve it. The problem comes when we try to measure participation. All too often this occurs once or twice a semester, and it is assessed through a subjective, recollective process. We sit down with a list of our students, and we try to remember how well they participated over a lengthy period of time. There are three problems with this subjective recollection:

1. The **recency effect** *is the tendency to remember what happened over the last few days rather than over the whole assessment period.* As much as you would like to remember what Diego has been doing for the whole nine-week period, you cannot get his inattention over the last week during reading period out of your mind.

2. Critical event bias *is the tendency to remember unusual or significant events more than routine events.* On the positive side you remember the great question Gretchen asked a month ago in science. On the negative side you cannot forget Gregory's disruptive behavior early in the term that got him sent to the principal's office.

3. The **halo effect** *is the tendency to remember good things about our good students and more negative things about our bad students.* If Jamie is usually attentive and does well on his tests, we may not notice that he never asks or answers questions. If Sarah is the class clown and frequently disruptive in class, you may fail to notice that often she asks very telling questions.

These problems are not just peculiar to teachers. They seem to be part of human nature. Business managers tend to remember the last few days, too. Clinical psychologists, trying to make decisions about clients who might be released from an institution, tend to remember big flare-ups that happened months before. Coaches tend to have good opinions of their better-behaved players than their less disciplined ones. Your building principal might remember big mistakes or what you've done recently when making her evaluations of your teaching rather than your overall good work.

To make our evaluations of student participation more reliable and valid, we might use aids to memory. One aid to memory is the teaching journal described in Chapter 19. Another more formal aid would involve occasionally making specific observations about students' participation in situations where you might expect high levels of participation, such as discussions.

Table 21.1 presents a possible aid to memory. This is an eight-item checklist of questions and comments made by various students during a discussion.

Q-R Questions asked about classroom routines ("Is this going to be on the test?")

Q-F Questions about facts (Knowledge and Comprehension) ("When was the trial of Galileo?")

Q-A Questions about applications ("When do you use the mean or the median?")

Q-H Questions about higher-order objectives (Analysis, Synthesis, or Evaluation) ("Why was slavery only questioned during the 18th and 19th centuries?")

A-M Students answered questions I posed.

C-F Comments about facts ("But Galileo did recant.")

TABLE 21.1 DISCUSSION PARTICIPATION CHECKLIST

	Q-R	Q-F	Q-A	Q-H	A-M	C-F	C-A	C-H
Jon		/			///			
Marie			///					
Justin	/	//						
June								
Kareem					/	/		//

C-A   Comments about applications ("If Galileo had dropped a feather, his results would have been different.")

C-H   Comments about higher-order objectives ("I think that it's important to remember that we are talking about 1650, not today when science is much more accepted.")

This scheme is useful because it produces two kinds of information: number of participations and kinds of participation. Jon participated four times; Marie participated three times; Justin participated two times; June did not participate; Kareem participated four times. On the basis of amount of participation, we can say Jon, Marie, Justin, and Kareem are satisfactory, but June needs to work on her participation. When we look at the nature of the participation, we learn about the students. Jon likes to answer questions; Marie likes to ask application questions; Justin wants to know facts and what will be on the test; Kareem tends to be a higher-order participator. This information helps us know our students' styles of learning, and it helps us provide feedback to students about how they might become more effective contributors to class interactions.

I had deliberately collapsed the two lower levels of the cognitive domain (Knowledge and Comprehension) and the three higher-order categories (Analysis, Synthesis, and Evaluation) because this is about as detailed as we can get when we lead a discussion. If we try to distinguish whether a particular question was Analysis or Synthesis, we will not be an effective discussion leader. For beginning teachers even this simplified scheme may prove difficult. Evaluating a performance such as a speech or a discussion requires us to simplify our recording techniques. If we try to capture everything, we will fail. This is an important concept to remember as we turn our attention to oral reports.

▩ CONTENT AND ORGANIZATIONAL OBJECTIVES IN ORAL REPORTS

The material in previous chapters on essay test items (Chapter 13) and written products (Chapters 17 and 18) should be useful in developing methods of assessing the content and organizational components of an oral report. The main difference between analyzing an essay for content and organization and analyzing an oral presentation is that an oral report occurs in time and then it is gone. Unless we videotape a student presentation, it is a genuine performance rather than a product. Although it is useful for both instructional and assessment purposes to videotape occasional student oral reports, teachers will not videotape every student's oral presentation. If a teacher does not record an oral report, then he needs to develop a simple method that can capture the main aspects of the presentation. Following are a few simple and reliable suggestions for getting to the main issues in an oral report.

Content

Suppose we are in a sixth-grade history class and we are listening to students give reports on famous figures of the Italian Renaissance. We anticipate the reports will each be about four minutes long. We have told our students we want them to tell the class four things about their person:

1. What was his/her family like?
2. How did he/she learn his/her craft?
3. What was his/her main contribution?
4. Show the class one specific thing the person did.

A student makes a report on Galileo and tells us (1) he studied philosophy and mathematics at the University of Pisa; (2) he was an astronomer and mathematician; (3) he advocated the theory that the Earth revolves around the sun, for which he got into trouble with the Inquisition; and (4) he discovered that two objects fall at the same speed regardless of their weight. She tells us what the Inquisition was and describes in excellent detail the experiment of dropping two different-sized balls from the bell tower in Pisa. If we are not keeping notes or using a checklist, we might overlook the student's omission of Galileo's family. We have created a simple checklist, which renders the following results:

_____ Family
__X__ Learned craft
__X__ Contribution
__X__ Specific

When we use rubrics such as this and a student gets three out of four checks, the student has not necessarily earned a 75 percent. We are looking for four kinds of information, but we might want to build in an extra point for exceptional detail. In this case we may want to make a brief note of what was exceptional:

_____ Family
__X__ Learned craft
__X__ Contribution
__X__ Specific
__X__ Extra _very good description of Inquisition and Galileo's theory_

If all we were interested in was content, we could stop at this point. But there are other things we will need to look for in an oral report, including organization and presentation skills.

Organization

It is more difficult to assess organization in a real-time performance than it is to assess content when we have very specific content objectives. For example, we probably want students to have something equivalent to a topic sentence, but we could imagine very different beginnings of a presentation on Galileo:

> Galileo was a famous astronomer and mathematician who discovered the moons of Jupiter and sunspots.
> Galileo was born in Pisa in 1564.
> Have you ever seen a picture of the famous Leaning Tower of Pisa? Did you know that one of the most famous scientific experiments took place there?

Each of these opening approaches dictates a different organization, which will unfold in front of us over the next three and a half minutes. Unless we have dictated a specific type of organization, we will probably want to use notes rather than a checklist rubric. We will use a more subjective kind of rubric:

_____ Very well organized _____

_____ Somewhat organized _____

_____ Organization needs improvement _____

The student who began with the statement of Galileo's contributions seems on the right track, but he goes back and forth in Galileo's life and works and ends without a conclusion. Perhaps this merits a *somewhat organized*. On the other hand the student who begins with Galileo's birth goes through the events of his life chronologically. Maybe it's not a snappy presentation, but it has coherence and merits a *very well organized*. We might want to give her feedback that an attention grabber would be appropriate up front. Perhaps the boy who began with the rhetorical question and then went on to give the events of his life (but somehow forgot to mention the famous Pisa experiment) was not well organized. By putting the content into a checklist which can be checked off as the elements appear in the speech, we can devote more time to paying attention to organization, the more ephemeral aspect of the presentation.

CONTENT		ORGANIZATION	
_____	Family	_____ Excellent _____	
X	Learned craft	X Good *Return to the opening question*	
X	Contribution	_____ Needs improvement _____	
X	Specific	_____	
X	Extra *Good description of the trial*		

▓ PRESENTATION OBJECTIVES

When a student makes an oral presentation, we have moved outside of the cognitive domain when we assess her presentation skills. We are now in the psychomotor domain. In the psychomotor domain (Simpson, 1972) we have seven levels of objectives in the taxonomy.

1. Perception Students receive information that will guide their performance.

2. Set Students are ready to take part in a motor activity.

3. Guided Response Students imitate a response by someone else. We would expect many errors during this phase.

4. Mechanism We have moved beyond learning the basic skills and students are working on making the response automatic.

5. Complex Overt Response Simple, well-practiced behaviors are combined to make more complex performances.

6. Adaptation Students learn to modify their performances to meet situational demands.

7. Origination Students develop their own creative performances.

I feel safe in saying that most teachers who want students to make oral reports omit the first three levels of the taxonomy and jump into oral reports at the level of Mechanism. We rarely present models (Perception) or help students learn what skills they need to focus on (Set) or give them simple oral presentation tasks for practice (Guided Response). Inclusion of these early components will benefit students' presentation skills.

One of the problems with the first three levels of the taxonomy is the deemphasis of lecture in the American classroom: Many students have experienced few formal presentations by their teachers, and therefore have few models to follow when we ask them to make formal presentations. Because of this lack of exposure to good models, another good use of taping oral presentations is to share excellent ones with students in the future.

Guided Responses

If we want our students to give excellent speeches, we may want to begin in earnest at the level of Guided Response. This may be equivalent to working on paragraph organization before writing multiparagraph essays. If we are working over a nine-week period on a presentation on a famous figure of the Renaissance, we may begin by having students do two weeks of research on their person. During this period we show them excellent examples of oral presentations (Perception). We discuss these presentations with them (Set), pointing out what makes some more interesting than others (e.g., making eye contact with the audience, speaking in an animated way, asking questions).

At the level of a Guided Response, we may want students to stand in front of the class and repeat fairly closely a speech made by the teacher. These minispeeches are important for students to gain confidence in speaking in front of groups. We have eliminated all the issues of content and organization by providing them for the student. We are now focused entirely on presentation issues. We stand in front of the class and make the following minispeech:

> Donatello was one of the first great sculptors of the Renaissance. We know very little about his childhood, except that he came from a very poor family and was born in 1383. Even when he became a famous artist he always lived like a poor man. Some people criticized his work because the figures that he carved always looked like poor people, not heroes.

The student rehearses this speech and then stands and gives it to the class. Under the level of Set, we have given the student several specific objectives to meet:

_____ Make eye contact with the audience

_____ Speak in an interested manner

_____ Show confidence

When students meet our expectations, we can simply check the corresponding part of our rubric. When we feel that children do not meet our expectations, we should make notes to give students feedback:

_X_ Make eye contact with the audience

_X_ Speak in an interested manner

_____ Show confidence _Didn't know material, lost place twice, should practice more_

Mechanism

In this level of the taxonomy, we divide the child's whole speech into segments, which are equivalent to paragraphs. We move from repetitions of our speech to the students' own speeches. We provided models for each of the segments, students practiced them, and now students begin to present their own similar components. If we want to focus on presentation skills, we may approve a written version of the minispeeches before the student's pres-entation to make sure of the content and organization.

These minispeeches are important for students to gain confidence in speaking in front of groups. We can use the same rubrics as we developed for the Guided Response.

Show-and-Tell Show-and-tell is widely used in the early grades and is similar to Mechanism-level presentations. There are many reasons for including show-and-tell activities in the classroom besides teaching students how to make oral presentations: Students get to share who they are with their classmates by bringing in items that are important to them, and they learn about the diversity of their fellow classmates. Such activities can also be a good way of introducing elementary presentation skills. Teachers often guide the content by asking students to bring in and tell about objects (family photographs, toys, something old, etc.), but they rarely help students develop skills. Show-and-tell activities, particularly in the kindergarten or first grade, work best if they develop a single skill at a time (make eye contact, demonstrate how to make something involving three steps, speak slowly). If you have a single objective, the assessment rubric is very simple, although you will want to give students specific feedback about that objective.

Complex Overt Response

We now ask students to assemble their whole performance. We may have divided a student's speech into three segments based on content: (1) general contribution and family life, (2) how they learned their craft, and (3) their specific contribution. Now the student puts them together in a whole speech.

We may have had different presentation objectives for each segment. Perhaps after practicing eye content and speaking in an interested manner during the first segment, we concentrated on speed during the second, and facial expression during the third. For the whole speech we may include all of these topics in the rubric:

_____ Made eye contact _____

_____ Used voice to convey interest _____

_____ Used face to convey interest _____

Pacing: _____ Good _____ Too fast _____ Too slow _____

_____ Remembered material _____

_____ Smiled _____

Adaptation

Students should learn there are different kinds of speeches: One size does not fit all. The presentation skills we would expect for a persuasive speech (eye contact, body language, emotion in voice) are quite different from our expectations of a demonstration (skillful physical demonstration, reassuring manner). Just as we have to teach students how to write different forms of prose (analysis, argument, narrative), we must teach students different speech performances in terms of content, organization, and the presentation skills necessary to be successful.

Many times, particularly in middle and secondary school, we expect students to make presentations of material to other students where we will be holding the class responsible for that material. This presentation illustrates the philosophy that the classroom is a community of learners. Children may make better presentations if they use slides on an overhead projector. In the near future we may even expect students to learn to use presentation software, such as PowerPoint®. Learning how to make well-organized and visually interesting overhead slides may be part of the presentation skills we expect from some presentations. We will need to instruct students on the elements of such presentations and assess their performance, partially in terms of the effectiveness of their visual aides.

Origination

The final level of the taxonomy is the hardest to assess because students show their own personal creativity in making oral presentations. Students may include music, role play, or involve their audience in ways that go beyond your expectations. Teachers are sometimes bewildered about what to do when students go beyond the objectives. A few years ago I observed kindergarten students making oral reports about the careers they were interested in. The general direction for this presentation was to tell at least three different things that the person holding that job would do. Most of the students stood up and told a few things they learned and then sat down. One boy came to class wearing khakis and a blue blazer. He handed out business cards for his father's soft drink distributorship, shook each student's hand, and urged them to drink Coke, not Pepsi. He asked the teacher if she would put up a Coca Cola sign on the bulletin board.

Then he sat down. He had not spent a minute behind the podium as all his classmates had done. He told them nothing, yet he clearly showed them several things a soft-drink salesperson does at work (making contacts, urging sales, placing advertisements). The teacher was unsure about how to assess this performance.

Although all teachers want to encourage creativity, it is often a surprise and an assessment quandary when it occurs. The goals for this presentation stressed content, and the content was there. I would encourage the teacher to assess the content high, and the presentation as original. The teacher might then have to step in to make sure that the other students learned what was expected by asking the student a few questions. Those questions would also assure the teacher that the child understood something about the behaviors he was modeling.

Putting It All Together

We have discussed content, organization, and presentation objectives. Eventually we will want students to put all these elements together and we will want to assess all three kinds of objectives. It is critical to develop a recording instrument, such as a checklist, that we can use while we listen to the presentation. Here is a short example. There are three items under content, organization, and presentation, a place for a specific comment, and an overall rating:

CONTENT	ORGANIZATION	PRESENTATION
_____ Family	_____ Good opening	_X_ Good eye contact
_X_ Learned craft	_X_ Good conclusion	_X_ Good pace
_X_ Contribution	_X_ Organized throughout	_X_ Used picture well

Comment _Need to work on the beginning, but very interesting after that!_
You have much improved your pace. Slower is better!

_____ Excellent _X_ Good _____ Satisfactory _____ Needs improvement

Confidence and Stage Fright

In several of the examples we have used the word *confidence*. Confidence is shown when the presenter knows what comes next, can pronounce all the words in the presentation, and can answer questions after a presentation. Confidence in speaking is something that develops slowly and with repeated practice.

The flip side of confidence is stage fright, or performance anxiety.

The best way of dealing with any fear is to expose ourselves to what we are afraid of, but that exposure should be gradual. Think about the best way of getting a child over her fear of dogs: Buy her a puppy! Few children are afraid of puppies, and the puppy will gradually change into a dog. A child who is afraid of standing in front of his classroom needs to approach the task step by step. Useful activities include the short Guided Response and Mechanism, having the student make his presentations from his own desk, and practicing in front of the teacher alone or in front of a video camera. You may help a child who exhibits stage fright if you get him to give more short, well-rehearsed speeches than you require for other children. At each practice he will become more confident and less anxious. Allowing him to skip the requirement will not help him overcome his fear.

Questions for Reflection

1. Conduct is another area, like class participation, where we often rely on our memories to come up with student grades. Develop a simple plan of aides to memory that will make your conduct grades more reliable and valid.
2. Develop a rubric for what you consider a good adult speech. Observe one of your professors for 15 minutes using this rubric and write an assessment report.
3. Use the rubric you developed in number two and watch a political speech on C-SPAN. Write an assessment report.

CHAPTER

22

Group Work

Collaborative work is the most vital topic in education, from nursery school through graduate school. The impetus for this emphasis comes from two very different sources, industry and feminist theory. Industry has long complained that the American educational system creates good independent workers, but it does not produce graduates who can work in teams. Feminist theory suggests that schools should foster cooperation and promote methods of working that are noncompetitive and nonhierarchical. With the blessings from the political right and political left, American education has plunged into cooperative learning. There is consensus that cooperative learning is good for students, and that it needs to be emphasized in the classroom. There is less consensus on where it best fits, and very little consensus on how to assess cooperative learning.

Richard Slavin (1979), at Johns Hopkins University, pioneered one emphasis on team work in the 1970s as a response to racial strife in the Baltimore school system. He developed a technique called Teams-Games-Tournaments in which interracial teams worked cooperatively on projects and then competed with other interracial teams. The technique seemed very effective in combating division in schools along racial lines and promoted achievement across the board. Industry wants group work that emphasizes interteam cooperation and intrateam competition. More recently, Slavin deemphasized the competitive component of his original model, saying most of the benefits were attributed to the cooperative aspects of the process. How one interprets these and other findings in this literature is likely based on one's view of competitiveness.

Assessing group work is a thorny issue. Whether one approaches it from an industry or feminist perspective, a basic assumption of group approaches is that individuals bear a responsibility to the group. Whether we teach cooperatively and assess individually, assess so that part of a student's evaluation is based on the group's accomplishment, or Assess *entirely* on group work, depends, in part, on our philosophy of teaching and assessment and the realities of the classroom situation. Many teachers and most parents take a dim view of evaluating students on the basis of others' work, but such practices are part of the theory behind group work. Before a teacher initiates group activities, she would do well to think through her attitudes about such practices and develop a strong rationale for her decisions.

As with many other topics discussed in this section of the book, we may want to return to the basic dichotomy between process goals and content goals. The teacher needs to determine whether her primary reason for instituting group work is to teach students how to work cooperatively or whether she believes that specific content can best be learned in a group context.

▨ ASSESSING GROUP PROCESS

From industry we have learned there are two basic models of how groups work. In the **interchangeable model** *each team member learns to do each job.* In the **expert model** *each person discovers the role for which he or she is best suited and becomes an expert in that team role.* The interchangeable model was pioneered in Japanese industry, and the expert model was developed in American industry. Suppose a teacher adopts a group strategy in teaching science and has students work in teams of three collecting data. One student makes observations; one student writes down the observations; and one student produces graphs of the observations. In the interchangeable model students take turns in each role. In the expert model students are assigned roles (either by the teacher or by team consensus) based on students' abilities or interests.

In educational writing on teamwork, it is not always clear which model the author is following. For example, sometimes team work is recommended because it allows students with different skill levels to become members of teams, even if they could not do some of the roles demanded of them. This approach seems to follow the expertise model. Other times team work is recommended because it allows students to practice undeveloped skills; by varying roles they can experience success somewhere in the overall process. A teacher must choose one or the other approach or mix them at different times.

What Are Important Process Skills?

Let's examine a specific group project. In a life-skills class, groups of four ninth-grade students are to research and make a group presentation, orally and in writing, about different kinds of postgraduate educational opportunities. The teacher wants students to learn about technical schools, community colleges, education and training opportunities associated with the military, and four-year colleges and universities. He also wants them to learn about the jobs each education prepares students for; what is necessary to get into them; what opportunities exist in their community; and what each kind of education is like. He also wants his students to begin to think about their aspirations of postgraduate experiences. At the end of a week of research in the library and the guidance office, he wants students to:

1. produce a six-page paper summarizing the differences among the four kinds of education/training experiences;
2. make oral reports about local opportunities (the teacher assigned two institutions to each of the six groups); and
3. write a one-page statement about his or her preferences for postgraduation education, based on a statement of his or her life goals.

As an English teacher he wants his students to learn to write accurately and effectively, do library research, learn computer skills, and learn to collaborate. He also has objectives for this project to help his students plan for their futures.

The Group Paper   The teacher is aware that most of his students have never written a paper like this cooperatively, and he breaks down the task into six components:

1. An introduction, giving an overview of the findings of individual students' research. This section is to be written as a group.
2–5. Sections on each of the four educational types. The topics are assigned to individual students by the group. Each student is to write a one-page summary on a computer file.
6. A conclusion, summarizing the main points.

The steps in writing the paper are:

1. Students do individual research.
2. Students write their individual papers.
3. Students share their findings with each other.
4. Students provide classmates with feedback.
5. Students revise their papers based on feedback received.
6. Students complete the introduction and conclusion.
7. Students merge their files by computer to produce a single paper.

The teacher develops a 20-point rubric to evaluate each student; 10 points are based on group work and 10 points on individual work. The decision to count group and individual work equally reflected the teacher's philosophical decision to count group work heavily, knowing both students and parents were somewhat uneasy about this process. The teacher also decided about half of the group part of the grade would be an assessment of each student's work in the group context.

The evaluation of the individual section is straighforward. The teacher told the students to look for five kinds of information: (1) a description of the education; (2) how one gets in; (3) what kinds of jobs it prepares one for; (4) local opportunities; and (5) the cost. For each of these a student would get 1 point if the information is accurate and one point if the writing is clear.

	ACCURATE	**CLEAR WRITING**
Description	_____	_____
Getting in	_____	_____
Jobs	_____	_____
Local	_____	_____
Cost	_____	_____

For the part of the assessment that deals with group process, the teacher asked each student to rate other students in his or her group on two traits. He used a form like this:

> For each student on your team, put a check beside that person's name if he/she gave you helpful feedback on your section and helped write the introduction and conclusion.

	GAVE GOOD FEEDBACK	**HELPED WITH INTRO AND CONCLUSION**
Alice	_____	_____
Benny	_____	_____
Chaz	_____	_____

Students could get a possible 6 points from their colleagues on their cooperativeness with the group part of the project. The teacher rated the introduction and conclusion on a 3-point scale:

0 = low content and organization

1 = low content with some organization

2 = good content and good organization

Put together, the individual assessment/feedback form might look this:

INTRODUCTION

___2___ ___X___ good content/ organization _____ needs more organization _____ needs content /organization

YOUR SECTION

	ACCURATE	**CLEAR WRITING**
Description	_X_	_____
Getting in	_X_	_X_
Jobs	_X_	_X_
Local	_X_	_X_
Cost	_X_	_X_
___9___ Total		

CONCLUSION

| 1 | _____ good content/ organization | _X_ needs more organization | _____ needs content /organization |

WORKED IN GROUP

	FEEDBACK	HELPED WRITE INTRO AND CONCLUSION
4	2	2

16 Grand Total   Grade B

You may wonder whether such a complex feedback system is necessary. The answer is yes, because the teacher had a complex set of objectives. The teacher who lent me this exercise says it takes about 45 minutes to read the papers and prepare individual assessment forms. There is only one paper per group, so to give feedback to students, some sort of individualized form is necessary. The teacher saves time filling out the individual forms because he reads five papers from his class of 20 rather than 20 individual papers. Each student has time to read the comments the teacher wrote on the paper and compare it to the feedback form. Each student reads the comments on the paper explaining why the conclusion got a rating of a 1, rather than a 2. The teacher needs to write these comments only once, if he uses a similar feedback form.

The teacher tells me that when parents see such a system, they are likely to accept it. Students like to discuss their work together so that they can do a better job the next time they have a group project. The teacher also tells me there is one major pitfall: Students who do not get all possible points on cooperativeness want to know who rated them down. He makes it very clear from the beginning that such ratings are absolutely confidential, and he removes them from the classroom as soon as possible so that there is no possibility of students finding out who gave them high marks and who gave them low ones.

The Group Presentation   The first time the teacher used this project, he did not give explicit instructions for making the presentations. Because each group reported on only two local institutions, some groups had only two members speak. He could not give individual presentation evaluations. The next time he required each student to make part of the presentation.

The teacher developed a simple checklist for evaluating the presentation. Six points were awarded, up to 3 each, for the factual material on the two institutions, and 4 points for the presentation. The checklist he used while the students were making the presentation looked like this:

	INSTITUTION A	INSTITUTION B
Type of institution	_____	_____
Admissions procedures	_____	_____
Careers prepared for	_____	_____

	STUDENT A	STUDENT B	STUDENT C	STUDENT D
Confident	_____	_____	_____	_____
Organized	_____	_____	_____	_____
Accurate	_____	_____	_____	_____
Interesting	_____	_____	_____	_____

As the presentations unfolded the teacher checked under each of the institutions when the three types of information he had required were presented. For each student he checked if each of the four qualities he was looking for were exhibited. He also made some notes on the form. He gave each student an individual feedback form that included the total number of content points the group earned and their own presentation score. Each student received at least one individual comment.

Group grade	_____
Your presentation	
Accurate	_____
Organized	_____
Confident	_____
Interesting	_____
Total	_____
Comment	_____

The final component of the project was the individual paper. This was also graded by a 10-point rubric, focusing on the student's logical connection of his goals with types of education. As this is not a group project, but an individual paper, you should refer back to earlier chapters on assessing individual student written work in Part II of this book.

Group Process Assessment

Group process is assessed in three basic ways: self-assessment, assessment by other team members, and assessment by the teacher.

Self-Assessment   One common method of assessing group process is to have students assess their own participation in the group process. Normally this approach is not recommended for children before the age of eight, and it is quite difficult for older children until they have had a good deal of experience in group work. Students must learn to work cooperatively and must learn to assess their contributions to group work.

How can students best assess themselves? Students can assess their effort; they can tell us how much time they put into the research component of a project; they can tell us what parts of the process they felt confident in and which parts they had difficulty with. Students can also tell us what parts they liked and did not like. (Students may want to tell us they are good at everything, but a rating they did not like on a component of the process may be pointing out a weakness.)

Teachers who are teaching students to work in groups earnestly can use students' self-assessments to help them learn about themselves by sitting down with students individually and comparing their self-assessments to the assessments made by others in their group. A student who tells her groupmates that she liked their part of the project may rate herself high in providing useful feedback. If she receives information that her colleagues did not find her perky comments helpful, she may adjust her behavior in the future to provide more constructive criticism.

Assessment by Team Members   Another common assessment approach is to have each team member assess every other team member. In theory this is the best approach because the other team members have the best vantage point for determining whether a student did his job and did it well. Of course there are problems inherent in this process: Students may assess their friends higher than they deserve and those students they don't like lower. Parents may have strenuous objections to other children assessing their sons and daughters.

There are two approaches to such ratings:

1. Global ratings *where a student gives a general rating of her groupmates' performance*

   John   was   1. very helpful in the process
                              2. helpful in the process
                              3. not helpful in the process
                              4. disruptive to the process

Global ratings are likely to be influenced by friendship and cliques, and in most cases students will give each other very high ratings.

2. Behavior-anchored ratings *in which a student decides where a colleague's behavior falls along a continuum of behaviors.*

   John   was   1. always helpful, always on time
                              2. always helpful, usually on time
                              3. usually helpful, always on time
                              4. sometimes helpful, sometimes on time
                              5. not helpful, usually late

Students will typically provide more constructive feedback using such ratings.

Teacher Assessment   Teachers are only present during group work for a relatively small part of the functioning of a team, which is a problem with teacher assessment of group process. This is particularly true in high school where there may be expectations that the teams will work outside of the school day. Even in elementary schools, where team work takes place in the classroom, if a teacher divides her 25 students into five teams of five students, she will only be able to be present, at most, 20 percent of the time.

Teachers also need to guard against positive and negative biases. A teacher who goes into the group work process probably wants the process to work well, and she may be prone to overlook many glitches in the process. The purpose of assessment is not to give students bad grades, but accurate evaluation and feedback. In other situations teachers may develop a negative bias because they are consulted only when things are not working well, so they see mostly the problems with group work.

What can a teacher assess best?

Teachers can assess more objectively than students, and they can assess those things which can be sampled. Let's say that students are doing a group experiment in science. Students are trying to compile their individual observations and come up with a conclusion. The teacher can stagger the timing of this task so that she sits in on each discussion for five minutes. She can see who is participating and who is not, who is offering good suggestions and who is off task. Teachers often are in a position to see who gets their work done on time, who assumes a leadership role, and who seems to fall out of the group process. Teachers may be needed to evaluate the participation of special needs students in groups.

▦ ASSESSING CONTENT

Content assessment of group work is very similar to assessing content in individual work. The main difference is that some of a product may be ascribed to the entire group, and other parts are ascribed to the individual student. The group paper is an example of this approach.

Suppose you have been studying books in language arts and you have given your third-grade class a project of producing a book in teams of five. The students must agree on a story, write a text, put the text in book form, and illustrate it. You have specific qualities you are looking for in the book, in addition to the group process skills you will be assessing by a different rubric. You want the story to have a beginning, a middle, and an end. In the beginning you want a description of the setting and the characters. In the middle, you want a problem to be resolved. In the conclusion, you want a resolution to the problem. You want illustrations representing the text to be colorful and detailed. You want the book to reflect what you taught them about bookmaking.

You now have two options as a teacher. Do you assess the book as a whole and give everyone the same evaluation, or do you attempt to discover students' roles and assess them for their accomplishments? Do you attempt to do both?

We must go back to the objectives. If we evaluate students only on their individual contributions, we will probably diminish cooperativeness. If the evaluation we give includes all students—and if that evaluation is somewhat low—we will probably get a lot of grousing from the students. (I have seen students confide in the teacher that they were responsible for the part that got the high ratings, but they had not been involved in the components that got less than perfect ratings. The teacher's response to this information is to ask the student why she wasn't involved in those other components, as this was a group project.) I prefer a mixture of group and individual assessment for group work.

▦ TALKING TO PARENTS ABOUT GROUP ASSESSMENT

Many teachers have indicated that parents are often concerned initially about group work. They are concerned particularly that their children's grades will be dragged down by the poor performance of another group member. They rarely are concerned that their child's grade might be dragged up by an outstanding collaborator, or that their child will drag down another child's grade.

As in most cases of innovation, teachers are better off taking a proactive rather than reactive position: It is better to anticipate and deal with problems before they occur than to correct the problem later. If you want to introduce group projects and group assessment into your classroom, and you know that your students and their parents have had little or no experience with group work and assessment, it is better to communicate what you will be doing before you undertake the group work. If group work is uncommon at your school, I would also recommend involving your principal in your planning process to ensure you will be backed up if there are complaints.

For the sake of the parents and the students, I would also ease into group assessment. You may allay many fears if you divide the first group assessments into three components: (1) a group assessment of the whole project; (2) an individual assessment of each student's contribution to the project; and (3) an assessment of each student's cooperativeness. I would recommend at first weighting the individual component the highest, cooperativeness the next highest, and the total product the least. This is not only politcally wise, but it also gives the greatest emphasis on those things students already know how to do, and puts less weight on those things that students are just learning to do. Parents can see the relative weight of their son's or daughter's grade in these components.

For example, Maria, a fourth-grade student, worked on a cooperative learning project on Japan. She received a grade of C+. Maria told her mother it was the other students' fault that she received this relatively low grade, and now Maria's mother wants to discuss this problem with you.

When the mother appears for her conference, you show her your grading rubric. The individual component was 60 percent, the rating of cooperativeness was 20 percent, and the group product was 20 percent. The individual component consisted of 20 percent of your evaluation of Maria's oral presentation; 20 percent for her illustrated description of a Japanese custom; and 20 percent for her score on a test. The cooperativeness grade was composed half of peer ratings and half of your ratings. And the group product rating was based on a book organizing the descriptions.

Here is Maria's evaluation breakdown. (You normally do this with points, but presenting the evaluation by letter grades may make more sense to her mother.)

Oral presentation	B
Illustrated description	C
Test	C
Cooperativeness (teacher)	C
Cooperativeness (peers)	B
Group product	B

Here you would be able to say that the C+ was consistent with her individual work (B, C, C); that her cooperativeness was also C+ (you rated her less cooperative than her peers); and, if anything, the group grade pulled her up a bit.

Sometimes the group grade will be lower than the individual grade. Your genuine commitment to group process will be necessary then, and you will have to explain how the student can learn to have a more positive impact on the group project.

Questions for Reflection

1. Write down every possible objection you can think of to group work. Now write a 500-word article for your class newsletter, adressed to parents, dealing with as many of those negative ideas as you can. This time, *don't* be positive. Think of ways of counteracting objections only.
2. Suppose your teacher went a little soft in the head and decided to throw out a final examination in this course and replace it with a group project. Design such a project. Now decide which you would really rather have: an individual test or a group project. Why?
3. What problems do you think you would encounter by having students rate each other's cooperativeness? Would there be differences among elementary, middle, and high school students? Explain.

23

Portfolios

*A*few years ago I was working with a principal in an elementary school on a project. During this period several of the teachers at the school attended a three-day workshop on portfolios. They each came back very enthusiastic about replacing the rather sterile grade book filled with numbers, with *a collection of student work*, or a **portfolio.** This would be authentic assessment. They had been writing down a series of numerical grades that had little meaning to the student, the teacher, the parents, or the teacher the next year. Now, for each child, they would collect examples of work showing how the student solved problems, wrote, drew, gave oral presentations, journaled, and understood science. This was November.

By April, each of the nine teachers had abandoned the portfolio process. The first defector came very quickly. She was a fifth-grade teacher who bought 24 expanding file folders for student work. She decided to pick one representative student paper each week in each subject area. After three weeks the file folders were nearly half full and she realized, by the end of the year, she would have hundreds of file folders brimming with student work. She wondered when she would have time to look over all this material and use it to make a reasoned decision about each student's achievement in each subject area.

The second defection came from a teacher who soon discovered her students wanted to take their best work home for their parents to see and were selecting their less worthy work to leave in the portfolio in the classroom.

The third defector was a teacher who was very organized in her classroom. The confusion of the dozens of portfolios seemed to distress her. The fourth defection came after a teacher had several uncomfortable sessions with parents who wanted to see tests and grades, not a collection of drawings and essays.

And so on and so forth. The history of portfolio use over the past decade is one of initial enthusiasm, followed by a period of realization that portfolios have three serious drawbacks:

1. They require space.
2. They require a great deal of teacher time.
3. They are difficult to interpret.

I do not want to be negative about portfolios. They, like gradebooks, have their uses and their disadvantages. I would caution that they need to be approached realistically and thoughtfully.

If you go to a database, such as ERIC or Educational Index, you will find references to literally thousands of articles on portfolios over the past decade and a half. There are articles about the use of portfolios in every conceivable subject at every conceivable age and ability level. I have included several excellent references in the bibliography (Bozzone, 1994; Hill, Hill, & Norwick, 1994; Nidds & McGerald, 1997; Karp & Huinker, 1997). I would like to present my own interpretation of how portfolios can be used in classrooms without becoming so unwieldy they are an eyesore in the classroom and the teacher never has the time or energy to consult them. One possible way of organizing this presentation is to discuss how portfolios are created and managed. The issues here are what goes into them and who makes that decision. Another presentation might talk about who will use them. There seem to be five possible audiences for a portfolio: the student, the teacher in his role of evaluator, the parents, the child study team, and future educators. I will try both of these approaches.

▦ CREATING PORTFOLIOS

Portfolios have been around a long time, primarily in the arts. People do not hire a graphic designer or a soprano on the basis of their GPA, but on the basis of what they can do. A friend of mine is an artist who has recently landed a job as an illustrator of children's books. She got this job by sending around a portfolio of her work to major children's book publishers. This portfolio consisted of 25 slides. Another friend is an aspiring opera singer. Her portfolio is a tape of her singing six very different arias from six operas where she knows the leading soprano roles, along with clippings of reviews of her recitals and other vocal performances.

In the arts, a portfolio is a focused collection of performances: drawings and paintings, vocal performances, clippings of published articles or poems, and so on. Educators who have jumped on the portfolio bandwagon seem to have forgotten in the portfolio process is the focus.

What Goes into a Portfolio?

Only numbers go into a gradebook; we include only things we can assess quantitatively. What differentiates a portfolio from a gradebook is that *anything* can go into a portfolio. One could imagine a portfolio that would consist primarily of tests. The difference in orientation between the gradebook and the portfolio is that the portfolio contains the tests themselves, rather than a numerical summary of a series of tests. Suppose we collect 18 weekly spelling tests and we put those same grades in a grade book. At the end of the semester we compute our spelling averages, and 20 of our 24 students have earned A's or B's, but four students are struggling to pass spelling. What does our gradebook tell us about why these students are struggling? Very little. For our four poor spellers, we can spend a few minutes with a portfolio looking for patterns of spelling mistakes. Perhaps for some students we will get clues about we need to emphasize next semester. For one student the pattern eludes us, so we take the tests to a learning disabilities teacher or a speech teacher. They may have some help to offer—help that they could not give by looking at grades in a grade book. This is the real advantage of portfolios—it contains rich data, in which we may find patterns or trends. The advantage of the gradebook is that it contains succinct data. For the students who have high grades, all we need is confirmation that they are meeting the objectives at a high level of performance. The portfolio will add little useful information in these cases.

For at least five decades English teachers have kept portfolios of students' writing. When I was in high school in the early 1960s, our writing consisted primarily of book reports. We wrote one book report every six weeks throughout five years of senior high school. By the time we had completed our senior year, each of us had 30 book reports that followed us throughout our secondary careers. We could look back to see the progress in our writing. At the beginning of each year the new teacher could read examples of our writing. Teachers getting ready to write letters of recommendation for college could review our work. This assemblage of products had uses.

What makes the portfolio a compelling idea to many is that we can also include things we assess qualitatively. At the elementary school level we can put in writing samples, drawings, photographs of projects, videotapes of oral presentations, songs, and other performances. As we try to understand each student, we can go back and reflect over their various performances and products. Again, strengths and weaknesses may emerge that will help us assess their performance and aid us in developing new instructional strategies to help them.

Usually at the secondary level, the variety of material in a portfolio is more limited. In an English class we may collect various writing samples or a specific kind of writing, as in the example above; in a speech class we may collect videos of speeches and written texts of speeches; in an art class we may collect drawings and slides of paintings and sculptures; in a science class we may collect lab reports. We can see progress (or lack of progress) in those limited performances that each academic discipline is interested in. When we review several examples, we can recognize in a complex performance, such as a lab report, if students are having problems in writing, logic, computation, graphing, or following directions. We see what we could not see by looking at one report at a time.

The major advantage of a portfolio—that we have many examples of the students' products—is also its major weakness. If one collects too much material or too diverse material, one may not ever have time to review it; if one does attempt such a review, it may be quite difficult to make sense of it.

Who Selects the Items in a Portfolio?

According to most of the articles in the literature on portfolios in the elementary school, students select what goes into them. When one reads the literature on secondary education, it is most often the teacher, sometimes in consultation with the student, who selects the items. Often, at the secondary level, certain materials automatically go into the portfolio, such as all lab reports in a science class or all book reports in an English class.

The issue of who determines what goes into a portfolio decides whether the portfolio is to be a serious method of assessment or an instructional activity. Let me give you an example to consider. Suppose you decided to use a portfolio as part of your assessment procedure in a fifth-grade language arts class. You decided to have the portfolio count 50 percent of the final grade. This grading period you are studying narrative forms, and you allow students to put material in their portfolio on their own, entirely unsupervised. Some students will take home all of their excellent work, and put their less satisfactory work in the portfolio (they want mom and dad to see the good stuff, but are quite willing for the other to remain in the classroom). You now sit down with a rubric looking for evidence of the main learning objectives in the unit. Some portfolios show little evidence of meeting the objectives, although you know the student demonstrated such learning. What do you do?

When students select materials for their portfolios they take responsibility for their own learning. Some of your students have not done so. Will you give them an unsatisfactory grade? I doubt it.

Assessment is a serious business, a professional business. In portfolio evaluation the selection of material for the portfolio is a critical component of the process. When the teacher gives up that responsibility to students, she has turned the process into an amateur one, and every step that takes place after selection is tainted. Hiding behind a slogan such as letting students take responsibility for their own learning is no defense. Ten-year-olds are incapable of taking total responsibility for their own learning. If they could, we would all be out of jobs.

In a unit on narrative form, when a teacher sees an example that meets the objectives, she will want to see it again in six weeks when she completes her assessment. She must take responsibility for assessing the child's work. She should put that material or a copy in the portfolio, or attach a note to it asking that it be returned after mom and dad look at it. When we assess a portfolio we want to assess the objectives rather than the child's recognition of what those objectives are.

If we are collecting a portfolio for reasons other than assessment—for example, to have examples of student work available during parent-teacher conference night—it is an interesting exercise to have students select work they would like to have up on the wall. Spending a few minutes with each child discussing his selection will tell us a great deal about the child's understanding of the curriculum and about his goals and standards.

Similarly, I would suggest that allowing students to help us make decisions about what goes into an evaluation portfolio is an interesting process, although the teacher must take professional responsibility for what is in the portfolio at the end of the day. Sit down beside a child for a few minutes with what you consider to be an excellent drawing. Show the child he understood the basic point of a book he has recently read, explain why you think it is an item that should go into the portfolio, and then listen to the child's comments. You have done your job to assist the child in taking some responsibility for his own education; if nothing else, he will begin to understand the purpose of the portfolio.

▦ MANAGING PORTFOLIOS

The teacher I described above who decided to select one piece of student work in each subject area each week was setting herself up for failure. In a class of 25 students who are studying writing, spelling, reading, arithmetic, science, social studies, art, health, and physical education, one item per week per subject means that each nine weeks a minimum of 2,025 pieces of paper need to be collected, organized, and reviewed. This is likely to be well over 10,000 items per year.

Teachers going into portfolio assessment may be well advised to begin slowly, perhaps in only one curricular area at first. Let's begin with writing. Each week the child selects one item to go into the portfolio, after consulting with the teacher. At the end of nine weeks the teacher reviews the portfolio for evidence of the four learning objectives she had during the grading period. Let's say that the objectives were as follows:

_____ Write a topic sentence.

_____ Include descriptive adjectives in the topic sentence.

_____ Include evidence for the main idea.

_____ Write a concluding sentence that is related to the topic sentence.

The teacher puts this checklist on the outside of the portfolio.

Hilary is an excellent writer. Any item she puts into the portfolio supports these objectives. At the end of the nine-week grading period, the teacher asks her to select one item to remain in the portfolio and the remaining eight items go home. The teacher puts a paper clip on Hilary's essay, checks off all the items on the checklist, and clips this to her essay.

Joe is a weaker writer. No one piece of his writing demonstrates all of these objectives, but the teacher can find one piece of writing that demonstrates each objective. The teacher keeps these four items in the portfolio and sends the other five items home. The teacher clips together Joe's first batch of essays and notes on his checklist that he needs to combine all the elements in one paper. The checklist stays on the outside of the portfolio because the teacher is still trying to get all of the objectives met in one piece of writing. The teacher puts the new objective sheet under this first sheet.

During the next nine weeks the teacher up the ante: She wants two kinds of supporting evidence, and she want details. When she reviews Hilary's portfolio both student and teacher look for one or two examples in her new writing that show she has met the objectives. The new essays are clipped together, along with the objectives sheet. Maybe this time Joe has one essay in the new batch that meets all of the first set of objectives. The teacher clips the first checklist to the material collected, but he has not satisfied all of the new objectives. The second set of objectives remains on the outside of the portfolio. The teacher can go on to introduce new objectives for Hilary, while Joe is still working on two types of evidence and supporting detail. If the teacher now has a parent conference, the portfolios are well organized and do not contain an overwhelming amount of material. This process individualizes instruction. At the end of the year, the teacher has a coherent, small collection of work, neatly tied to the writing program objectives, which Joe and Hilary's new teacher can review during her August planning week.

Perhaps at the beginning of the second semester, the teacher feels comfortable with the writing portfolio and can begin a portfolio in a second area. This process is well managed and focused. The strengths of portfolio assessment will probably be maintained because the teacher is not overwhelmed by data collection and maintenance. Assessment is enhanced, but not overwhelmed by too much information.

▨ AUDIENCES FOR PORTFOLIOS

A wide range of materials in a portfolio is useful because there are many audiences for them. If we keep everything, or at least a great deal of material, there should be something in the portfolio to serve every need. But will we have the time and energy to scan through literally hundreds of bits of information and then review them to see if they meet our immediate needs? Probably not. Following are some brief comments about what kinds of materials might be collected in a portfolio, depending on the various audiences who may need to review them, including the students themselves, parents, child study teams, and future teachers, or assess them for instructional purposes.

Portfolios for Students

Portfolios help students take responsibility for their own learning, one of the most common justifications for them. A common translation is "children learn the purpose of their instruction" or "students learn to see their progress." Following are examples of each of these purposes of portfolios.

Understanding the Goals of Instruction In a unit on different cultures, in seventh-grade social studies, you are studying Japan, Australia, South Africa, and India. Students do library research on each country and produce various types of products, including oral reports, essays, annotated collections of photographs, and a three-dimensional project. Your overarching goals for the total unit are to learn about:

_____ differences in dress, related to climate and religion

_____ differences in food, related to climate and health beliefs

_____ differences in holidays, related to religion and national history

_____ differences in schooling, related to economic conditions

Each student collects his or her various projects and products into a portfolio; then you sit down with the student and decide which items should remain in the portfolio and which should be eliminated. Tony has written the following short description of a Japanese festival, as a caption for a photograph he found in the *National Geographic:*

> I learned that in Japan, near the old capital of Kyoto, in the fall, people set fires on the surrounding mountains which take the form of different characters in their language. One of the characters is fire, and so it is often called the Festival of Fire. People come from all over Japan for this festival.

You bring out your set of objectives and ask Tony which objective is met by his little essay. He says, "Holidays."

You say, "But you haven't related this to religion or national history. This is a good start, but you need to do a little more research to tell me why the Japanese do this."

Tony can then either revise his product or, if he has demonstrated this objective elsewhere, he can eliminate this item from the portfolio. Tony will have learned to pay closer attention to the objectives of an assignment, and he will learn about selecting items that meet or do not meet the objectives.

Seeing Progress When one is teaching a complicated process, such as writing, music, or working with a child with learning difficulties, portfolios are an enormous boon when the child's stamina or confidence is strained. When I was an eighth-grade English teacher, I had one class of remedial students. I did not keep formal portfolios, but I kept writing samples from earlier in the year. When my students occasionally gave up, I pulled out a piece of their writing and asked them to make corrections. After the students made corrections, I pointed out that all of those corrections represented things they had learned during the year about the writing process.

Having actual samples of students' work is important in this context. As the year goes on we may raise our grading standards. The student may continue to make C's on his written work, and he may become disappointed that all of his hard work seems to be getting him nowhere. Comparing older work to their new work or present skill level will show students they are learning. I remember when I was learning to play the French horn how reassuring it was for my teacher to play me a few seconds of tapes he had recorded months earlier. While I still could not produce beautiful mellow notes from that hateful piece of brass, I no longer made ear-splitting squawks and bleeps as I had been doing fairly recently.

Portfolios for Parents

Selecting work for a portfolio we intend to share with a parent depends on the message we want to convey to the parent. If you are satisfied with a student's progress, the normal portfolio material you are collecting for assessment purposes will be the most useful. If you have some specific issues you want to bring to the parent's attention, you may also want to include a small amount of additional material that demonstrates the issue. I emphasize small amount because parents do not like to be sandbagged at parent conferences. Teachers may want to share with parents that homework often comes late, is done sloppily, or is incomplete. One or two items will make the point. (It is only fair, for the next conference, to collect evidence that the problem has been addressed, as well!)

Portfolios for a Child Study Team

One of the more important uses of portfolios is collecting materials for referral to a child study team because a teacher suspects the student has a serious learning problem or is gifted or talented. Usually this will involve keeping a second portfolio in addition to the one used for assessment.

Child study teams are the first step in the referral process, and they are made up mostly of classroom teachers. These individuals will be more impressed by examples of the student's actual work than they will be by standardized test scores.

Portfolios for Future Educators

One excellent use of portfolios is as a means of communicating with a student's future teachers. As a fifth-grade teacher prepares to teach her new class, she would profit by seeing work from her students during the fourth grade. We need to ask what kinds of materials are useful for her.

As the teacher prepares for a school year, we need to consider how much time she will realistically be able to devote to looking at a portfolio. The probable answer to this question is she would prefer information she could review in a matter of hours rather than days. We might think a teacher could devote three to four hours looking over portfolios. For a fifth-grade teacher who will have 25 students, this suggests that each portfolio should contain information that could be reviewed in 5 to 10 minutes. This might include a few writing samples from different subject areas, a rubric indicating how well each student works in groups, or oral reports. It may include a few tests, drawings (along with a description of the assignment), and more creative items, perhaps even photographs of projects. This teacher will also be looking at grade reports, and maybe standardized tests. Often teachers include narratives about the student's classroom behavior.

There are two approaches: standardized portfolios, containing the same material for every student, and individualized portfolios, with items that portray the individuality of each student. Standardized portfolios may seem bland, but they keep the playing field level. If you produce individualized portfolios, you allow your impression of the student to influence the next year's teacher. I would particularly caution against trying to convey individual negative information to the next teacher. One advantage of getting a new teacher every year, from the student's perspective, is that it gives her a fresh start. If you convey messages such as *gets work in late*, or *does sloppy work*, you take away the child's ability to start over with a clean slate.

Of course the portfolio might be referred to later in the semester by the new teacher, so the previous teacher may include a little more information than can be looked at in this short time. I suspect if teachers pass on huge amounts of material, they will be ignored. The most relevant material here is from the last quarter of the year, and the previous teacher should include the student's best work, rather than representative work. It's a good idea to consult with the teachers to see what information they would like to have.

Portfolios for Evaluation

There are two basic ways in which portfolios are assessed: **gatekeeping assessment,** *for which material is added to a portfolio as objectives are met*, and **retrospective assessment,** *in which a teacher reviews a collection of material at the end of a grading period to determine which objectives have been met.* The gatekeeping approach is highly managed and focused but lacks some richness in detail; the retrospective approach is more time consuming but has a wealth of material in it. Let's consider an example from a middle school art class.

In the gatekeeping approach the teacher wants the student to collect 10 items that show she has worked with five different media and worked on five different types of composition. On the front of each student's portfolio is a checklist:

MEDIA	COMPOSITION
_____ Graphite	_____ Abstract design (black and white)
_____ Ink	_____ Abstract design (color)
_____ Pastel	_____ Still life
_____ Watercolor	_____ Landscape
_____ Tempera	_____ Human figure

Students add items until each of the categories is covered. Then they are permitted to replace items with later work which they consider better, usually in consultation with the teacher. Such replacements are an excellent teaching opportunity. The student approaches the teacher with a new ink line drawing. The student explains why she thinks it is better than what is in the portfolio already. The teacher comments on her interpretation, and they jointly decide whether to replace the drawing. At the end of the semester the teacher has a limited number of products to assess, and she needs not assess whether the technical objectives of using all different media and all composition types have been met. The teacher can go on to assess the artistic qualities of the portfolio.

In the retrospective procedure materials are put into the portfolio under guidelines that these exercises should be represented. But there are no limitations on the number of items in the portfolio—they accumulate. At the end of the grading period the teacher will take the same checklist and determine whether each type of material is present or not. After that phase of assessment has taken place, the teacher proceeds through the material looking for artistic qualities.

▦ THE RELIABILITY AND VALIDITY OF PORTFOLIO ASSESSMENTS

The topic of the reliability and validity of portfolio assessment has not been frequently addressed in the literature on the use of portfolios. When it has been addressed, some doubt has been raised, particularly about reliability.

Let's return to the example above where we are looking for cultural differences in a group of products about Japan, South Africa, India, and Australia. Recall the objectives:

_____ differences in dress, related to climate _____ and religion _____

_____ differences in food, related to climate _____ and
health beliefs _____

_____ differences in holidays, related to religion _____
and national history _____

_____ differences in schooling, related to economic conditions _____

_____ Japan   _____ India   _____ Australia   _____ South Africa

We made a complex checklist here. We want students to observe differences among the cultures in dress, food, holidays, and schooling, and we also have specific cultural issues we want them tied to (such as climate, religion, health beliefs, national history, and economic conditions). We would also like students to make observations about each of the four cultures.

We review the materials in each student's portfolio, checking off each item as we discover material. In the example of Tony's description of the Fire Festival, we might check off *Japan* and *holidays*, but we would not check off its relation to either religion or history. At the end of our review we may have checked the following:

__X__ differences in dress, related to climate __X__ and religion __X__

__X__ differences in food, related to climate __X__
        and health beliefs _____

__X__ differences in holidays, related to religion __X__
        and national history _____

_____ differences in schooling, related to economic conditions _____

__X__ Japan   __X__ India   _____ Australia   __X__ South Africa

As far as content is concerned, Tony addressed one issue (dress) completely; two incompletely (food and holidays) and one not at all; he addressed three of the four cultures. We conclude that this is Needs Improvement using the following grading rubric:

Excellent	Student addresses each component of culture and relates each to cultural background issues.
Satisfactory	Student addresses each component of culture and usually relates each to cultural background issues.
Needs Improvement	Student addresses most components and relates some to cultural background issues.

As you will recall from Chapter 4, one way of establishing the reliability of such an assessment is to have another teacher evaluate the same portfolio using the same rubrics. A second teacher comes up with a very similar checklist:

__X__ differences in dress, related to climate __X__ and religion __X__

__X__ differences in food, related to climate __X__
        and health beliefs _____

__X__ differences in holidays, related to religion __X__
        and national history _____

__X__ differences in schooling, related to economic conditions _____

__X__ Japan   __X__ India   _____ Australia   __X__ South Africa

Only in one case (dress and religion) is there disagreement, but this difference tips the balance in the second teacher's evaluation, which is Satisfactory. If this were the case in a real assessment, we would say that there is considerable unreliability in the process.

As teachers move toward portfolio assessment, enlisting a colleague in such exercises, with perhaps a dozen portfolios, will help them develop reliable methods of assessment.

Validity, however, is a somewhat different story. In a portfolio, we are not trying to predict one thing with another: We have the thing itself in the portfolio. Most often the issue of validity is moot in a portfolio. We are not concerned whether a score on a spelling test predicts that students will actually spell correctly when they write because we are dealing with spelling in their actual writing.

Questions for Reflection

1. Identify several different grade-level and subject areas and make lists of possible portfolio materials that could be included.
2. Make a list of at least a dozen kinds of materials you could collect in this course in a portfolio.
3. Suppose that instead of filling out an application for a job as a teacher, you were asked to select one example of five different kinds of materials, place it in a portfolio, and then write a rubric showing that you have all the qualifications to be a teacher. What would you select for your portfolio? What would your rubric look like?

CHAPTER

24

Authentic
Assessment

*A*t the beginning of this section I rejected the term *authentic assessment* to describe performance-based assessments, although this is a common name in the current assessment literature. The reason I rejected this label was two-fold: First, it implies that other kinds of assessments, specifically paper-and-pencil tests and standardized tests, are in some way unauthentic. Second, it implies that if one uses something other than traditional tests, the method is automatically authentic. If we want to use the word *authentic* to describe assessment, authenticity is embedded in the process, not the specific kind of assessment procedure. **Authentic assessment** *measures educational objectives as directly as possible.*

Some objectives can be measured directly by paper-and-pencil tests. If a Spanish teacher wants her eighth-grade students to be able to recall 20 vocabulary items, a fill-in-the-blanks test measures this objective directly. It would be a waste of her time and an overextension of portfolios' usefulness to hunt through a series of writing exercises to see whether each student used these 20 words accurately somewhere. A tenth-grade world history teacher may want his students to recognize modern nations that occupy the locations of the ancient countries his students are studying. Here, even the dreaded multiple-choice test has its authentic purpose. Students might complete a map project, which some teachers might prefer. Students who have completed the project have not necessarily committed the facts to memory. If the teacher wants students to remember that France was Gaul, Romania was Dacia, and Bulgaria was Thrace, it seems an authentic instructional activity for students to memorize these facts and for them to be assessed through an objective quiz.

Assessment runs into problems when it becomes indirect. If our objective in a first-grade music class is for students to produce a rhythmic pattern portrayed in musical notation, the authentic way of assessing is to give students a pattern such as:

and ask them to reproduce it by clapping or playing a percussion instrument. Sometimes teachers will use a multiple-choice item to measure this knowledge.

The dotted half note is equal to:
a. 3 quarter notes
b. 6 eighth notes
c. 12 sixteenth notes
d. all of the above

It would seem the knowledge necessary to clap out a rhythm and to answer this question overlap a good deal. But they are not the same performance, and one (clapping out a rhythm) directly meets the objective as stated, while the second (the knowledge multiple-choice item) assesses something close to the objective. Technically, clapping out a pattern assesses an Applications objective, and the multiple-choice item measures a Comprehension objective. If we want to use the multiple-choice item, we should go back and revise our objective down (students will show their understanding of the musical notation system).

Authenticity is not just a problem with objective items. Suppose a teacher wanted to allow children to be creative in their demonstration of knowledge of musical notation, and she asked each child to write down a pattern using notation. Although this is interesting, it misses the mark as surely as the multiple-choice item. It does not assess the objective as written. Would it be possible for a child to complete this exercise without any Comprehension of musical notation and without the Applications ability of being able to read a rhythmic pattern? Certainly. A student could take an existing pattern of four bars and reverse the middle two:

He has created a new pattern, but he may not understand the meaning of the various note values or be able to clap out his new pattern. The teacher in the first example has dropped a level in the taxonomy, and the teacher here has gone to a Synthesis objective. Without making sure that the underlying Comprehension and Application skills are there, the process has been subverted. This looks like an authentic assessment activity, but it may not be. (The teacher might see whether the child can clap out his new pattern, in which case she would be assessing Applications; if she wants students to produce original patterns, she should add this higher-order objective to her unit objectives.)

▓ BEYOND UNIT OBJECTIVES

Let's consider an interesting problem posed by the adoption of the portfolio as the method of measuring high school students' learning. A decade ago a magnet school that emphasized the arts in a major northeastern city decided to abandon grades and tests in favor of portfolios of students' work. At the beginning of the senior year, students from this school had only a collection of video and audio tapes of oral presentations, dance and musical performances, and photographs of art projects to describe their accomplishments in high school. These students wanted to apply for jobs or college admissions.

Those students who wanted to get jobs in the arts immediately after high school graduation and those who wanted to go to professional schools were very well served by the emphasis on portfolio development. I was on the admissions committee at a liberal arts college at the time, and we received several bundles of materials from this school. I remember sorting through this material for several students, taking at least half an hour per student. The other members of the admissions committee refused to even look at the material. We had over 900 applications to our program, and although we had majors in art, design, music, and theater, all of our students would have to take almost three years in liberal arts courses, as well. These courses involved taking tests, writing papers, and the usual activities of college courses. The major was only about one-fourth of the requirements for the degree. The bundles of portfolios were returned. We needed more evidence of the students' achievements in a wide variety of courses, such as course grades and SAT scores. We needed evidence that these students would be able to perform well on tests and write traditional essays. We believed the portfolio did not provide that information. In other words, for admissions to a liberal arts college, a portfolio that focused almost exclusively on the students' achievement in the arts was an unauthentic assessment procedure.

This example leads us to realize that the unit goals and objectives we set for our students are not the only ones which count in students' lives. The unit is part of a whole process of education called a curriculum. Education in the sixth grade prepares students for the seventh grade, college, and life. We may believe norm-referenced tests are not good for students (I do not believe this, myself), and we may not give anything like a timed test to our students, but students will leave our classrooms and have teachers with quite different philosophies. They will need to take tests to gain employment and to get into higher education. We may not want to get bogged down in facts when we teach American geography, but as we create our unit goals, we need to consider whether learning state capitals or the names of the Great Lakes might not be useful or even essential information in our students' future lives. Some teachers do not believe that in the age of calculators and computers it is necessary to learn math facts, but I find it frustrating when a cashier cannot make change when the system is down.

▣ INTEGRATING TRADITIONAL AND PERFORMANCE-BASED ASSESSMENT

Thirty years ago the schools relied heavily on paper-and-pencil tests. When I was in high school (a bit more than 30 years ago), we had six-weeks' tests, which counted as half of our six-weeks' grades, and semester exams, which counted as half of our semester grades. At most, nontests counted as 25 percent of our grades. As tests needed to be graded a day or two before report cards were handed out, objective items were the most common. (Multiple-choice items are easy to grade quickly.) There were some short-answer questions on these tests and even an occasional essay, but the structure of the evaluation system in place at my school made it necessary for teachers to emphasize objective tests.

As I talked with teachers in preparation for writing this text, I discovered that many school systems still have procedures in place which, despite an official authentic assessment orientation, made teachers rely heavily on traditional tests. Most middle and high schools still have six-weeks' or nine-weeks' tests that are assigned a required percentage in the grading formula, and teachers rarely have much time between their administration and the deadline by which grades have to be developed. Teachers who want to include less emphasis on tests may feel there is little they can do, except to lobby their administrations for more time between test administration and dates grades are due, but teachers can do things that will emphasize performance-based assessments.

The major modification in emphasizing performance-based assessment is taking the long view. Suppose when we plan a nine-week unit in sixth-grade language arts, we have two dozen objectives, divided into three units. Of those 24 objectives, we determine that seven can be authentically assessed by objective tests. Two are best assessed by student journals; six by individual projects; and six by written products, during each of the units. A group project can assess the remaining three objectives.

The first thing we must consider is our own limited capacity for assessing student work. We cannot do all of this assessment in the last three days of the grading period. We must pace ourselves, which means pacing the assignments. How many tests and quizzes should we have and when should we have them?

Let's say several of the objectives we have revolve around students learning the spelling and definitions of words used in their reading activities. Each Friday we could have a spelling and vocabulary test. But instead of taking home a bundle of tests every weekend, we now try a plan where we do not count weekly quizzes. These are merely practice for students. We will assess spelling and vocabulary only through the final nine-weeks' test. After students take their weekly quizzes, we give them the answer key and have them copy the words they missed into a notebook, which they will review for their nine-weeks' test. We do not have to grade the tests or take time putting all of these scores into a gradebook or a computer database. Moreover, by not counting these tests, we will not inflate the percentage of our final because of the number of paper-and-pencil tests.

I'm sure you have thought that if you don't count these tests, students will not study for them. That problem can be overcome by counting one or two of them. Usually have students grade their own quizzes, but occasionally collect them and take a set home.

Although we might want to include the journals the students write over the whole nine weeks, we have to compromise. If you have students develop two journal entries to be submitted to you, have one due during the first four weeks and one during the second four weeks. You can look these over and have them back to students and your assessments completed well before you have to deal with the nine-weeks' tests. This will save you stress, and it will emphasize the importance of keeping the journal every day to students, not just before you collect them. Projects and written exercises should be coming in, giving you adequate time to assess them and to give students quality feedback, maybe one per week. Structure the group project with a grading rubric that is easy to use and which provides clear results.

Because you have had plenty of time to evaluate all the student performances, you should have little difficulty in integrating your performance assessments with your nine-weeks' test. Because you have already assessed the higher-level objectives, the nine-weeks' test can be focused on Knowledge, Comprehension, and Applications objectives. You may include an essay question because you think it is good for your students to get used to writing under pressure, but it will not have much weight.

The only remaining problem is that some of your performance-based assessments are qualitative and some are quantitative, and you must put these together into a quantitative letter grade. How do you combine things such as an 88 on a test and a *met all objectives* on a project to produce a grade?

There are two answers to this question, neither of which is satisfactory for a teacher. The first is that *you can't*. That would be the position of some measurement theorists. The second is the pragmatic approach, or *any way you want*. The fact is, you have to.

Let me give you one possible solution. Let's assume your school district requires that the nine-weeks' test counts for one-third of the final grade, and your district uses a 10-point spread (90–100 = A; 80–89 = B, etc.). You let your test count 100 points; everything else will count a total of 200 points. You divide up the other activities:

#	Activity	Points Each	Total Points
2	Journal entries	20	40
3	Individual projects	25	75
3	Written products	20	60
1	Group project	20	20
1	Spelling quiz	5	5
Total			200

Let's look at your grading rubric for the first journal entry. During the first unit you were studying fables and tall tales from different cultures. You asked students to write each day about their reading, and then you asked them to select one entry and develop it, addressing the issue of how different cultures influence different aspects of tales. You ask them to think about how a tale might be different if it were an American tale. Your directions were:

> Look through your language arts journal and find an entry which you can expand. I want you to think about a specific story and tell me at least one way it reflects the culture in which it was written. Write this answer in a complete paragraph.
>
> Now imagine that you were telling this story to your own children. Tell me how you might change the idea you discussed in the first paragraph to make it an American story. Answer this question in a paragraph.

This is a pretty hard task for sixth-grade students. While you were discussing each fable, you brainstormed about these ideas, and usually you pointed out to students several details that made the story specific to its culture. You might expect them to remember these ideas. But the idea of changing a detail to make it American is a hard one. One student wrote the following:

> I liked the story of the Peach Boy. This is a Japanese tale about a boy who is discovered by two, old, poor, people floating down a river, inside a giant peach. They are hungry and they cut the peach open. What a surprise. The boy grows up and becomes very brave. He goes on a mission against some monsters who live on an island. He is helped by a monkey, a dog, and a bird. He beats the monsters.
>
> If this was an american story I don't think the people would eat an old peach that comes down the river. Also, I don't think he would take a monkey, because there are no wild monkeys in america like in Japan.

You have developed a checklist of content and process skills.

	EXCELLENT	GOOD	ABSENT
Process			
_____ Topic sentence	2	1	**0**
_____ Paragraph organization	4	**3**	0
_____ Spelling and punctuation	4	**3**	0
Content			
_____ Details of story	**3**	2	0
_____ Identifies Japanese elements	3	**2**	0
_____ Changes elements	**4**	3	0

As for processes skills, although there is no topic sentence in either paragraph, the paragraphs have reasonable organization. There are some spelling and punctuation errors, but this is a reasonable piece of work. For content the student includes details of the story and then changes two elements. He only identifies one Japanese element, the monkey, at the end. I have developed a scoring system here where we can directly add up points. This student gets 15 points translating to a C+.

Having an assessment rubric translate directly into points is one way of proceeding. Please notice I have weighted the points positively, so that an *excellent* for *changes elements* gets a 4, and a good gets 3 (not 2). You need the points to turn into reasonable grades. This student got two *excellents*, three *goods*, and one *absent*: Perhaps a C+ is too low. We might want to adjust our grading system:

	EXCELLENT	GOOD	ABSENT
Process			
_____ Topic sentence	2	1	**0**
_____ Paragraph organization	4	**3.5**	0
_____ Spelling and punctuation	4	**3.5**	0
Content			
_____ Details of story	**3**	2.5	0
_____ Identifies Japanese elements	3	**2.5**	0
_____ Changes elements	**4**	3.5	0

The student would have 16.5, which is equivalent to a 83 percent or a B. Although the paragraphs could have been better organized, this was a pretty good response, which may have merited a better grade.

During the second unit, on fairy tales, we asked students to invent a monster that had magical qualities, terrifying qualities, and a vulnerability. We wanted a written description and either a picture or a three-dimensional model. We evaluated the projects by the following qualitative rubric:

_____ Met three objectives; showed substantial work

_____ Met two objectives; showed substantial work

_____ Met two objectives; showed some work

_____ Met one objective; showed some work

_____ Met no objectives; showed little work

_____ Did not do the project

This project is worth 25 points. We might assign point values to each of the classification thus:

_____ Met three objectives; showed substantial work	25	100%	A+
_____ Met two objectives; showed substantial work	23	92%	A
_____ Met two objectives; showed some work	21	84%	B
_____ Met one objective; showed some work	19	76%	C
_____ Met no objectives; showed little work	17	68%	D
_____ Did not do the project	0	0	F−

We can now translate this qualitative assessment into our point system and include it into our grading point system.

▒ THE ROLE OF STANDARDIZED TESTS IN AUTHENTIC ASSESSMENT

For most writers who use the term *authentic assessment,* the idea that standardized tests, such as the SATs, the Praxis Examination, the Stanford-Binet intelligence test, or the Iowa Tests of Basic Skills (ITBS), could be part of an authentic assessment process is heresy. Individuals who write about authentic assessment typically reject norm-referenced testing ideas. Authentic assessment is the comparison of student achievement to the learning goals of the classroom, measured in a way that matches the objectives as directly as possible. Standardized tests are often indirect measures of achievement.

Let me give you an example of this direct and indirect issue. In a writing curriculum, we want students to learn to write a well-organized paragraph. We find out whether they have met this objective by examining their written work. On most standardized writing tests, students analyze writing, identifying various features that are regarded as necessary to organized paragraphs. Clearly this is something different from producing a piece of writing. We only call these tests writing tests because of a statistical relationship between scores on these items and the ability to write a paragraph. The relationship is much like the musical questions asked at the beginning of this chapter. They are related, but often not of the same quality.

I like to think of standardized tests as having a getting-back-to-reality function in the assessment process. They help us understand how well our specific objectives relate to national norms. Consider the issue of invented spelling. Suppose we decide not to teach spelling in the second and third grade because we believe attention to spelling hurts students' ability to write. Freed from worrying about correct spelling, we reason, students will learn a great deal about writing. This may be true, but we need to be concerned about spelling, too. If we postpone spelling until the fifth grade, will those who have used invented spelling catch up by sixth grade? (We expect students in an invented spelling curriculum will do less well on standardized spelling tests in the fourth grade.)

The results of standardized tests are equivocal on this issue. By sixth grade, students who had an invented spelling curriculum in first through fourth grade are still behind, but not by much. The invented spelling approach is too new for us to answer the question of whether gains in writing skills are worth the loss in spelling ability.

Part IV deals with standardized tests and how they are useful to classroom teachers.

Question for Reflection

1. You should now be in a position to write a statement on your approach to classroom assessment. Suppose you are asked, as part of a job application, to write such a statement. Keep it under 400 words and make it as specific as possible.

2 5

The Normal
Distribution

$\mathcal{L}$ et's begin by flipping a coin. If we flip it 100 times, we would expect it to come up heads 50 percent of the time and tails 50 percent of the time. If we designate heads as 0 and tails as 1, we could graph this result as follows:

Now, suppose we flip two coins at the same time. There are four possible outcomes, each equally likely:

HH = 0 (25%)
HT = 1 (25%) ⎫
TH = 1 (25%) ⎬ 50%
TT = 2 (25%) ⎭

We could graph the total. Twenty-five percent of the time we would expect to get 0 (two heads = 0 + 0); 50 percent of the time we would expect to get 1 (HT = 0 + 1 or TH = 1 + 0); and 25 percent of the time we would expect to get 2 (two tails = 1 + 1):

We can now flip three coins:

HHH = 0 (12.5%)

HHT = 1 (12.5%)
HTH = 1 (12.5%) } 37.5%
THH = 1 (12.5%)

TTH = 2 (12.5%)
THT = 2 (12.5%) } 37.5%
HTT = 2 (12.5%)

TTT = 3 (12.5%)

If we were to graph these results we would expect 12.5 percent of the time to get 0; 37.5 percent of the time to get 1; 37.5 percent of the time to get 2; and 12.5 percent of the time to get 3:

We will go one step further, flipping four coins:

HHHH = 0 (6.25%)

HHHT = 1 (6.25%)
HHTH = 1 (6.25%)
HTHH = 1 (6.25%) } 25%
THHH = 1 (6.25%)

HHTT = 2 (6.25%)
HTHT = 2 (6.25%)
HTTH = 2 (6.25%)
THHT = 2 (6.25%) } 37.5%
THTH = 2 (6.25%)
TTHH = 2 (6.25%)

HTTT = 3 (6.25%)
THTT = 3 (6.25%)
TTHT = 3 (6.25%) } 25%
TTTH = 3 (6.25%)

TTTT = 4 (6.25%)

Here we expect to get 0 6.25 percent of the time; 1 25 percent of the time; 2 37.5 percent of the time; 3 25 percent of the time; and 4 6.25 percent of the time:

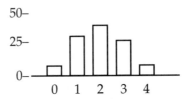

If we kept doing this for more and more flips of the coin, eventually we would get a distribution that looks like a bell. Specifically, this graph would be symmetrical (you could fold it in half and one side would be the mirror image of the other); the numbers would bunch up in the middle and become much lower at both ends (called the tails). This graph is called the normal distribution.

▨ PASCAL'S TRIANGLE

Here's another way of thinking about this. Maybe you remember this from eighth- or ninth-grade mathematics class:

$$
\begin{array}{c}
1\ 1 \\
1\ 2\ 1 \\
1\ 3\ 3\ 1 \\
1\ 4\ 6\ 4\ 1 \\
1\ 5\ 10\ 10\ 5\ 1 \\
1\ 6\ 15\ 20\ 15\ 6\ 1 \\
1\ 7\ 21\ 35\ 35\ 21\ 7\ 1 \\
1\ 8\ 28\ 56\ 70\ 56\ 28\ 8\ 1
\end{array}
$$

This is the beginning of Pascal's triangle. You begin this with 1 and 1. The second line is formed by beginning with 1 and then adding the numbers in the previous line together, in this case $1 + 1 = 2$. You end with 1. So the second line is 1 2 1. You begin the third line with 1. You add together the first two numbers from the line above, $1 + 2 = 3$; then you add the second numbers together, $2 + 1 = 3$; and you end with a 1. Always begin and end with a 1. Always add together pairs of numbers from the previous line.

Perhaps you notice the results are related to the flipping coin problem. When you have:

    1   1

the total is 2. We have:

    1/2   1/2

    50%   50%

When we have:

   1   2   1

the total is 4. We have

   1/4   2/4   1/4
   25%   50%   25%

And when we have:

   1   6   15   20   15   6   1

the total is 62. We have

1/62	6/62	15/62	20/62	15/62	6/62	1/62
1.6%	9.7%	24.2%	32.2%	24.2%	9.7%	1.6%

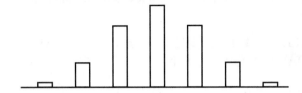

▓ PROBABILITY AND BIOLOGY

Gender   Let's go back to the very first graph, the one-coin, 50-50 graph. This graph can represent the relationship between biology and gender. As you know a girl has XX chromosomes and a boy has XY. During cell division the mother always contributes an X (because she has two X's herself), but there is a 50-50 chance the father will contribute an X (producing a girl) or a Y (producing a boy). Therefore this graph represents the probability of the distribution of genders in the population (50-50).

Eye Color   Now let's consider a second characteristic, eye color, which will be similar to the two-coin, 25-50-25 distribution. Here you must consider the contribution of both parents. Consider the situation with blue eyes, which is a recessive trait, and hazel eyes, which is a dominant trait. If you receive a hazel gene from one parent and a blue gene from the other, because blue is recessive you will have hazel eyes. But you will be a carrier of blue eyes because you will have one blue gene that you will give to half of your children. Suppose two carriers of the blue trait (BH) marry. They will produce the following children:

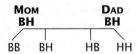

Children: BB   BH   HB   HH

(The first comes from Mom, the second from Dad.) Twenty-five percent will have blue eyes (BB) 50 percent will be carriers (BH or HB), and 25 percent will be pure hazel. This is identical to the second graph.

Intelligence We suspect intelligence is affected by dozens, or hundreds, or maybe even thousands of genes, so we expect the distribution of intelligence will be very similar to the normal distribution.

We know intelligence is substantially influenced by genetics, but many other things influence intelligence. Complications during pregnancy and birth; high fevers during early childhood; and abuse and neglect can lower a person's intellectual capability. Conversely, growing up in stimulating homes and attending excellent schools can enhance intelligence. We may still want to think intelligence is distributed like the normal distribution: Most of us cluster around the center, with only a few extraordinarily smart individuals in the upper tail and, fortunately, only a few individuals in the lower tail.

▦ THE NORMAL DISTRIBUTION AND THE STANDARD DEVIATION

The normal distribution has a remarkable relationship to the standard deviation (see Chapter 4), and understanding this relationship is crucial to understanding much of the information on standardized tests. Many students who are not mathematically inclined find this relationship difficult. In my experience in over 20 years of teaching this idea, I found that many students eventually have what psychologists call an "Aha" experience—suddenly they see the relationship clearly and simply. Students sometimes try to make this harder than it is.

When we talk about the normal curve, we are in the realm of calculus. We must think about the area under the curve. If you have not studied calculus, the idea of area under the curve is foreign. I will begin with a cumulative frequency (bar) graph (Table 25.1). There are 100 x's in this graph, each one representing one student who scored below the dashed line on the 20-item test. There was one student who got a score of 4, ten who got a score of 8, and two who got a score of 15. This meets the properties of the normal distribution: The graph is symmetrical (there are the same number who scored 4 as who scored 16, 5 as 15, 6 as 14, etc.), and there are many in the middle, but few in either tail.

Just by looking at this distribution, we see the mean is 10.0. (Remember the mean is the balance point.) The median is 10: If you count the scores from either end, you will find the middle person (50th or 51st person) received a score of 10. And the mode is 10. (More students score 10 than any other score.) That is another important property of a normal distribution: mean = median = mode. If you need to have the mean calculated for you, we can do this using a frequency distribution chart (Table 25.2).

TABLE 25.1 A NORMAL DISTRIBUTION

4	5	6	7	8	9	10	11	12	13	14	15	16
						X						
					X	X	X					
					X	X	X					
					X	X	X					
					X	X	X					
					X	X	X					
					X	X	X					
					X	X	X					
			X	X	X	X	X					
			X	X	X	X	X					
			X	X	X	X	X					
		X	X	X	X	X	X	X				
		X	X	X	X	X	X	X				
		X	X	X	X	X	X	X				
	X	X	X	X	X	X	X	X	X			
	X	X	X	X	X	X	X	X	X			
	X	X	X	X	X	X	X	X	X	X	X	
X	X	X	X	X	X	X	X	X	X	X	X	X

Rather than adding up 100 separate scores, we can multiply the number of individuals who got each score by the score, and then add up those products. For example, there were 10 people who got an 8 on this test. So instead of adding 8 up 10 times, you can multiply 8×10. We can do the same thing to calculate the standard deviation (Table 25.3).

You may remember from Chapter 5 that the standard deviation equals $\sqrt{\sum d^2/N}$ and d equals the scores minus the mean. In column 1 in Table 25 we have the scores. In column 2 we have the number of individuals receiving that score. In column 3 we subtract the mean to find the deviation score. We square the deviation score in column 4, and in column 5 we multiply the squared deviation scores by N. At the bottom of column 5, we add all these up, giving us $\sum d^2$. We then divide by N (100) to get 6.04. To find the standard deviation we take the square root. The square root of 6.04 (approximately 6) is going to be between 2 and 3, very close to 2.5. We need not concern ourselves about decimal points here because the test is scored in units. (It doesn't make any sense to talk about tenths of a score on a 20-point test.) Let's consider the

TABLE 25.2 FREQUENCY DISTRIBUTION CALCULATION OF THE MEAN

SCORE (x)	N	SCORE x N (Nx)
4	1	4
5	2	10
6	4	24
7	7	49
8	10	80
9	17	153
10	18	180
11	17	187
12	10	120
13	7	91
14	4	56
15	2	30
16	1	16

$$\Sigma x = 1{,}000$$
$$\text{Mean} = \Sigma x / N = 1{,}000 / 100 = 10.0$$

TABLE 25.3 FREQUENCY DISTRIBUTION CALCULATION OF THE STANDARD DEVIATION

SCORE (x)	N	d (DEVIATION [SCORE − MEAN])	d^2	$N \times d^2$
4	1	−6	36	36
5	2	−5	25	50
6	4	−4	16	96
7	7	−3	9	63
8	10	−2	4	40
9	17	−1	1	17
10	18	0	0	0
11	17	+1	1	17
12	10	+2	4	40
13	7	+3	9	63
14	4	+4	16	96
15	2	+5	25	50
16	1	+6	36	36
				$\Sigma d^2 = 604$

SD to be 2.4%. Now we are ready to discover the relationship between standard deviation and the normal distribution

The standard deviation has to do with scores, and we can talk about it above or below the mean. In this case we are talking about a mean of 10 and a standard deviation of 2.4. If we go up one standard deviation, we would include those scores between 10 and 12.4, or 10, 11, and 12. If we go down one standard deviation, we are talking about scores of 10, 9, and 8. In the mathematical relationships between a normal distribution and the standard deviation we should find 68 percent of the scores between one standard deviation below the mean (7.6) and one standard deviation above it (12.4). In this case we found 10 + 17 + 18 + 17 + 10 = 72. This is a little high, but close enough. We should find 95 percent between two standard deviations above the mean (14.8) and two standard deviations below it (6.2). In this case we found 4 + 7 + 10 + 17 + 18 + 17 + 10 + 7 + 4 = 94, which is excellent. If we had 1,000 scores on a 100-point test, we would expect the scores to be more accurate. But the usual expectations are these:

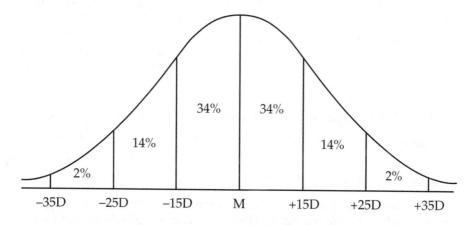

On a test that is normally distributed (please note, not all assessments are normally distributed), we expect about two-thirds of students to fall between one standard deviation above the mean and one standard deviation below the mean; we expect about 95 percent of all students to fall between two standard deviations above and below the mean, and about 98 percent to fall between three standard deviations above and below the mean.

What does it mean to score at the mean?

Fifty percent of those who took the test will score above you, and 50 percent will score below you. It also means your percentile score is 50.

What does it mean to score at one standard deviation above the mean? Thirty-four percent of people who took the test will score between you and the mean, and 50 percent will score below the mean; you scored above 84 percent of people who took the test, and 16 percent scored above you.

What does it mean to score at two standard deviations below the mean? Forty-eight percent of people scored between you and the mean, and 50 percent of people scored below the mean. You scored above 2 percent and below 98 percent.

These percentages are approximate, but they are the most useful ones in understanding the relationships between the standard deviation of normally distributed test scores.

If you score at half or quarter units, you will have to use tables to convert scores to determine *the percent of people you do better than,* or your **percentile score.**

▩ Z-SCORES

Finally, we can use standard deviations to convert scores on one normally distributed standardized test to scores on another test, *if the two tests are highly correlated.* We do this with **z-scores,** which are *scores on an assessment expressed in standard deviation units.* Suppose you scored 115 on an IQ test. Most IQ tests have a mean of 100 and a standard deviation of 15. This is one standard deviation above the mean. The z-score is +1.0. (The statistician who worked this out was German, and in German, the word for standard deviation begins with the letter z.) If your IQ was correlated with a score on a test with a mean of 83 and a standard deviation of 21, what would be your likely score on that test?

Just add one standard deviation unit to the mean on the second test:

Mean = 83

SD = 21

Mean + 1 SD = 83 + 21 = 104

Let's do three more problems. Let's assume that scores on an intelligence test and SAT scores are correlated. (They're not closely correlated, but for the sake of argument, let's say they are.) The mean of the Verbal test of the SAT is 500 and the standard deviation is 100. The mean on most intelligence tests is 100 and the standard deviation is 15. Let's say you got a Verbal score on your SATs of 600. What's your IQ?

A score of 600 on the Verbal SAT is 100 points above 500 (the mean). The standard deviation is 100. That is +1 z-score. If we go up 1 z-unit from the mean (100) on the IQ test (with a z-unit of 15), then your IQ would be 115 (100 + 15 = 115). You go up one standard deviation on one test, and you go up one standard deviation on the other. This is simple.

Let's say that two tests of mathematics are correlated. One has a mean of 50 and a standard deviation of 10; the other has a mean of 80 and a standard deviation of 20. Your score on the first is 45. What is your score on the second?

Forty-five is one-half standard deviation unit below the mean of 50, so your score would be half a z-score below the mean on the second test. The mean on the second test is 80, and the standard deviation is 20. Half of 20 is 10. If we subtract 10 from 80, we get 70.

Finally, suppose that Test A and Test B are negatively correlated. That would mean a z-score above the mean on Test A would result in a z-unit below the mean of Test B. (Refresh yourself in Chapter 4 if this does not make sense.) The mean of Test A is 50 and the standard deviation is 10; the mean of Test B is 100 and the standard deviation is 16. You got a score of 45 on Test A. That means you scored one-half z-unit below the mean. Because the two tests are negatively correlated, you should score one-half z-unit above the mean on Test B. The mean of Test B is 100, and the standard deviation is 16. Half of 16 is 8, so you should score 8 points above 100 = 108.

Questions for Reflection

1. You have a 130 score on an intelligence test with a mean of 100 and an SD of 15. IQ is correlated with a test of creativity with a mean of 10 and a standard deviation of 5. What creativity score would you expect to get?
2. SAT scores are correlated with GPA. At your college the mean GPA is 3.0 and the SD is .45. What is your predicted gap, if you had a verbal SAT of 400?
3. GPA at the college in question 2 is negatively correlated with the number of close friends you make at college. The mean number of close friends is 6 and the standard deviation is 2. If you had a GPA of 3.90, how many friends would you expect to make?

Answers:

1. 20 (mean = 10 + 2 z-units [5 × 2]
2. 2.55 (mean = 3.00 − 1 z-unit [.45]
3. You are two standard deviations above the mean, so you will score two standard deviations below the mean, 6 − 4 = 2.

PART IV

■

Standardized Tests

*T*his final section deals with norm-referenced, standardized tests, such as intelligence tests and achievement test batteries. These are less a day-to-day concern of teachers than classroom tests and performance assessments, but on occasion, teachers are expected to be able to use the information they convey. Teachers sometimes think of standardized tests as the enemy. They worry about whether these tests will take over the curriculum; whether the tests will misidentify their students in terms of such labels as learning disabled or mentally retarded; and whether the tests will be used to evaluate their effectiveness as educators.

There is a slogan in education: Knowledge is power. Knowing about standardized tests will help teachers gain control over their classrooms, if tests are illegitimately used; they will help teachers identify students for special education and other special programs; they will help teachers explain test scores to worried parents; and they will help teachers understand how to use standardized test scores to their benefit in their professional evaluations. Standardized tests can be a powerful information source for teachers. They convey information about individual students and about groups of students that can be used to assist in individualizing the curriculum.

In Chapter 26 we discuss the origins and nature of intelligence tests, and in Chapter 27 we describe how intelligence tests are used in the procedures for identifying students for special education. Classroom teachers are an integral part of this identification process, and they need to know the strengths and limitations of intelligence tests.

In Chapter 28 we discuss achievement test batteries, the lengthy tests given to students to compare their performance in the entire curriculum to national norms. We also briefly describe the use of such tests in educational research and innovative program evaluation. In Chapter 29 we discuss more limited achievement tests, particularly those that involve reading. We contrast standardized approaches to reading assessment with classroom assessments. In the final chapter we will discuss two practical considerations for classroom teachers: how to interpret test scores to parents and the use of standardized tests in teacher evaluations.

CHAPTER

26

Intelligence Tests

*W*hen I began my student teaching in first grade 25 years ago, my cooperating teacher was engaged in a battle with the local school psychologist. She had referred a boy in her class to be tested because she thought he had mental retardation. The school psychologist tested him and discovered that he was not mentally retarded, and he got a score on the intelligence test indicating he was somewhat above average. The teacher was convinced the school psychologist either made a mistake or was incompetent.

My cooperating teacher was a distinguished educator. She had taught for nearly 20 years at the same school. She was loved by her students (including the boy she thought had retardation), and she showed a keen interest in each of her students as individuals. In her gradebook it was obvious in every subject this boy was squarely at the bottom of the class, rarely rising to passing work in comparison to his classmates. She pointed to some standardized tests she had administered, indicating the boy was significantly behind his fellow students: On a reading inventory, this child had scored only at the first-grade level, while every other child in the class was reading on a third-grade level or above. He was two years or more behind the other students on every subject, which she remembered from an education course she had taken when she was in college as a sign he might have a serious learning problem.

I hope you noticed that as a first-grade student he was reading on grade level, which would not be an indicator of mental retardation. But he was two to four years behind the other children in his class in every subject. How could this happen?

The school where I did my student teaching was near a biochemical research facility. Of the 22 children in my first-grade class, 18 had fathers or mothers who held PhDs in biology or chemistry. Most of these children came from very bright families who stimulated their children by reading to them and engaging them in all sorts of activities. Most of the children in this neighborhood had been to academically oriented nursery schools and kindergartens. Eventually, a third of these students were identified for gifted and talented programs. Compared to these students, the little boy was not doing very well. But the boy was not mentally retarded, and it took a score on an intelligence test to make this clear. In her 20 years of teaching at this exceptional school, my cooperating teacher had had very little experience with average students.

Intelligence tests are now used in education to confirm or disconfirm hunches that teachers, counselors, physicians, and parents have about the intellectual functioning of children.

▒ ORIGINS

As described briefly in Chapter 2, intelligence tests originated with the efforts of French educators to predict as early as possible which students would not learn from traditional educational methods. If a child had failed to make substantial progress in learning to read, write, and do mathematics by the end of the first grade, these educators wanted to determine whether this lack of progress was due to **mental retardation,** *relatively permanent low intellectual functioning;* **a learning disability,** *low functioning in one or more important verbal areas, but not an overall disability, which is more or less permanent;* **a developmental delay,** *a significant lag in normal development, which may correct itself with time and intervention;* **disadvantagement,** *low level academic skills because of understimulation before coming to school;* or **other disabilities,** such as undetected hearing or vision problems.

The psychologist Alfred Binet, who devoted much of his career to research on children's abilities to solve problems, was asked in 1904 to see if he could develop a method of differentiating these groups. For nearly two decades before this, efforts to develop assessment that could differentiate among these groups had been unsuccessful. These earlier assessments were based on the idea that children who failed to learn had sensory problems. (Children who failed to learn to read did so because they could not see the difference between a *d* and a *b*, for example.) Binet thought success in school was based on higher-level skills such as the ability to understand cause-and-effect relationships, to detect similarities and differences, to understand word meanings, to remember complex ideas, and to solve problems. Almost immediately it became apparent that children who we would now say had mental retardation had difficulty with all of these tasks, and children with learning disabilities (a very recent term) and other kinds of problems have difficulty with only some of these tasks.

Compared to today's intelligence tests, the Binet test was short. It only had 40 items on it. Interestingly, it contained many types of items that we still use today. Children were asked to define words such as *horse* and *mama*; they were asked to repeat long sentences and groups of numbers; they were asked to count, compute arithmetic facts, and solve simple arithmetic problems; they looked at pictures that had important parts missing; and they told how things were alike and different.

Binet developed norms for his tests. He determined how many problems the average five-year-old, the average six-year-old, the average seven-year-old, and the average eight-year-old got correct. If an eight-year-old scored like a five- or six-year-old, Binet suggested the child had a significant learning problem. A few years after Binet died, a specific ratio of **chronological age,** *the child's actual age,* to **mental age,** or *the age group to which the student's scores were similar,* was developed. This is called the **intelligence quotient,** or **IQ.**

Binet felt that if a child was a year or a year-and-a-half behind, the problem might well correct itself, but his research suggested that if a child was two or more years behind, the child was better served by placing him in a special classroom. The special classroom would have the advantage of a specially trained teacher, few students so instruction could be individualized (typically there were 40 or more students in an elementary school classroom at the time), and special methods of teaching children with learning problems. Among the special methods of teaching were manipulative, hands-on materials and a curriculum that proceeded by smaller steps than in the regular classroom. The goal was to help students catch up, although many students were unable to do so.

By 1913 the results of the Binet tests excited an American researcher, Lewis Terman. Terman had two additional insights. First, he recognized that many of the items on the Binet test were very specific to France, and he developed an American version of the Binet test (which he called the Stanford-Binet after his university, Stanford). For example, question 40 on the Binet test was "Tell the difference between Catholicism and Protestantism," a topic of common discussion in French society at the time but not in America in 1913. Second, he recognized that some students were very good at these kinds of tasks. In fact, they were many years ahead of their classmates. He coined the term *gifted* to describe them.

Terman's interest in the gifted arose from the conditions of his own life. He had grown up in a poor farming community that could not support a high school. It was only through a series of lucky and unlucky breaks (such as developing tuberculosis) that he received more than a sixth-grade education. Terman reasoned there were many gifted and talented children throughout the United States whose promise was stunted through the bad luck of being born in a county that did not have secondary schools. Terman wanted to develop a way of assessing students of promise so that they could be given opportunities to continue their education past elementary school.

Today's intelligence tests are based on the work of Binet and Terman and the work of the psychologist David Wechsler. Wechsler was the chief psychologist at New York City's Bellevue Hospital. Wechsler had to determine whether the 30 to 40 individuals who were acting unusually when they were picked up off the streets in New York were mentally ill or mentally retarded, or both. Unlike Binet or Terman, Wechsler was dealing primarily with adults, and many of the people he dealt with were not native English speakers or had little formal education. The tests developed by Binet and Terman were composed primarily of verbal items because they were designed to predict school performance. In contrast, half of the items on the Wechsler tests were verbal and half were nonverbal, such as solving mazes, putting together puzzles, and identifying the incomplete pictures that Binet had developed.

▓ TYPES OF ITEMS ON INTELLIGENCE TESTS

Many of the items on today's intelligence tests were created by Binet, Terman, and Wechsler. Below are some items that are similar to the items on the Wechsler tests. The Wechsler tests are the most commonly used tests in education today, so we will use Wechsler's division between verbal and performance items.

Items on intelligence tests are presented orally and face-to-face by a trained school psychologist. Normally the test takes between an hour and an hour and a half. Although there are clear procedures, the psychologist establishes rapport with the student informally at first and will often ask follow-up questions when an answer is unclear. Within each category, the process begins with easy items and proceeds to harder and harder items until the examinee misses a specified number in a row. Then a new category of item begins. Some items are timed, and quick responses get more credit than slower responses.

Verbal Items

1. *Information*

   This subtest measures how much a person knows about important facts in the culture.

   Easy: What are the seasons of the year?

   Hard: What is the main theme of *Hamlet?*

3. *Digit Span*

   To test for basic memory, seven series of digits are presented and are to be repeated in the same order by the examinee. Testing begins by presenting three digits at a rate of one digit per second. There are two sets of digits in each series, up to nine digits. Testing is discontinued when the examinee fails both sets of a particular length. A second part of this test consists of seven series, from two to eight digits, where the examinee must repeat the series in reverse order: Psychologist: 3-9-5-1; Examinee: 1-5-9-3. Testing on the second part is discontinued if the examinee misses both sets at one length.

   Easy: (Say this forward.) 4-5-9

   Hard: (Say this backward.) 6-3-7-3-8

5. *Vocabulary*

   Almost all intelligence tests have vocabulary items. Some answers are incomplete and earn one point; others are complete earn two.

   Easy: What is a hand?

   1-point answer (a body part)

   2-point answer (a body part you grasp things with)

   Hard: What does "recitative" mean?

7. *Arithmetic*

   Teachers are sometimes surprised to learn that arithmetic items are included in the verbal part of the intelligence tests. Students are asked relatively simple questions, but they are not allowed to use paper and pencil to solve them. In the harder items quick responses get more credit than slow answers.

   Easy: How much is 3 plus 3?

   Hard: If three persons earned $90 for working for a full day, how much money would you have to pay 13 persons for working two days each (extra credit given for quick responses)?

9. *Comprehension*

   This subtest consists of questions designed to measure practical knowledge and common sense.

   Easy: Why do we pay taxes?

   Hard: What does the expression "A stitch in time saves nine" mean?

11. Similarities

    Another way of understanding a child's verbal ability is to ask questions about similarities and differences.

    Easy: How are a robin and a wren alike?

    Hard: How are smiling and frowning alike?

Performance Items

2. *Picture Completion*

   Drawings, each with some part missing, are presented to the examinee on cards:

4. *Picture Arrangement*

These items look very much like the frames of a comic strip presented out of order. The examinee is asked to put them into an order that will tell a story:

6. *Block Design*

Ten red and white designs on cards are presented to the examinee, which he is to reproduce using either four or nine identical one-inch cubes. The faces of the cubes are either solid red, solid white, or half red and half white, divided down the diagonal:

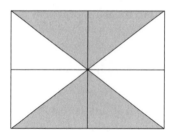　　　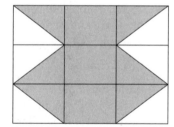

8. *Object Assembly*

These items are jigsaw puzzles that form common shapes such as an animal or a face.

10. *Coding*

These items ask examinees to code a long series of nonsense forms with numbers. This section is timed, and students get a score based on the number of correct responses:

1	2	3	4	5	6	7
╤	╁	⊤	Γ	⅃	╁	⊐

1	3	7	5	2	3

Current Tests

Three intelligence tests are primarily used today to test elementary and secondary school students: the Weschler tests, the Stanford-Binet, and the Kaufman ABC. Tests based on Wechsler's work are the most commonly used tests: the WPPSI-R, for children under the age of six; the WISC-III (Wechsler Intelligence Scale for Children, third edition), for elementary and middle school children; and the WAIS-R (Wechsler Adult Intelligence Test, Revised Education), for adolescents and adults. These tests produce verbal and performance IQ scores.

The Stanford-Binet, now in its fourth edition, is the extension of Terman's work. It produces a single score, and its content is mostly verbal. The Stanford-Binet is often used to identify gifted students.

The Kaufman ABC is used with minority children. The content of the test is deliberately multicultural. This test is also specifically geared toward the identification of learning disabilities and has a number of innovative items that measure different memory problems.

▓ INTERPRETATION OF SCORES

Although the legal definition of the different categories of scores on an intelligence test may vary from state to state, and the terms used vary slightly from school district to school district, intelligence tests normally divide students into five levels:

1. Gifted — Scores above 130
2. Normal — Scores between 70 and 130
3. Educable Mentally Retarded (EMR) — Scores between 55 and 70
4. Trainable Mentally Retarded (TMR) — Scores between 40 and 55
5. Severely and Profoundly Handicapped (SPH) — Scores less than 40

Originally, the IQ was computed by comparing the child's test score to his age. The test score was reported by mental age (MA). For example, on the original Binet-Simon test, there were 40 items. The typical eight-year-old would get 20 items correct, so if you got 20 items correct, you got an MA score of eight years. The MA was divided by your actual age (CA = chronological age) and multiplied by 100 to produce an IQ. If you were four years old and got 20 items correct, then your IQ was 200 (IQ = MA/CA × 100 = 8/4 × 100 = 200). If you got an MA score of 8 and you were 16, your IQ would be 50 (8/16 × 100 = 50). Actually, the German psychologist William Stern developed the notion of IQ; Binet, who mostly tested seven-year-olds, was concerned primarily if the MA was two years behind the CA.

Intelligence tests measure crystallized intelligence. Our crystallized intelligence usually stops developing at around the age of 16; one way of understanding the meaning of these different levels is to think of the IQ as the percentage of 16, the highest level of intellectual functioning a person would achieve as an adult. If a child has an IQ of 100, when he is an adult he will have the intellectual ability of a 16-year-old. If we think about the limits of EMR (55 and 70), the individuals will function somewhere between an 8-year-old and an 11-year-old when they are adults: They may read at a second- to fifth-grade level, do second- to fifth-grade mathematics (arithmetic and measurement), and understand social studies and science at that level. We use the word *educable* to indicate that the goals of a child's schooling will be similar to those of other children's—reading, writing, arithmetic—salthough we will expect the child to make slower progress.

If we think of TMR, the limits are from six-and-a-half to eight. As an adult the individual will function at the level of a first or second grader. They will not be able to read, although they may recognize some words; they should be able to count but not do much beyond addition and subtraction of one-digit numbers. The term *trainable* indicates we have different goals for a child's schooling. TMR classes focus on self-management skills and basic competencies, not reading, writing, and mathematics. Many children with TMR never really acquire spoken language, even by age 21.

Another way of thinking about the meaning of these classifications is to consider Piaget's stages of intellectual development. A child who is in the Educable Mentally Retardation range will be a life-long Concrete Operator, while a child in the Trainable Mentally Retardation range will be operating on a preoperation level throughout adulthood. A child who is classified in the Severely and Profoundly Handicapped range will remain in the sensori-motor period.

Finally, we may want to consider the reasonable life expectations for individuals in various levels of retardation. We expect individuals with EMR to live independent lives. They can hold down jobs with high levels of routine and high levels of supervision—such as working in the fast-food industry—marry, raise children, and live normally within the community. They will need some assistance in some aspects of their lives. They will not be able to fill out income tax returns. They will have difficulty in dealing with unusual circumstances at work.

Individuals with TMR will need assistance in most aspects of their lives but not constant supervision. Many individuals with TMR work in sheltered work settings. Many will live in group homes where a professional will be available to see that their needs are met. If they have children, they will have great difficulty raising them.

Individuals with SPH will need supervision in all aspects of their lives. If they work it will be in sheltered workshops specifically designed for them, and they will need supervision 24-hours-a-day for life. Most persons with SPH will spend most of their lives in institutions because many of them have other problems as well, including vision and hearing problems, and physical disabilities. Most individuals in this range of ability have experienced severe trauma, such as injury, poison, or disease.

▨ BIAS IN INTELLIGENCE TESTS

One of the persistent criticisms of intelligence tests is that some ethnic and linguistic groups do significantly less well on the tests than other groups. In the United States African-American students and first- and second-generation Latino students score, on average, 10 to 15 points lower than the norm. Some would interpret these findings as bias in the tests. Others would say the scores register the disadvantages in our society of belonging to various minority groups and argue that by blaming the test, we are opting for a quick solution to a far more serious problem.

Ethnic Minorities

African-American students score all over the range of intelligence, but if we plot the normal distribution of their scores, it will be centered around a mean of 88, not 100, as it is for white students. There have been many interpretations of these data.

Although intelligence tests predict potential, they also reflect the homes, communities, and schools where children grow up. Socioeconomic problems in each area can affect intelliegence test scores. For example, children growing up in working single-parent families have less stimulation by an adult than those who grow up in two-parent families, and more African-American children grow up in single-parent families than do white children. Parents' educational levels affect their children's intelligence test scores, and in many communities, African-American parents have less education than their white counterparts. Unfortunately, many African-American children attend schools that are less adequately funded than schools for white children.

The real culprit seems to be poverty. If we compare the scores of African-American and white children growing up in poverty, both groups have lowered means on intelligence tests. When we compare African-American children who are not in poverty to white children not in poverty, most of the differences in intelligence test scores disappear. But because there is a much higher percentage of African Americans growing up in poverty than white children, when we look at all African-American children compared to all white children, we discover the differences in mean IQ scores.

How does poverty affect IQ? First, poverty affects the health of children and parents. Poor parents may not be able to afford proper prenatal care, routine medical checkups, or medical care for even serious childhood diseases. Many children in poverty have inadequate diets. These medical problems may affect general intellectual functioning. Second, there are many things which are good for children that require money: books, magazines, newspapers, educational toys, vacations to stimulating learning environments, quality day care, and preschools. Third, children living in poverty often live in dangerous communities and often spend much time unsupervised in their homes while their parents work. Finally, most poor parents work at strenuous jobs, often more than one job, and when they are not working, have little energy to devote to their children's development.

Blaming intelligence tests for the message they convey about inequality in our society will not solve the problem of poverty. Children from poverty do less well in school, on average, than middle class children, and intelligence tests were developed to predict how well one will do in school. Intelligence tests convey an unpleasant message to us about part of our culture, and getting angry at the tests and claiming they are biased will only sweep the problem under the rug.

Linguistic Minorities

Children who come from families where a language other than English is the primary language spoken in the home can be at a disadvantage on the verbal items on intelligence tests. This appears to be the case for many Latino students where Spanish is the main language in the home; this does not appear to be the case for Asian students, particularly those from Vietnam, Japan, and China, due in part to typical beliefs regarding English. Many first- and second-generation Latino families continue to speak Spanish in the home, live in communities where Spanish is the primary language, and work in Spanish-speaking workplaces. Asian parents are far more likely to encourage their children to learn English and to speak English themselves in the workplace and, to some extent, at home. Asian students actually are at an advantage over white students on IQ tests, scoring, on average, about 10 points higher.

When we were describing the kinds of items on typical intelligence tests, you may have noted that many items involve ordinary vocabulary and even linguistic idioms. Consider the item: How are a wren and robin alike? A child whose everyday life is conducted in Spanish might well know the answer to this question if the question was asked in Spanish. Maybe he knows *wren* but not *robin*. He cannot answer the question. Although there are Spanish intelligence tests, there are also items that use technical, academic vocabulary such as *plagiarism*. The same child might be at a different disadvantage on the Spanish version on different items.

There is no clear-cut solution to this problem. Most school psychologists are aware of this problem and will interpret scores on intelligence tests differently for bilingual children. If such a child receives a verbal IQ score of 50 on a Wechsler test and a score of 90 on the nonverbal part of the test, although this child might technically fall into the level of EMR, the psychologist knows not to make this classification. A bilingual student who receives a VIQ (verbal IQ) score of 115 and a PIQ (performance IQ) score of 140, although not technically scoring above 130, may be placed in a gifted class, nevertheless. IQ test scores are guides, not rigid determiners of placements.

▓ INTERPRETING IQ TESTS TO PARENTS

The classroom teacher does not interpret the results of an intelligence test to parents. That job is in the hands of the school psychologist and the principal of the school. Parents, however, may have questions about what they have been told, and if they have established a good working relationship with a teacher, they may ask the teacher for clarification of their conversations with the psychologist and principal.

Often, at the end of a process that has involved the administration of an intelligence test, parents will receive news about their child that is emotionally difficult for them. A mother may have thought her child was gifted and hoped to have the child placed in a special program, but the test reports the child is high-ability normal. Others may have thought their child had a mild learning problem, but the outcome of the process identifies the child as having a learning disability or, even more emotionally distressing, retardation. The parents may come to the other person who knows their child intimately, the teacher, for assurance, support, or confirmation.

Teachers should exercise a great deal of caution about using technical classifications when talking to parents at any stage of the process. For example, if a teacher were to say to a parent at the beginning of the process, "I want to have your child screened to see whether he has a learning disability," the parents could demand the school put the child in a program for learning disabilities immediately.

The teacher is an agent of the school system, and when she applies such a formal label, it carries the weight of the school system. Rather than use labels teachers should describe the child's behavior: "Judy is almost failing this year, and our achievement tests indicate she is reading two years behind grade level. I think it would be worthwhile seeing why that is," is a much safer approach to take than throwing around terms like *learning disabilities* or *retardation.*

Likewise, if you disagree with the final outcome of the identification process, you should never short circuit the formal process by expressing your reservations to parents, unless you are willing to put your career on the line. Teachers are significant members of the identification process. You will be consulted in every step of the process, but the final diagnosis is based on medical, sociological, psychological, and educational information. You may have thought Wendy had a learning disability, but the final weight of accumulated information is that she has educable retardation. If you have misgivings about that determination, make your concern known to your principal, not Wendy's parents.

Sometimes parents have misgivings about the outcome of the process. They realize their son is having difficulties in school, but they are unprepared for the outcome identifying him as having mental retardation. Teachers sometimes offer so much support and sympathy that distressed parents interpret this sympathetic support as a confirmation of their doubts. Even if you share these doubts, your primary job is to support the decision of the team of which you were a member. You can remind parents who have misgivings that the process of identification is not irrevocable: The placement of the child is reviewed each year. Placing a child in a small group with specially trained teachers and aides may provide the student with the kind of learning experiences she needs to catch up after a semester or a year. You may also remind parents that they, too, are part of the decision-making process. Parents have sigificant rights in special education, and they will have been given information about them. You can make sure that concerned parents understand those rights.

Questions for Reflection

1. Suppose you are talking with a parent about the process of identification. Their son has just been identified as having a learning disability. Part of the definition of *learning disability* is that a child is behind in achievement but has normal intelligence. Write out an explanation you think would help a parent understand this definition.
2. A child you thought was gifted has received a score of 128 on an IQ test. What questions would you ask the psychologist during the child study team meeting?

27

The Role of Intelligence Tests in Special Education

*I*n the past, students were placed in various forms of special education solely on the basis of IQ test scores. You are certainly aware of examples of tragic misdiagnoses of individuals that surface from time to time. Most of these come from a time when children who were identified as having mental retardation were placed in institutions. Later it was discovered the child had an undetected hearing loss, a transitory emotional disturbance, or a speech problem that produced a low score on the test.

Such misdiagnoses are far less likely to occur today for three reasons. First, the intelligence test score is now only part of the identification process. Convergent information from other sources, including the classroom teacher, must all come together before a student is labeled mentally retarded. Second, few children with mental retardation are institutionalized today. Public Law 94-142, the Education for All Handicapped Children Act of 1975, now requires students to be taught in the "least restrictive environment," which in most cases will be a neighborhood school. Third, no child is diagnosed only once. The child's progress is evaluated every year, and major reevaluations take place every three years. Children who are placed in special education classrooms and who make significant progress may be reevaluated within a year or two and taken out of special education.

We often think identifying a child for special education and placing him in some sort of special program is a bad thing. Although a teacher may occasionally refer a disruptive child with the hopes of getting rid of him, the real purpose is to place the child in an environment where he can maximize his potential. It is not some purgatory in which an atypical child is punished.

When I was teaching the course that led to writing this book, I used to bring in a panel of high school students who had been diagnosed with learning disabilities to discuss their experience. Often my students would ask them questions that took the general tenor of "Weren't you embarrassed by being labeled as having a learning disability?" Always, the students said emphatically *no*. Most said they knew that something was wrong, and they wondered before the diagnosis whether they were lazy or stupid. Some even said before the diagnosis their teachers or parents had used those exact labels for them. When they got to the special education classroom, they began to understand their problem, and they began to learn techniques to help them overcome their problems. One boy, who had just been accepted to college, summed up their collective experience:

> Why would finding out I had a learning disability be a problem? I couldn't read at all in the fourth grade. I thought I wasn't trying hard enough or that I hadn't figured out the secret. I thought I was stupid. Then I learned that I had a condition like thousands of others and that there was a way that I could learn to read. It wasn't magic when I went to the resource room, but after I'd been there for four months, by God, I could read. . . . Actually, reading wasn't that much of a problem for me at the time. What I really hated was when the other kids told me I was 'fat.'

▓ THE IDENTIFICATION PROCESS

Children are put into special education through a lengthy and comprehensive identification process. At each step in the process, the odds are loaded against identifying students for special education. One of the major changes that PL. 94-142 effected was that school districts have to pay for the education of students identified as having a disability. Gone are the days when a school district could say a child had a hearing problem or retardation, and the child was shipped off to a special school, which was paid for by the state. While the federal government supplies some money for special programs, the local school districts must also pay for part of the costs, a financial disincentive for placing children in special programs.

Below we will briefly discuss the general procedures in the identification process for the major categories of special education that require intelligence tests. Other classifications, such as hearing disability, visual disability, speech disability, emotional disturbance, orthopedic handicap, and chronic disease do not always require an intelligence test, although in determining the specific program for an individual student, an intelligence test may be administered. Before describing the specifics of the major disabilities that involve IQ tests, we will summarize the steps in the identification process.

Referral

Critics of the special education process often forget that for a child to be involved in the special education identification process, someone must suspect there is a problem. For the most serious problems, such as Trainable Mentally Retarded and Severely and Profoundly Handicapped, parents and physicians are the most likely referral agents. These problems often come to the attention of the schools when children are infants or toddlers. Schools must provide services for children with these problems as early as age two. The less severe problems are more likely to be diagnosed in the school context, either by parents or teachers. Learning disabilities often are diagnosed only in third or fourth grade when children's problems begin to seriously affect their performance. We often think of a learning disability as synonymous with **dyslexia,** or *reading problems,* but there are other kinds of learning disabilities. Many children have memory problems; others have difficulty in processing spoken language; still others have difficulty with mathematical computations.

Child Study Team

The first real step in the referral process is sending the child's case to a local child study team. Usually this team consists of regular education teachers within the school, a special education teacher, a school psychologist, and the principal. They will sometimes involve a physician and a social worker. If the teacher is making a referral, he will describe the child's behavior, both academic and social, in explicit detail. It is normally a good procedure to avoid suggesting diagnoses at this point. In Chapter 23 I suggested that the teacher who is making the referral might collect samples of the child's work that he thinks shows the kinds of problems the student is exhibiting.

The child study team will often make suggestions to the referring teacher about ways of modifying her normal procedures. A child may not be paying attention; her work may be sloppy and inaccurate; she may be developing disruptive behavior in the classroom, cafeteria, and playground; she may be turning in a lot of work late or not at all. The child study team may suggest that the child be moved to the front of the classroom and that more formal discipline techniques be tried. A parent conference may be recommended to see whether there are problems in the home that could account for these developments. The team may suggest the teacher try these techniques for two months and report back.

If the initial ideas fail, the child study team may initiate a more formal diagnostic process. Normally the referring teacher will be part of the team, although another teacher who has taught the child may be included, particularly in referrals made early in the school year. At this point the child's parents become directly involved in the process, and they must give permission for the diagnostic phase to begin. (In some extreme situations, the school may get a court injunction to supervene a parental decision.) When a child turns 18 he replaces his parents on the team, if he is capable of participating in the process.

Diagnosis

Once the diagnostic phase has been set in motion, the child will be evaluated by a number of specialists, and the results will be presented to the team within a legally binding period of time. Usually a suggested diagnosis is made by the school psychologist, but this diagnosis must be accepted by the team. Teams quite often modify the diagnosis in significant ways.

The Individual Educational Plan (I.E.P.)

The outcome of a diagnosis of a handicapping condition is a document called an individual educational plan, or I.E.P. The **I.E.P.** is *a document that describes the diagnosis, a year-long set of instructional objectives, and instructional and assessment accommodations that are legally binding on the school.* Often this document is 10 to 20 pages long and sets forth a complete educational plan for the child. For a child diagnosed with retardation, the plan covers all academic areas, describing step-by-step the educational plans for each subject. For a child with a learning disability, some areas are covered by the plan, although in other areas the child is expected to remain in regular educational settings and experience the normal curriculum. **Level of services,** or *the site of the delivery of education* is extensively described.

Level of services range from special residential schooling, which is the most restrictive, to consultation, which is the least restrictive. The various levels are:

Residential schools—The child is placed in a special school where he will live; this schooling may be for 12 months, 9 months, or, occasionally Monday morning through Friday afternoon. The amount of time children will live at home will be specified in the I.E.P.

Special nonresidential schools—Some school districts have special schools for difficult-to-teach handicapped children; SPH students and emotionally disturbed children are the most likely to be placed in such schools. Children do not live in such schools.

Self-contained classrooms—These are special classrooms in a regular school where children spend the entire day with other handicapped children.

Resource rooms—These are special classrooms where handicapped children spend part of the day, from which they are mainstreamed into regular classes for the rest of the day.

Inclusion classrooms—These are regular classrooms where handicapped children are placed full-time; during part of the day, special education teachers, aides, and nurses come to the classroom and assist the regular teacher.

Consultation—This is the lowest level of services: A special education teacher consults weekly or monthly with the regular education teacher to assist her in providing individual programs for the handicapped child. This level of service is typical for senior high school children with learning disabilities.

The I.E.P. is signed by parents and is legally binding on the school and the family for a year. It is reviewed annually.

▨ CLASSIFICATIONS INVOLVING INTELLIGENCE TESTS

Giftedness

Giftedness is not a handicapping condition, of course, but an intelligence test is central to the diagnosis of giftedness. The definition of giftedness is left up to each state. The most common definition is that children score above 130 on an intelligence test and show evidence of special abilities in any academic area. Sometimes evidence of creativity is included, but as we have discussed earlier, creativity is hard to define.

Retardation

Retardation is the most serious of the intellectual handicapping conditions. In order for there to be a diagnosis of retardation, the child must have performed below 70 on an intelligence test, and other possible explanations for the child's low score need to be ruled out. A thorough medical examination is needed to rule out undetected hearing and vision problems or illness. A social worker must visit the home and determine that there are no disadvantages. Convergent information from an **adaptive behavior assessment,** often *a checklist of everyday behavior such as dressing and feeding,* will confirm the child's overall low functioning.

Please note that intelligence tests are not used in the diagnosis of the Severely and Profoundly Handicapped. These individuals do not respond in testing situations. Few have any linguistic skills, and they do not respond to any types of test items, particularly at the very young ages when the diagnoses are made.

Learning Disability

The most common type of disability classroom teachers will see is a learning disability. In order for a child to be identified as having a learning disability, three criteria must be met:

1. The child must be at least two years behind grade level in one or more important verbal areas.
2. The child must have a normal level of intelligence as measured by an intelligence test.
3. Other possibilities, such as medical conditions and sociocultural disadvantagement must be ruled out.

If a Wechsler-type test is used in the identification process, there will likely be a very large difference between VIQ and PIQ, with PIQ the higher of the scores. Interestingly, children can be diagnosed as having both a learning disability and being gifted.

Developmental Delay

Before third or fourth grade it is impossible to identify a child as having a learning disability because the idea of being two or more years behind in achievement is impossible. What would it mean to be reading two years below a first-grade level? Yet, many first-grade students are incapable of distinguishing shapes or colors, cannot begin to write their names, and cannot count to 10 reliably, despite the fact that they have been in school for two years.

If a child with such problems is found to have an IQ within the normal range, he may be identified as having a developmental delay. Often such children are put into special classes that stress basic learning through sensorimotor means. Sometimes such programs are year-round and include after-school care.

Many children identified as having a developmental delay do not progress rapidly within their special classes and will be evaluated again in the third or fourth grade for a learning disability. Others will make rapid advancement and then be returned to regular classrooms. An intelligence test will typically find these children in the low normal range.

Cultural Disadvantagement

During the process of identification of a student suspected of having retardation or a learning disability, it may be discovered that the environment in which the child is living is not supportive of normal development. In these cases, poverty and neglect may be the main reasons for the child's low performance. Scores on intelligence tests may indicate a learning disability or mild retardation, but because of the environment of the child, these results are put on hold.

These children are not identified for special education. There are a number of other programs, such as in Chapter 1 programs, available for these children. These programs are meant to be remedial, with the expectation that children will eventually move out of them into regular education.

Questions for Reflection

1. Suppose you are about to have a conference with a parent whose child has just been identified as having a learning disability. (a) Anticipate five questions that the parents may ask you. (b) Write a two- or three-sentence response to the parents' concerns.
2. If you have children with learning disabilities in your classroom, would you prefer them to be sent out of your classroom for resource help, or would you prefer the special education teacher to come to your classroom? Make a list of pros and cons for both approaches.

CHAPTER

28

Achievement Test Batteries

$\mathcal{W}$e all can recall from our own educational experiences the week or so when, every two or three years, we had to take achievement tests. We had to come to class with two sharpened, number two pencils, and we would spend several hours a day, over three or four days, taking tests on the major subject areas of reading, writing, social studies, science, and mathematics. We would be admonished to do our best, but the reasons for these tests were often obscure. These are achievement tests, and because they measure many different subject areas, they are called achievement test batteries. Unlike an intelligence test, which attempts to predict future behavior on the basis of general questions, an **achievement test** *measures what one has learned*. In this chapter we discuss complex tests, called **batteries,** which *measure a variety of content areas*. In the next chapter we discuss achievement tests that focus on a single area, such as reading. In Chapter 30 we discuss some practical implications of achievement tests.

We will describe briefly two of the most widely used standardized achievement test batteries for elementary and secondary students, the Iowa Tests of Basic Skills (ITBS) and the Stanford Achievement Tests (Stanford-9). Before going on to these two tests, we describe a test that may be familiar to most teachers, the Praxis I: Academic Skills Assessment of the National Teacher's Examination, a test that most states require of preservice teachers.

▦ PRAXIS I

The Praxis I is designed to be taken early in a preservice teacher's college education to measure reading, writing, and mathematics skills. This test is used to eliminate students whose basic skills are not up to the standards we expect of potential teachers. There are currently two versions of the test available, a traditional paper-and-pencil version, administered several times a year under highly secure conditions, and **adaptive testing,** a computer version that follows a new form of testing and that begins with relatively difficult items. If an examinee can answer those questions, it is assumed she will be able to answer questions that are less difficult within the same area. For example, if examinees can multiply three-digit numbers with carrying, it is assumed that they can multiply two-digit numbers without carrying. If the examinees get the first question right, the computer goes on to other difficult items. If the examinees get the difficult item wrong, then they are presented with less difficult items. In most cases, adaptive testing requires fewer items and less time to measure the same content. Computerized versions of the Praxis can be taken on demand throughout the year, so they are much more convenient. Scores can be obtained relatively rapidly.

The reading test measures the ability of potential teachers to understand and analyze three kinds of prose. It measures longer passages of over 200 words, whole paragraphs of about 100 words, and one- or two-sentence statements. The content comes from a variety of subject areas, and students are expected to be able to focus on main ideas, supporting details, and the organization and language in a passage. Here is an example of an item in this area:

> Lewis Terman was the American Binet. He transformed the nature of intelligence testing by concentrating on both ends of the ability continuum, retardation and giftedness. Terman's concerns are clearly embedded in the fabric of American political life and education of his time. His major contributions occurred at the same time that America was reinventing itself as a world leader and an exemplar of the egalitarian state. Terman rejected the idea of a hereditary elite. He believed that children of promise should be given the advantages of the children of the wealthy. While he believed that intelligence was largely genetic, he did not believe that family wealth and prestige were inevitably indices of genetic advantage, nor did he believe that poverty was a sign of incompetence. Each child should be judged on the basis of his accomplishments and potential. The son of an industrialist may not have the "right stuff," while the daughter of a sharecropper might be the next Nobel prize winner.

1. Which of the following best describes the main point of this passage?
    (a) Terman was a supporter of women's rights.
    (b) Terman was a product of his times.
    (c) Terman supported the genetic basis of intelligence.
    (d) Terman did not believe in an elite.
    (e) Terman lived in awe of the wealthy elite class.

The writing test consists of two different tests. The first is a multiple-choice section in which the best expression is selected. For example:

2. *Having collected the tickets from each of the passengers,* the conductor re-
tired to his berth.
  (a) The tickets having been collected
  (b) After collecting tickets from every passenger
  (c) Having collected tickets from each passenger
  (d) The tickets were collected
  (e) After each passenger gave him tickets

There is also a general-topic essay question on this part of the test. An
example given by the publisher, the Educational Testing Service, is:

> Which of your possessions would be the most difficult for you to
> give up or lose? Discuss why.

The mathematics test covers five areas: (1) conceptual knowledge (order,
equivalence, numeration, operations); (2) procedural knowledge (computation, estimation, ratio and proportion, probability, algebraic equations, and
algorithmic thinking); (3) representations of quantitative information and
interpretation of graphics; (4) measurement and informal geometry; and (5)
formal mathematical reasoning. Here is an example of the last kind of item:

3. *Some values of* x *are greater than 50.* Which of the following is NOT consistent with this sentence?
  (a) 40 is a value of x.
  (b) 60 is a value of x.
  (c) All values of x are greater than 50.
  (d) Some values of x are less than 50.
  (e) 50 is a value of x.

The Praxis I is a relatively short test, taking only three hours in its paper
form and potentially less time in its adaptive computer format. It can be this
short because it is a **screening test,** *which is used to divide a group of candidates
into two groups, those with high enough achievement to continue in teacher education and those without the necessary skills.* The test is not designed to make fine
differentiations about the level of performance. The later tests in the Praxis
series, those that measure content knowledge in teaching fields and general
pedagogical knowledge, are lengthier and designed to make those kinds of
rankings.

▓ IOWA TESTS OF BASIC SKILLS (ITBS)

The Iowa Tests of Basic Skills (ITBS) is a traditional standard of achievement
test battery. Although the ITBS continues to evolve as testing theory develops, most of the items are multiple-choice. There are supplemental tests that
have students construct responses in workbooks, but these tests are time-
consuming to score and expensive, and most school districts do not use

them. A writing sample is also optional and more often included. The term *basic skills* does not imply that the test does not measure higher-order skills, such as interpretation, classification, comparison, analysis, and inference.

The test produces scores in the areas of language, mathematics, social studies, and science, and a number of subscores under language and mathematics. There is also a fifth area on sources of information, sometimes abbreviated as work study, which consists of subtests in the use of reference materials and visual materials, such as graphs, maps, and tables. There are several different forms of the test for different age groups.

The test produces four kinds of scores: a raw score (the number correct), a percentile score (the percentage of test takers that the examinee did better than), the developmental standard score (DSS), which is primarily used by school district personnel in program evaluation, and a grade equivalent score, which is an estimate of the level of a student's performance in terms of academic years. A student who receives a grade equivalent score (GE) of 7-4 on spelling has the spelling ability of a typical student in the third month of the seventh grade. Remember that achievement test scores are norm-referenced, so the percentile, DSS, and GE scores compare the students' scores to those of others taking the test. It is also useful to know that school districts can tailor the tests in certain ways, including the comparison group. The percentile scores may rank a student's achievement to national norms, state norms, or school district norms. National norms are often considered the best norms, but there may be political or other reasons for choosing different comparison groups.

Here are examples of the six kinds of items used in the language test:

A. Reading Vocabulary
Decide which of the four words has most nearly the same meaning as the word in **bold.**

   3. He seemed **perplexed** by his predicament.
      1) confused
      2) happy
      3) angry
      4) sickened

B. Reading Comprehension

> The Pitti Madonna is often regarded as one of Rafael's most beautiful works. It shows the Virgin holding a plump Infant in her arms. She is wearing expensive, Renaissance clothing with an Eastern flavor to them, rich in color and texture. It is an elegant work, fit for the home of a rich patron, but unrealistic in showing the actual economic status of Mary and Jesus.

   4. Which of the following is true of the Pitti Madonna?
      1) It makes Jesus look too fat.
      2) It makes Mary look too wealthy.
      3) It was painted for ordinary people.
      4) It shows the Christ child wearing baby clothes.

C. Language Spelling

5. Indicate which of the following is a spelling mistake:
1) dawn
2) night
3) train
4) yeer
5) (no mistakes)

D. Capitalization

6. 1) This novel is about princess Di
2) and her friends. It has been a
3) very popular best-seller on the *New York Times* list.
4) (no mistakes)

E. Punctuation

7. 1) The letter was signed by
2) the Dean of the College. His
3) name was Harold L Dodsworth
4) (no mistakes)

F. Usage and Expression

8. Find the error:
1) Me and Bobby had a good time.
2) Sinclair Lewis is my favorite author.
3) Terman was born poor.
4) (no mistakes)

Evaluation of the Test

The ITBS has high reliability and reasonable validity. As with any test, reliability and validity are much lower for young children than for older ones. The test is widely used because of its good test qualities.

The test was designed to provide information that is useful for both groups and individuals. Teachers should be able to use the results in placing students in different levels of instruction. It is generally agreed that the test does this better in the areas of mathematics, social studies, and science than it does in language. The emphasis on the language test is more on mechanics—spelling, grammar, capitalization, and punctuation—than on more complex reading and writing skills. Teachers might well proceed with caution in using the overall scores to place individual students in the language arts, although the detailed subscores in mathematics are regarded as very helpful in that area.

The test can also be used for group assessment. Teachers can use class scores to determine a general level of instruction, and the test is often used to evaluate curriculum innovations.

▦ STANFORD ACHIEVEMENT TEST (STANFORD-9)

The Stanford-9 is rapidly replacing the ITBS as the achievement test battery of choice for many school systems. Stanford-9 refers to the ninth edition of the Stanford Achievement Test, but it is a radical departure from earlier editions of the Stanford Achievement Test. It has a number of qualities that recommend it:

(1) It has been recently updated in terms of content to reflect major changes in curriculum.

(2) More thoroughly than the ITBS, it has integrated student-constructed responses and open-ended questions. In a **student-constructed response,** *student work is captured in the testing process.* In an **open-ended question,** *students provide a response rather than select a multiple choice.* In the area of mathematics, a student-constructed item might describe the steps a student used to solve a deductive geometry problem. An open-ended question might be a computation problem to which the student provides an answer rather than selects a correct answer from a list of possible answers. In a student-constructed response an evaluator would rate the student's process of coming up with an answer. The open-ended question primarily eliminates guessing. Both, of course, require an actual reader rather than a computer to score the test; they are therefore more expensive for the school district, and it will take a good deal longer to return test scores.

(3) There are many options which school districts may take. One reviewer noted that the various options available to school districts would stack up over three feet tall.

The Stanford-9 has high reliability. Not unexpectedly, the computer-scored multiple-choice parts of the test have higher test-retest reliability than the rater-scored tests have inter-rater reliability. If children take the test on two occasions over several months, the evaluation of their performance changes very little on the multiple-choice parts of the test. Evaluations of writing samples and problem solving, however, have enough inconsistencies in them that caution must be used in using them to make important decisions about students. Many reviewers* suggest high-stakes decisions should not be made on the basis of the performance tests.

Here we find a conundrum about the new breed of achievement tests. Everyone admits there are limitations to what multiple-choice tests can tell us. But when we move to more complex responses, such as looking at how a student solves a geometry problem or writes an essay, there is enough disagreement among raters that we must be careful about using those judgments. Multiple-choice tests produce limited information, but that information is highly reliable. More complex tests produce richer responses, but there

---

* The reviewers referred to here are those writing in the encyclopediae of tests, *Test in Print,* and the *Mental Measurement Yearbook.* The specific references are included in the annotated bibliography.

is a large element of subjectivity in scoring those tests. Part of the problem is inherent in measuring lower- and high-level objectives. When we are measuring Knowledge and Comprehension objectives, we generally can agree on what constitutes a correct answer. As we move into Analysis, Synthesis, and Evaluation objectives, there is less agreement. Subject-predicate agreement is easier to assess than whether a student has used vivid language.

Reviewers of the Stanford-9 and other tests that use the newer, open-ended and student-constructed formats, urge caution when deciding if the new kinds of information are cost-effective. A computer can score a complex multiple-choice test quickly, reliably, and inexpensively. An open-ended test, and even more, a student-constructed test, takes a great deal of time, effort, and expense. If the information produced by these more expensive techniques is not reliable, using them may not be worth the expense.

▧ COMPETENCY TESTING

Many states are moving toward constructing their own achievement test batteries, often called competency tests. Although the ITBS and Stanford-9 construct their levels based on an examination of textbooks, state guidelines, and the recommendations of professional societies, most state competency tests are based on specific sets of statewide objectives. Competency tests are more likely to include student-constructed responses and open-ended questions.

Another difference between competency tests and achievement test batteries like the ITBS and the Stanford-9, is that they are deliberately high-stakes tests. School districts that do not meet state goals may have their funding reduced. Students who do not meet minimum scores may be held back at certain points in the curriculum, often before moving to secondary school or before graduation. These tests and the creation of the minimum passing scores are highly contested issues in education today, but political pressures seem to make the movement toward these tests inevitable.

▧ PROGRAM EVALUATION

One reason we need to administer standardized tests is to get a reading on how our program stacks up, either to district, state, or national goals. Every year when test scores are reported, they become an occasion for a great deal of commentary in local newspapers. Critics of education wonder why scores are so low, and school district personnel interpret the scores in the best possible light.

Scores tending to remain near average is one of the most common complaints of school critics. Most of these critics do not understand the nature of norm-referenced tests. A school district that has a variety of students from different socioeconomic and cultural backgrounds should find an average score highly satisfactory. If the typical fifth-grade student is achieving on a fifth-grade level, the schools are doing their job. Sometimes more affluent districts' average score is above average, and nearby districts will be criticized for failing to achieve this higher level.

Other times, an average score will drop a point or two, and critics rush in to decry the failure of the school system. There will always be year-to-year fluctuations. Concern should be forthcoming only when scores decrease steadily over several years. Likewise, schools should not take too much credit if scores go up one year. The next year they are likely to have to explain why the scores went down.

▣ EDUCATIONAL RESEARCH

Standardized tests are often useful when we do research in education. Here is the basic idea behind educational research: We treat one group specially. We call this group the **experimental group,** *the group exposed to the special experimental treatment.* We want to contrast the outcomes of the experimental group to *a group that gets the usual treatment,* often called the **control group.** If we can assume the two groups were the same at the beginning of the experiment, then any difference in outcomes can be attributed to the experimental condition. Here's an example from early history (which may or may not be true). An Egyptian pharaoh was riding through a city and saw a poor woman sitting on the side of the street. He observed a venomous snake rise up and bite the woman. She immediately ran to the local market and bought some citron and ate it. The pharaoh asked her why she did this. She said that citron was an antidote to the snake's poison.

The pharaoh then had two pits dug in the sand outside of the city. He threw 100 people in each pit and threw in dozens of these venomous snakes. He gave citron to one group (experimental manipulation) and no citron to the other (control condition). Two days later, he came back and counted the dead. All those in the pit without citron were dead; all those who ate citron were still alive. He concluded that citron was an antidote for snake bites.

We can imagine a similar situation in the classroom. Suppose you are a middle school science teacher. You have two classes of students who are below average on their science scores on the ITBS. You have an idea about how you might teach science better. Instead of following the normal curriculum, which consists of reading three to four pages of the science textbook every day and supplementing lectures with demonstrations and videos, you decide to throw out the textbook and have students conduct real experiments every day. You go to your principal, and he is halfheartedly behind you. "Try it out in one class," he suggests, setting you up to do educational research.

You decide to use the ITBS science tests scores as your measure of the effectiveness of your new approach. You administer the test at the beginning of the year and again at the end of the year. You compare the changes in test scores between your two sections. You look at two of the kinds of scores produced by the ITBS: raw scores (the number of items correct) and the percentile scores (the relative standing of each student in terms of other students). Here is what you find:

	RAW SCORES		PERCENTILE SCORES	
	PRE	POST	PRE	POST
Experimental class	21	34	43	51
Control class	20	26	42	41

Remember that raw scores refer to the number of items correct. In your experimental class the average scores changed from 21 to 34, while in your control class they only changed from 20 to 26. You can use some statistical tests to determine whether the experimental class changed more than the control class, but we can assume the change of 13 points is bigger than the change of 6 points. The percentile scores for the control class decreased by 1 point, while the percentile score for the experimental class increased 8 points.

Although this is an excellent study, sometimes you do not have the funding to have both a pretest and a posttest. In this case, if you can assume both groups are the same at the beginning of the study, you do not need to administer the pretest. In our example both groups were at about the same place at the beginning of the study. If we only used the posttest, we would see the same results. Often, however, the groups are not the same at the beginning. For example, if this school grouped by ability, and the experimental group was the high science group and the control class was the medium science group, then only using the posttest would give you results you could not interpret. Whatever strategy you used you might expect the high-ability group to do better than the low-ability group.

Another approach is to have your control group be a historic control group—for example, last year's students. Instead of trying out a new idea in one class and comparing it to another, you change your approach for all classes and compare their scores to the scores from last year. There are some problems with this approach. (The test may have changed, for example.) But if you found that over two years your students did better with the new approach than students did the previous two years, you may be confident that the new approach works better.

Questions for Reflection

1. Design an educational experiment. Specify what the control condition is and what the new experimental condition is. Indicate what test you might use as the measure of the innovation's effectiveness.
2. Find a newspaper report of your state's testing program, either using standardized tests like the ITBS, or the state's own competency tests. Read the article and comment on it: Does the reporter know what he or she is talking about? Write a letter to the editor critiquing the article.
3. Make a list of the pros and cons of competency testing.

29

Special Achievement
Tests and the
Assessment of Reading

*M*att, a new student, comes to your fifth-grade classroom with no folder from his previous school. You have your students divided into several levels of language arts, mathematics, and social studies, while you do science in multi-ability groups. What do you do with this student until his file arrives?

At the fifth-grade level, the most common concern is determining a student's reading level. Teachers may accomplish this task by using a standardized reading inventory or by constructing an informal reading inventory (IRI). Formal reading assessments take many forms, from word lists that students pronounce to lengthier paper-and-pencil tests similar to the reading subtests of an achievement test battery. Originally IRIs were developed to place students in instructional materials such as basal readers. When most teachers used basal readers, developing an IRI was straightforward. Many basal readers had reading inventories the teacher could administer, or he could develop one of his own rather quickly by taking several graded passages (for Matt, a passage on the fourth-, fifth-, and sixth-grade levels) and determining how well the student deals with each in several aspects of reading. This assessment would tell us (1) on what level the student could read independently; (2) in which group he should be placed for social studies based on his reading level; and (3) in which reading group he should be placed.

In this chapter we discuss readiness tests, reading tests, and other skill-specific achievement tests teachers may use. We conclude this chapter with a brief outline of sources of information about tests.

▨ READINESS TESTS

Readiness tests are used in the early grades to determine who is ready to begin instruction in an area and who needs to remain in prereading and prearithmetic. Although a number of such tests exist, the Metropolitan Readiness Test (MRT) is the most commonly used.

There are two versions of the MRT. Level 1 is appropriate for assessing students at the beginning of kindergarten; level 2 is developed for use in the middle or end of kindergarten. The MRT level 1 consists of six subscales that are administered to small groups of kindergarten students. Normally, one subscale at a time is administered over a period of several days. Each subscale takes between 5 and 25 minutes to administer. The subscales on MRT level 1 are Auditory Memory, Beginning Consonants, Letter Recognition, Visual Matching, School Language and Listening, and Quantitative Language. Level 2 adds Sound-Letter Correspondence, Finding Patterns, and Quantitative Operations. On the Beginning Consonants subscale, examinees are asked to pick which picture begins with the sound the examiner has made. Quantitative language asks examinees to pick out the number of objects spoken by the examiner or the numerical representation of that number.

Although the MRT is technically reliable, there is more controversy about its validity and test-retest reliability. Short-term (two-week) test-retest reliability is acceptable, but the test-retest reliability over a period of several weeks is relatively low. Test-retest reliability for any test of young children is lower than would be expected for older children and adults. This may be the first standardized test children are exposed to, which may further lower its reliability over time. In addition, children's skills change rapidly during this period. The group administration of the test probably has the major effect on its low reliability. A group of 10 active kindergarten students taking their first standardized tests may not be the best situation for determining skill levels. The low reliability of tests in general have led a few states to ban the use of standardized tests in preschool. Other states require them.

The second issue, the MRT's validity, is a more complex issue. The test, originally developed in 1933, was based on the thinking at the time about what skills students must have before being taught to read, count, and add (e.g., Adams, 1990). Research shows that several of the subscales still remaining on the test are not good predictors of early reading. These subscales include Auditory Memory, Visual Matching, and Finding Patterns.

▦ READING TESTS

Standardized reading tests are primarily used to match students to reading materials and to group students together for small-group instruction. Assessment of reading generally involves consideration of two criteria that involve a number of different techniques: word recognition and passage comprehension. For example, individually administered tests may have students pronouncing words in graduated lists, pronouncing words in context, and reading whole sentences out loud; group tests focus on silent reading and usually have students answer questions about material they have read, varying in tasks from word definitions to questions about the content of the material. Oral tests often focus on errors such as refusals, omissions, reversals, mispronunciations, and substitutions, although experienced teachers will make other observations as children read.

In addition to determining the grade-level equivalent of the student's ability, most reading assessments further divide the student's performance into different skill levels. A system of reading levels, developed by Emmett Betts in 1946, is still considered useful. (See Table 29.1.) Betts said the highest level of comprehension (independent reading) required students to recognize most of the words and to be able to comprehend most of the information (90 percent). The independent level was necessary for recreational reading and home reading. A lower level of word recognition and comprehension was necessary for a second level (instructional reading), reading in content areas. Teachers need to explain a good deal of the material in class at this level. Frustration level, where a child may recognize only 90 percent of the words and comprehend as little as 50 percent of the content, would be appropriate for reading instruction: The teacher is there to help students decode the written material as well as understand the content. Understanding content depends on word recognition: If the student does not understand the meaning of a key word in a passage, he will not understand the content. We need to identify a reading level for children for each of these various reading tasks.

There have been criticisms of this system since its inception, but it has been found generally useful by teachers.

In classrooms where the teacher has deliberately excluded basal readers, the teacher's task of selecting appropriate materials for students' reading is more complex. Suppose that a teacher wants to determine whether a recently published book is appropriate for use with a specific student for independent reading or a group of students in an instructional context. To determine the suitability of the text for a reading task, the teacher may construct a **cloze test,**

TABLE 29.1 BETTS' LEVELS OF READING

		% WORD RECOGNITION	**% COMPREHENSION**
Independent reading	the level that can be used for at-home reading	99+	90
Instructional level	the level that should be used in subject-matter instruction	95	75
Frustration level	the level that should be used in reading instruction	90	50

which *measures students' ability to read a text that has important words elimi-nated.* Such a test assesses whether there are enough context cues for a child to understand the gist of the material. Developing a cloze test involves three steps:

1. Select a passage of about 250 words from the text.
2. Leave the first sentence intact and select at random any one of the first five words of the second sentence. Drop that word from the text, and every fifth word thereafter.
3. Reproduce the text. For every fifth word type 15 underlined spaces until 50 underlined blanks have been included. A passage from *Moby Dick*, a relatively difficult text, might look like this:

> Stubb was the second mate. He was a _____ of Cape Cod; and hence _____ to local usage, was _____ a Cape-Cod-man. A happy-go-lucky; _____ craven nor valiant; taking _____ as they came with _____ indifferent air; and while _____ in the most imminent _____ of the chase, toiling _____, calm and collected as a _____ joiner engaged for the _____. Good-humored, easy and careless, _____ presided over his whale-boat _____ if the most deadly _____ were but a dinner, _____ his crew all invited _____.

(The missing words are native, according, called, neither, perils, an, engaging, crisis, away, journeyman, year, he, as, encounter, and, guests.)

In a cloze test, a score of 0 to 38 percent is the frustration level; a score of 40 to 56 percent is the instructional level; and a score of 58 percent or above is the independent level. There were only 16 blanks in this passage; if you got five or fewer, *Moby Dick* is written at your frustration level; if you got six to nine correct, it is at your instructional level; if you got a score of 10 or higher it is at your independent reading level.

Readability formulae, which are based on a number of criteria such as the average number of syllables or letters in words and average sentence length and complexity, analyze a student's ability to read a particular text. Different formulae will produce distinctly different scores, and there is much controversy about which, if any, to use.

▓ OTHER SPECIFIC ACHIEVEMENT TESTS

There are literally hundreds of specific achievement tests available to class-room teachers. Perhaps the most useful of these are tests of mathematics. One of the most widely used is the Key-Math Test, which is useful for students

ɟarten through ninth grade. The test is individually administered
to 50 minutes to give. The test covers basic concepts in numera-
l numbers, and geometry; arithmetic operations; and applica-
reas of measurement, time, money, estimation, interpreting data,
anu problem solving. The test produces a number of norm-referenced (percentile) and criterion-referenced (grade equivalent) scores. Except at the
kindergarten level, reliability and validity are acceptable. The Key-Math test
is useful for both our situation with the new student, Matt, as well as assessment with special needs children.

Another test, which has been used often because of its ease of administration, is the Wide Range Achievement Test. This might be called a quick-
and-dirty test. It is extremely quick to give. Its major disadvantage is the low
quality of the information it produces. It includes reading, spelling, and
arithmetic subscales. The reading subscale consists only of a graded list of
words that the student pronounces, producing a grade-equivalent score.
This test would likely be used only to get a preliminary level of student ability (before Matt's record from his previous school arrives) and has some use
in educational research.

▨ SOURCES OF INFORMATION ABOUT TESTS

There are three main sources of information about standardized tests: test
manuals, research, and test encyclopedias.

Test Manuals

The most specific information about tests can be found in their manuals. Test
manuals are available for almost all commercial tests. These manuals include information about their use, technical qualities (reliability and validity), standardization samples, and administration procedures. As you read
the test manual, keep in mind that the manuals are designed to sell tests and
sometimes omit major concerns about the tests.

Research

Teachers who are interested in specific tests may want to consult the research literature on tests. To access this literature teachers may want to go
on-line to various databases. The most useful database for classroom teachers is ERIC, a huge repository of information about education sponsored by
the federal government. ERIC contains published information about tests
(and other topics relevant to education), and it indexes unpublished sources
of information such as conference papers and government reports. Published documents are coded as EJ (Educational Journals) and unpublished
resources are indexed as RIE (Resources in Education). Most universities
that offer graduate degrees in education have a complete microfiche file of
all of these resources. If you do not have access to a university library, each

report also has a detailed abstract on the database. Often the information on the nature, reliability, and validity of a test is included in these abstracts.

Research on specific tests is most often about the validity of a test; that is, how useful a test is in a particular context. This information is often the most helpful for a teacher in determining whether to use a specific test or not.

Test Encyclopedias

The most complete information about a test can be found in test encyclopediae. The most respected of these encyclopediae are *Tests in Print* and *Mental Measurement Yearbook.* These two sources summarize the nature of tests and also include two reviews from authorities in the field that assess the strengths and weaknesses of the tests. These reviews also include a full listing of the research on the tests. As most tests undergo revisions, tests are reviewed from time to time in these encyclopedias, so you might have to consult more than one volume to get a complete perspective on a particular test. Only the most important tests are included in these volumes.

Question for Reflection

1. Select a test. Find its manual, an ERIC research report, and a review from *Mental Measurement Yearbook*, then write a one-page report about its uses and limitations. *Mental Measurement Yearbook* is now available on line in most college and university libraries.

CHAPTER

30

Interpreting Standardized Tests to Parents and Standardized Tests in Teacher Evaluation

*M*ost teachers have strong opinions about the whole language approach to teaching language arts. Whatever your opinion of the approach is, you would probably agree it has been a case study in poor relations with parents and citizens. Although there are many different versions of whole language teaching, the idea behind it is to make students like reading and writing before saddling them with all of the problems of learning to read and write correctly. Whole language teachers usually use basal readers sparingly, if at all, focusing on works of children's literature. The idea here is that children are more interested in literature than the often-bland stories in basal readers. Also, children will be exposed to good writing rather than the constrained writing in basal readers, which use only the vocabulary children have already mastered. Whole language teachers usually encourage students to use invented spelling and ignore misspellings and grammatical errors for the sake of getting children to enjoy writing about topics that interest them. Whole language teachers believe that after children learn to like reading and writing, they will be more motivated to learn the rules.

Many school districts that adopted the whole language approach continued to use standardized tests based on phonics-method basal reading. Whole language teachers would expect children taught by the whole language method to be behind their agemates who had been taught completely in the phonics tradition. Parents, however, have reacted very negatively to their children's low reading scores, and in district after district, parents have demanded the whole language approach be discontinued. If nothing else, these parents' reactions tell us parents care about their children's scores on achievement tests. The experience of the whole language controversy also reminds us how interwoven curriculum, instruction, and evaluation are. If you change your objectives, you need to change your assessment procedures.

▨ PARENT-TEACHER CONFERENCES

Beginning teachers report one of the most stressful parts of teaching is dealing with parents. All too often the ideal alliance between home and school turns into an adversarial relationship when the child is experiencing difficulty.

Most school districts will schedule parent-teacher conference nights shortly after the results of standardized tests have been returned. First-time parents may be overwhelmed by a page full of numbers reporting their child's progress. Below is a report of the eighth-grade scores for a student on the Iowa Tests of Basic Skills (ITBS).

As we look at the ITBS report, we are faced with 68 numbers. The one thing the parents want to know is "How is my kid doing?" Where do they look in this maze of numbers?

To simplify this set of numbers for parents, explain to them what each column of numbers means. The first column is headed with the label NPCT, which stands for *national percentile*. This school district chose to compare

TABLE 30.1   A STUDENT'S ITBS PROFILE (EIGHTH GRADE)

DESCRIPTION	NPCT	DSS	RAW	GE
Reading vocabulary	89	192	33	10-7
Reading comprehension	66	174	38	9-5
Language				
Spelling	57	170	25	9-0
Capitalization	85	193	23	11-2
Punctuation	90	199	26	11-3
Usage and expression	87	191	34	11-1
Total Language	83	188	108	10-6
Visual materials	83	188	26	10-6
Reference materials	88	196	37	10-9
Total Work Study	86	192	73	10-6
Math concepts	85	185	35	10-6
Math problem solving	88	188	26	10-4
Math computations	57	169	26	8-8
Total Math	81	181	87	9-9
Complete Composite	85	186	339	10-3
Social Studies	92	213	32	12-2
Science	95	216	33	13-0

students' performance against national norms. They could have decided on state norms (SPCT) or local, district norms (LPCT).

The second column is called DSS, which is a standard score, not particularly useful to anyone expect the evaluation experts at the central office of the school district. Likewise, RAW refers to the number correct, also not useful unless you are highly familiar with the test content. Children in the eighth grade may be taking a test designed for eighth-, ninth-, and tenth-grade students, so they are not expected to get all of the answers correct. Also, remember that an ideal item on a standardized, norm-referenced test is one that will be missed by half of the students. Many parents are not familiar with this idea. They just want their children to get all the answers right. The fourth column is GE, or grade equivalent, often the most meaningful score for students and parents. Here's how I would explain this material to parents.

First, I would tell parents to pay attention to percentile scores and GE scores and ignore the other scores. I would tell them these other scores are primarily for research purposes. That eliminates half the information.

I would then explain that a NPCT percentile score is the percentage of all other eighth-grade students their daughter did better than of the hundreds of thousands of students who took the test, and that GE scores tell me what level their daughter is working on. The first number is the grade and the second is the month. 10-6 means tenth grade, sixth month. Their daughter took this test during the fifth month of the eighth grade. She is working two years ahead of expectations.

Then I'd look at the total score, which is the Complete Composite. I can tell this student's parents she did better than 85 percent of the students nationally who took the test, and she is functioning overall like a tenth-grade student. That is, she is almost two years ahead of the average student.

Next I would look at the total math, total language, social studies, and science scores. This student's profile looks like this:

Math   81   9-9
Language   83   10-6
Social studies 92   12-2
Science   95   13-0

She is about a year ahead in math, two years ahead in language, four years ahead in social studies, and almost five years ahead in science. This is excellent news.

Yet, I would bet that the parents of this student will focus on spelling (57th percentile) and math computations (57th percentile). Fifty-seven sounds like a failing grade, doesn't it? I might want to reassure the parents this is not what 57 means. It means she is above average. I can point to the grade-equivalent scores. She is about half a year ahead in these two areas.

These are her weak areas, but they are above average. Interestingly, both involve rote memory, which is a relatively easy area to improve: Perhaps she needs to practice math computations and spelling a little bit every day. If she does this, over time, she will improve. There is little cause for concern because she is above grade level. I would caution these parents against putting their daughter into a focused program to improve these basic rote-memory skills and emphasize how well she is doing on the higher-level skills.

I began with this student because there is no bad news here. Your primary job is to help parents understand what the scores mean. But there will be many other times when the news is not as good.

Suppose that you have an eighth-grade student whose summary profile looks like this:

Math	43	6-8
Language	33	5-3
Social studies	39	5-9
Science	31	5-1

This child is nearly two years behind in math and three years behind in language, social studies, and science. As you help the parents understand what these scores mean, each number will convey bad news about their son's academic achievement.

There is a tendency when such information is conveyed to parents for assigning blame to become the focus of the discussion. Is it the school's fault? Is it the parent's fault? Is it the student's fault? Or, most conveniently, is it the test's fault? Parents want to be assured it is not their fault, and few teachers will decide it is theirs.

One of the first things you might want to consider in such a situation is the information you have been sending the parents throughout the year. Test scores usually come out in the spring, so you have sent home a great deal of graded work and several report cards. If you have been sending home all A's and Excellents, the parents will have some reason to be critical of you. "Why did we not see this coming?" is a legitimate question. If you have been sending home more C's and Needs Improvements, the parents have little to criticize.

Likewise, if you have seen this coming, but never requested a parent conference nor sent home requests for the parents to become more involved in supervising the student's homework, it would be inappropriate for you to question whether the parents have been doing their job. Nor can you blame the student if you have not alerted the parents to some shortcoming in the student's attention to his work.

Assigning blame is a waste of time in most cases. Blaming the child in this situation is risky, particularly if the parents are upset by his scores. They might punish him severely or they might impose a harsh study regimen that will teach him to hate school work even more than he already does. Blaming the parents will probably have no good result, even if they have ignored your requests for conferences. Blaming the test is usually a cheap shot. Of course, there may be situations where something did go wrong with the testing procedure. My very first paid day of teaching came when I was substitute teaching and I had to administer the Stanford Achievement Tests. I had several students who had just returned from being absent with the flu for several days. These kids were still somewhat sick. I complained to the guidance counselor, but she said to give the test to them anyway. That was a mistake, and if such a thing has happened, the problem should be acknowledged. But if the tests confirm what you have known about the student's level of achievement for some time, trying to get out of an uncomfortable situation by dismissing the test scores will do no service for the student.

A more productive strategy is to focus on what information the tests provide that can serve as the basis for a remedial approach. Although the student's mathematics score is also low, his main problems seem to come from those areas that rely on language. We can then look at his grade-equivalent subscores in language:

Reading vocabulary	5-4
Reading comprehension	5-1
Language spelling	4-5
Capitalization	6-2
Punctuation	6-1
Usage and expression	4-8

These scores tell us his problem is likely one of decoding reading: He's relatively strong in the skills of capitalization and punctuation, but every subscore that has to do with understanding words in context is low. Parents can help by knowing more about their student's habits at home. First, you might ask whether the boy reads at home and what he reads. Second, you might ask about his TV viewing habits. Third, you might ask whether the parents read to him, subscribe to a newspaper, or have a library card. These will give you hints about possible avenues of remediation.

Often the best suggestions involve asking the parents to do something that correlates with your plans. You will go with him to the library every two weeks and help him select a book if the parents will make sure he spends 30 minutes every night reading that book. You will send a section of a newspaper home with him every week if the parents will read one article with him every night. You will send home an extra 10 spelling words every week if the parents will agree to have him rehearse for 10 minutes on Monday, Wednesday, and Thursday evenings. Rather than trying to decide who is responsible, such a strategy suggests everyone, you, the parents, and most of all, the student, will be making some changes that are likely to lead to improvement. If you can get this child to read half an hour a night more than he does, and if you can get the parents more involved in his learning, there is a good chance he will do better.

Sometimes scores are so low they suggest a child needs to become involved in a review by the child study team. This boy's scores are at that level. Whether this conference is the time to make this suggestion, is a judgment call. If the parents are upset and angry, this may not be the time. You might suggest a new approach be put in place for nine weeks, after which you will assess his reading with a reading inventory and have a follow-up conference. You can, of course, consult the child study team on your own. If parents inquire about special programs, this might very well be the time to discuss the child study team. Keep in mind that parental cooperation with the child study team process is critical and try to avoid making it unpleasant.

▨ STANDARDIZED TESTS IN TEACHER EVALUATION

One of the nightmares beginning teachers think about is the possibility that after what they consider a successful year of teaching, their principal calls them in to discuss their annual performance. After describing the teacher's challenges and successes, the principal puts the students' standardized test scores in front of the teacher and asks why their eighth-grade students have not done better.

Suppose she puts down a computer printout of the average scores on the ITBS for the students in your class and the results are as follows:

	NPCT
Math	48
Language	42
Social studies	51
Science	46

Your students are scoring below national norms on mathematics, language, and science, and just barely above national norms on social studies. "Explain yourself," she says.

There are several responses you might make at this point. The first is to resign in a huff, preserving whatever dignity and career options you may still have. The second might be to protest that the tests did not measure the objectives you had for your class. After reading this book, you should be able to do this, but be sure you can justify it. The third might be to spin an explanation of why 46, 48, and 51 are not really that bad and to promise to work at language arts harder next year. A fourth might be to assert proudly that you are not teaching to the test and hope the principal agrees with you. Finally, you might want to claim that, because you are a first-year teacher, you got the lowest ability group, and these results are not actually that bad.

Each of these responses has some merit. But none of them has a realistic, completely professional tenor to them.

In general, it is not appropriate for an individual teacher to be held responsible for the achievement of his or her students on an achievement test battery. If a test is administered every three years, then the test measures the students' learning over the whole period, not just the year in which the tests were administered. The teacher may have met her objectives, but the curriculum was at fault: Perhaps there was a heavy emphasis on the math test with squares and square roots, but no one had covered them. Isn't the curriculum the responsibility, at least to some extent, of the principal? However, trying to blame the principal at this point is probably the least effective defense.

In over 25 years of working in and with public schools, I have found this kind of situation very rare. Yet, we do want teachers to be responsible for their students' learning, and many educators find achievement tests useful in assessing how well students are doing. Every test I know of includes a statement in the test manual that it is not appropriate for teacher evaluation. On the other hand, I have known teachers whose students have done particularly well on tests who would like to use those test scores as part of their evaluations.

If a school district wants to use standardized test scores as part of teacher evaluation, two considerations need to be addressed. The first has to do with pretesting. An eighth-grade teacher cannot be responsible for the accumulation of learning between the fourth-grade administration of the ITBS and the eighth-grade ITBS. A few school districts administer these tests every year, though. Would it not be fair to hold teachers accountable for their students' learning in this situation? Even more to the point, on state competency tests, shouldn't school districts hold teachers accountable for their students' progress on such tests?

The second issue has to do with the scores we use. Suppose we are in a school district that gives the ITBS every year. Shouldn't we expect at least a year's progress on the tests in a year?

We might expect a year's progress every year if the students were performing at a grade level. Suppose you had a group of students who were average. They began the year at 8-0; it would be reasonable to expect them to make a year's progress while they were in your classroom. But what if your eighth-grade students at the beginning of the year were on average at 6-5. Over the course of their first seven years of education, this group had been making about 80 percent of a year's progress. Why should you be accountable to a higher standard?

If we were to use standardized tests to evaluate teachers, we should use percentile test scores. The expectation should be that the average percentile scores should stay the same or make some progress. We hope teachers of lower-ability students make a whole year's progress, but the expectation of competence would only be that the students maintain their relative ranking. The percentile score, rather than the grade-equivalent score, should be used to make that determination.

That said, there are much better ways of measuring teacher effectiveness than on achievement test batteries or state competency tests. Throughout this book I have made some suggestions about how teachers might accumulate useful evidence for evaluations: samples of individual student work that show how the instructional objectives have been met; tests keyed to the teacher's objectives; tables showing how the teacher's objectives are tied to state or district objectives; and so on. This evidence is more impressive than scores on tests developed to measure general, national objectives.

▦ TEACHING TO THE TEST

When we read op ed pieces in newspapers or discussions of education in professional journals, we frequently encounter a slogan. For example, opponents of state competency tests often claim such tests will force teachers to *teach to the test.* This is a bad thing, right?

In this book I have advocated an approach to teaching and assessment that is sometimes called seamless teaching. In seamless teaching the curricular objectives are translated into carefully crafted instruction and measured authentically by assessments designed to directly assess whether the objectives have been met. In this case one teaches to the test and tests to the teaching.

Teaching to the test is not a bad thing if it is the right test. That's seamless teaching. Teaching to the test is only a bad thing if the test does not reflect the goals of the curriculum. Teachers have a professional responsibility to make sure the assessments that evaluate their students and themselves adequately measure what students should be learning and what teachers should be teaching. Teachers need not agree with each objective, nor do they need to feel as if district, state, or national objectives are the only ones that need to be met. There is always room for additional objectives, both from the state, district, and teacher. Teachers, like students, are responsible for mastering the objectives given to them to master. If they have not mastered them, they should have a plan for doing better.

Questions for Reflection

1. With another student in the class, role-play a parent-teacher conference using the two sets of test scores in this chapter. In both cases the parent should play a concerned parent who wants to understand his child's performance and what can be done to improve it. Write a summary of your role play.
2. Suppose you have a group of students in your class who are one year behind in mathematics and one year ahead in social studies. What would you consider a fair level of accountability for your students' achievements for the school year? Make a contract with your principal about the expectations for your students at the end of the year.

■

Accommodations (15) Legally binding changes in normal classroom procedures required for individual handicapped children by their I.E.P.

Achievement Test (2; 28) a test which is primarily designed to determine what a student has learned.

Adaptation (21) the sixth level of the Psychomotor Domain in which students learn to modify their performances to meet situational demands.

Adaptive Behavior Assessment (27) a checklist of routine behavior (dressing one's self, self-care behaviors) used in assessing degree of retardation.

Adaptive Testing (28) computer-assisted testing in which higher-level objectives are first assessed; if higher-level objectives are met, then lower-level objectives are assumed to have been mastered.

Affective Domain (8) that portion of the taxonomy of instructional objectives that measures emotional outcomes, such as attending to and valuing.

Aids to Memory (21) notes that will help us develop assessments of student class participation and conduct.

Alternate-Form Reliability (4) if two versions of a test are to be used interchangeably, they should show high correlations with each other.

Analysis-Level Objectives (8) the fourth level in the cognitive taxonomy. Analysis objectives ask students to find the basic structure of complex material; for example, outlining a story or discovering the premises on which an argument is built.

Answer Bank (10) a technique often used with fill-in-the-blanks tests at the elementary school level; potential answers are given by the teacher. This technique changes the fill-in-the-blank item from a supply-type assessment to a recognize-type item.

Application-Level Objectives (8) the third level in the cognitive domain. In Applications-level objectives, students must demonstrate their ability to use information in a new context or develop original examples.

Aptitude Test (2) a test used to predict future academic performance.

Arithmetic Mean (6) an average computed by adding all scores together and then dividing by the number of scores ($\Sigma x/N$); often called the average.

Assessment (1) a sample of behavior taken under standard conditions.

Authentic Assessment (24) a process in which educational objectives are measured as directly as possible.

Authorship (4; 20) the question of who made a particular object or wrote a particular writing sample.

Battery (28) a test consisting of a number of different subtests.

Behavior (1) observable activity.

Behavior-Anchored Ratings (22) in rating other's performance, behaviors are described along a continuum for rating, rather than using global ratings.

Chronological Age (26) actual age (since birth).

Number in parentheses refers to chapter where term is discussed.

Cloze Test (29) a procedure used to determine a student's level of reading in which a passage of known reading level has every fifth word eliminated and students attempt to supply the missing words.

Cognitive Domain (8) that part of the taxonomy of instructional objectives that deals with thinking.

Complex Overt Response (21) the fifth level of the taxonomy of the psychomotor domain in which simple, well-practiced skills are combined into complex performances.

Composing (18) see Drafting.

Comprehension-Level Objectives (8) the second level of the cognitive domain. Students must be able to demonstrate they understand factual material, often by stating information in their own words.

Concurrent Validity (5) a form of criterion-related validity in which the assessment is compared to the criterion at the same time

Content Validity (5) an estimate of the relation between a test and a set of objectives. Content validity can be assessed using a table of specifications.

Control Group (28) in educational research, those who receive the typical educational intervention.

Correlation (7) the degree of relation between two variables.

Correlation Coefficient (7) a numerical representation of the degree of relation between two variables. A low relation (0.00 to 0.30) indicates a small relation; a moderate relation is indicated by a value between 0.30 and 0.70; a strong relation is indicated by a relation above 0.70. A positive value indicates that as one variable increases, so does the other; but a negative value indicates while one increases that the other decreases.

Criterion-Referenced Tests (1) tests that score against a standard (or criterion). For example, an acceptable passing score on a professional licensing examination may be 90 percent; 90 percent is the criterion. Criterion-referenced tests are contrasted to norm-referenced tests.

Criterion Validity (5) the degree of relationship between a test and a standard the test has been developed to predict. For example, IQ tests were originally developed to predict how well students would do in school, so scores in IQ tests were com-

pared to overall school grades (criterion). See Concurrent Validity and Predictive Validity.

Critical Event Bias (21) in making assessment based on memory, a tendency to remember big events rather than routine ones. We may remember one explosive conduct problem more than 44 productive days.

Curving (14) a norm-referenced grading procedure in which the distribution of scores is based on a theoretical curve, such as 2 percent F's, 14 percent D's, 68 percent C's, 14 percent B's, and 2 percent A's, based on one interpretation of the normal curve.

Descriptive Rubrics (16) see Rubric.

Descriptive Statistics (6) a number that summarizes a set of numbers. Examples of descriptive statistics are means, medians, ranges, and standard deviations.

Developmental Delay (26) low intellectual functioning in primary grade students of unknown origin.

Deviation Score (6) the distance a particular score is from the mean. A score above the mean is given a positive score; those below it are given a negative score. With a mean of 9, a score of 11 has a deviation score of +2. With a mean of 200, a score of 100 has a deviation score of −100.

Diagnostic Assessment (1) tests given before instruction to determine what students already know or can do.

Difficulty Index (11) the percentage of students getting an item correct.

Disadvantagement (26) low intellectual functioning due to family and cultural issues.

Discrimination Index (11) the difference between the percentage of top students getting an item correct and the percentage of low-scoring students getting the item correct.

Distractor (10) one of the wrong answers to a multiple-choice item. The term *distractor* implies the answer should be reasonable in some way.

Drafting (18) the first stage of the writing process.

Dyslexia (27) disruption of reading.

Editing (18) see Revision.

Evaluation (1) the use of assessment information to make administrative decisions about students, teachers, and programs.

Evaluation-Level Objectives (8) the highest level in the cognitive domain of the taxonomy of instructional objectives in which students are expected to evaluate a complex event by some external criteria.

Experimental Group (28) in educational research, the group that receives the new procedure that will be compared to a control group.

Expert Model of Group Work (22) the idea that students should work in the area of their ability when working in a group. See Interchangeable Model of Group Work.

Face Validity (5) the extent to which test takers believe the test is useful.

Fluency (20) a quality of creativity. Creative individuals often are able to make many different responses in the same situation.

Formative Assessment (1) tests given to see how well instruction is going.

Frequency (20) a quality of creativity. Creative responses are relatively rare or infrequent.

Gatekeeping (23) in portfolio assessment, adding items to the portfolio only under two conditions: (1) they show that a new objective has been met or (2) they show that an objective has been met better than material already in the portfolio; in the latter case, the original material is purged and replaced with the new material.

General Ability Tracking (2) see Tracking.

Gifted (26) having an IQ at least two standard deviations above the mean (> 130).

Global Ratings (22) in opinion research, asks for a ranking based on overall categories (strongly agree, agree, disagree, strongly disagree).

Goal (3) a general statement of the expectations of instruction. In contrast to objectives, goals are often global and hard to pin down.

Grade-Equivalent Score (11) a score on an achievement test indicating typical level of achievement in terms of grade and month.

Grading (1) the process of assigning a letter or number to a product or group of products. Grading is based on assessment but is not synonymous with assessment.

Halo Effect (21) a tendency to remember good things about good students, and bad things about bad students.

Heterogeneous Grouping (2) the practice of placing children together in classrooms irrespective of their ability.

Inclusion (15) the practice of having special education teachers come into a regular classroom to assist the teacher's work with handicapped students.

Individualized Educational Plan (15) see I.E.P.

I.E.P. (15; 27) (Individualized Educational Plan) the official document prepared by the child study team for a handicapped child, which includes a diagnosis, an annual set of educational objectives, and a list of instructional and assessment accommodations.

Inferential Statistics (6) statistics used to make decisions; for example, a correlation coefficient used to determine whether a test is reliable or valid.

Informal Assessment (1) sometimes used to describe teacher-made assessments, particularly in the area of reading.

Interchangeable Model of Group Work (22) the approach that in group work students should learn to perform all group roles.

Intelligence Quotient (26) $MA/CA \times 100$ (mental age/chronological age)

Inter-rater Reliability (4) the extent to which two or more raters will give the same product the same assessment.

Item-Based Rubric (16) see Rubric.

Knowledge-Level Objectives (8) the first level of the cognitive taxonomy. Knowledge-level objectives involve only memory; for example, remembering all the words to a poem or being able to answer the question $4 \times 6 = ?$. Technically, the student does not need to understand what the facts mean.

Labeling (2) the concern that once an official label is applied to a child, the child will conform to the expectations of that label (e.g., if a child is labeled emotional disturbed he will engage in more acting-out behavior to conform to the label he has been given).

Learning Disabled (15; 26) an official designation given to a student who has a lag of two or more years in one or more verbal skill areas, although the student has overall normal ability.

Mainstreaming (15) the practice of keeping handicapped children in the regular classroom as much as possible and only sending them out to a special education resource room for skill training.

Mean (6) the arithmetic average, computed by the formula $M = \Sigma x/N$, where M = mean, Σx is the sum of all the individual scores, and N = the number of scores.

Mechanism (21) the third level of the psychomotor domain taxonomy in which the student is beginning to repeat a response so that it becomes automatic.

Median (6) the middle score in an ordered set of numbers. If the set of numbers has an even number, the median is the average of the two numbers in the center.

Mental Age (26) age equivalent on an IQ test. One's pattern is similar to typical test takers at this age.

Mental Retardation (26) overall low intellectual functioning, two standard deviations below the mean.

Mnemonic (12) a memorization key, such as ROY G. BIV for remembering the colors of the spectrum in order (red, orange, yellow, green, blue, indigo, and violet).

Mode (6) the most frequent score in a group of scores. Sets of numbers may have more than one mode or none.

Multiple-Choice Item (10) a recall item in which students select the correct answer from among a group of possible answers.

N (6) the symbol that indicates the number of observations in a statistical calculation.

Negative Scoring (16) a procedure in which points are lost when certain errors are observed on a student product or performance, such as when a teacher deducts points for each misspelled word.

Normal Distribution (25) a bell-shaped curve, with mean = median = mode.

Norm-Referenced Tests (1) an assessment on which scores are derived from each student's standing within a group; a teacher who always gives the highest-scoring three students an A, regardless of their numerical performance, is using norm-referenced grading.

Objective (3) a statement of curricular expectations written in terms of the behavior that students would be able to exhibit after instruction.

Objective Item (10) a recall item in which scoring is objective; that is, little decision-making is required from the test scorer.

Open-Ended Question (28) a question to which students provide answers rather than select one from a multiple choice.

Origination (21) the highest level of the psychomotor domain taxonomy in which children develop their own creative performances.

Parallel Form (4) a specific kind of alternate form test, in which items are constructed so that very similar items appear on each test; that is, items 5 on both test would be about very similar content.

Percentile Score (11; 25) the percentage of individuals one has done better than on a norm-referenced test.

Perception (21) the lowest level on the psychomotor domain taxonomy in which the student receives information that will guide his or her performance.

Portfolio (16; 23) a collection of student products assembled for summative evaluation.

Positive Scoring (16) the procedure of awarding points when specific items on a rubric are observed in a student product or performance. See Negative Scoring.

Predictive Validity (5) a form of criterion-related validity in which the test and the criterion are separate in time. The test is used to predict the criterion, which will be measured in the future.

Psychomotor Domain (8) that part of the taxonomy of instructional objectives that deals with physical performances, such as writing, sports, or public speaking; the prefix *psycho* implies the motor performance is guided by mental processes.

Qualitative Assessment/Grading (1, 14) assessment procedures that result in a verbal result.

Quantitative Assessment/Grading (1, 14) assessment procedures that result in a numerical result.

Random Sample (1) a random sample objective has an equal probability of appearing on a test as any other objective.

Range (6) the distance between the highest score in a sample and the lowest.

Rational Sample (1) selecting the content of a test on the basis of the importance of certain content appearing on the test.

Recency Effect (21) in evaluating responses based on memory, we are more likely to remember more recent events that more remote events.

Reliability (4) a measure of the accuracy of a test. See Alternate Form Reliability; Interrater Reliablity; Test-Retest Reliability.

Retrospective Assessment (23) (1) the practice of recalling information about assessment categories such as class participation or conduct; (2) in portfolio assessment, the practice of accumulating material and later seeing whether the objectives have been met (in contrast to gatekeeping).

Revision (18) the second state of writing in which changes are made to a first draft.

Rubric (16) an assessment system for awarding classifications, comments, or grades to a complex student product or performance. There are two principal kinds of rubrics: item-based rubrics, which give points for different components of the performance, and descriptive rubrics, which give a general description of the level of performance.

Sample (1) objectives assessed on a test.

Sample Size (6) see N.

Satisfaction Assessment (1) methods used to determine whether students are enjoying their education, such as asking students to rate the books they have been reading.

Scaling (14) a method of correcting scores on a test before awarding grades. Most frequently this process involves adding a number of points to each student's score.

Screening Test (28) a test that divides candidates with prerequisite skills from those who do not have those skills.

Set (21) the second level of the psychomotor domain taxonomy in which a student indicates readiness to take part in a motor activity.

Short-Answer Item (12) a supply-type item that does not require organization.

Standard Deviation (6) a measure of dispersion with unique statistical properties. The formula is $\sqrt{\Sigma d^2/N}$; the standard deviation is the basis for z-scores.

Student-Constructed Response (28) an item in which the process of student work is captured; for example, students write down all steps in a multistep math problem.

Subject-Ability Grouping (2) the process of grouping students for instruction by ability, subject by subject; this is in contrast to general ability tracking and heterogeneous grouping.

Summative Assessment (1) the final phase of assessment at the end of an instructional unit or grading period.

Swiss Cheese Item (12) a fill-in-the-blanks item with too many blanks.

Synthesis-Level Objectives (8) the fifth level of the cognitive domain. Synthesis-level objectives ask students to combine two or more complex ideas to form original ideas.

Table of Specifications (9) a graphic that shows the relation among curricular objectives, instructional strategies, and assessment instruments.

Taxonomy (8) A hierarchical classification system.

Taxonomy of Educational Objectives (8) a system of writing objectives based on an analysis of cognitive, affective, and psychomotor learning.

Test (1) see Assessment.

Test-Retest Reliability (4) a form of reliability in which a test is administered twice to the same students, both administrations either before or after instruction; if the test is reliable, the scores should be very similar in both administrations and the correlation between scores should be high.

Tracking (2) grouping students for all of their instruction on the basis of their overall ability; for example, placing students in high school in the college-bound track or the vocational track.

True-False Item (10) a recall item in which students must determine whether a statement is either completely true or has errors in it.

Unweighted Mean (6) see Arithmetic Mean.

Validity (5) the extent to which a test is useful in a particular situation. See Construct Validity; Content Validity; and Criterion Validity.

Weighted Mean (6) an average in which different scores are given different weights; for example, a final examination score may count three times that of a weekly test.

Z-Score (11; 25) a norm-referenced measure of where one falls in a distribution of scores based on standard deviation (z) units. A person who falls one standard deviation above the mean has a z-score of +1, while a person who falls two standard deviations below the mean has a z-score of −2.

ANNOTATED BIBLIOGRAPHY

■

General

1. Anastasi, Anne, & Urbina, Susana. 1997. *Psychological Testing* (7th edition). Upper Saddle River, NJ: Prentice Hall.

   In any edition, the definitive text on testing. For questions about tests properties, this is the book to consult. Unfortunately, it is heavy on standardized tests and light on teacher-made tests and educationally relevant tests.

2. Gardner, Howard. 1982. *Frames of Mind: The Theory of Multiple Intelligences*. New York: Basic Books.

   Still probably the best introduction to how Gardner's ideas can be applied to classrooms can be seen in the third part of this early book. Gardner has developed a new "intelligence" or two since 1982, but his ideas on instruction and assessment were never as clearly put as here. Not everyone will agree with his assumptions.

3. Popham, W. James. 1998. "Farewell, Curriculum: Confessions of an Assessment Convert." *Phi Delta Kappan, 79,* 380–384.

   A personal statement about one educator's transition from an exclusive focus on curriculum issues to an understanding of the importance of assessment after working on developing statewide, high-stakes assessments.

History of Testing

4. DuBois, P. H. 1970. *A History of Psychological Testing*. Boston, MA: Allyn & Bacon.

   A comprehensive history of psychological testing. This book gives excellent accounts of the Chinese origins of achievement testing and includes background on tests other than educational assessments, such as normal and abnormal personality assessments.

5. Lane, Harlan. 1976. *The Wild Boy of Aveyron.* Cambridge, MA: Harvard University.

   This remains the most readable account of the story of Victor, the wild boy of Aveyron. Lane puts the case study in historical perspective and traces its lasting influence on the education of handicapped children. For those who would like to learn more about the case, but are not committed to reading an entire book, the 1970 film *L'Enfant Sauvage* by the French director Francois Truffaut is limited to the early part of Victor's life in the civilized world, but is highly accurate and moving.

6. Linden, K. W., & Linden, J. D. 1968. *Modern Mental Measurement: A Historical Perspective*. Boston, MA: Houghton Mifflin.

   A short and accessible history of testing, focusing on achievement and aptitude testing.

7. Worthen, Blaine R. 1993. "Critical Issues That Will Determine the Future of Alternative Assessment." *Phi Delta Kappan, 76,* 444–454.

   This is a very balanced statement about the problems authentic assessment faces, which includes a thorough statement of what authentic assessment is and what its goals are. Professor Worthen focuses on the feasibility, financial and teacher effort costs, and whether various groups of test users, including parents, employers, and colleges, will buy into the new approaches. He also discusses whether the authentic movement has built into it enough self-criticism to be able to sort between excellent and not excellent practices. There is a short follow-up article by the same author that lists 10 issues schools should consider before moving into authentic assessment.

Reliability and Validity

8. Wainer, Howard, & Braun, Henry I. (eds.). *Test Validity*. 1988. Hillsdale, NJ: Lawrence Erlbaum.

A comprehensive approach to a variety of issues of validity. Particularly of interest are chapters by Warren Willingham on the problem of validity when dealing with handicapped individuals; an extended commentary on the importance of construct validity in intelligence testing; and a basic chapter on concepts and definitions by Lee J. Cronbach.

9. Mangano, Nancy G., Willson, Victor L., & Rupley, William H. 1986. "Practical Suggestions for Increasing the Reliability of Classroom Observational Research." *Reading Research and Instruction, 25,* 184–191.

This article is about research, but all of the suggestions are useful for classroom teachers as well. There are many practical ideas about making your class notes of children more accurate. There are also some very practical suggestions about observing teachers, which would be useful for any teacher who has a student teacher—or any teacher who is about to be observed.

10. McCleary, William J. 1979. "A Note on Reliability and Validity Problems in Compositional Research." *Research in the Teaching of English, 13,* 274–277.

This article will be of most interest to middle and high school teachers who use written essays, both on and off timed tests.

11. Murphy, Meg. January, 1981. "What's Your Classroom Testing Validity Quotient?" *School Shop, 40 (5),* 18–20, 27.

The article addresses the issues of reliability and validity from the perspective of a very performance-based discipline, school shop. This article is of particular interest for the development of an example of a table of specifications in a discipline that does not rely heavily on traditional tests.

12. Froman, Robin D., & Owen, Steven V. 1991. "Teaching Reliability and Validity: Fun with Classroom Applications." *The Journal of Continuing Education in Nursing, 22,* 88–94.

This may not seem like an article on the "must" list, but it is very provocative on the issues of reliability and validity. In nursing, particularly in continuing education, the issue of performance assessment and the validity of paper-and-pencil tests are critical: We want nurses to be able to *do* procedures, not answer multiple-choice questions about them.

Objectives

13. Mager, Robert F. 1962. *Preparing Instructional Objectives*. Palo Alto, CA: Fearon.

This little book (60 pages) remains the best introduction to the philosophy and procedures of objective-based education. It can be read in two hours and may be a transforming experience. A second edition was published in 1975.

14. Bloom, B. S., Englehart, M. D., Furst, E. J., Hill, W. H., & Krathwohl, D. R. 1956. *Taxonomy of Educational Objectives, Handbook I: Cognitive Domain*. New York: Longmans Green.
    See 16.

15. Krathwohl, D. R., Bloom, B. S., & Masia, B. B. 1964. *Taxonomy of Educational Objectives, Handbook II: Affective Domain*. New York: David Mckay.
    See 16.

16. Simpson, E. J. 1972. *The Classification of Educational Objectives in the Psychomotor Domain. The Psychomotor Domain, Volume 3.* Washington, DC: Gryphon House.

Along with number 14 and 15, this volume represents the best introduction to the taxonomy of educational objectives. These are not lively reads, but they are clear and comprehensive. Prospective teachers would do well to spend an hour or two with each of these volumes, particularly those with which they will be primarily working.

Statistics

17. Edwards, Allen L. 1976. *An Introduction to Linear Regression and Correlation*. San Francisco, CA: W. H. Freeman.

More about correlation than most teachers will ever want to know, but for the adventurous (or mathematics teachers) Chapters 4–6 offer a wealth of information. The approach is algebra-based, not calculus-based.

18. Vissa, Jeanne M. 1988. "Probability and Combinations for Third Graders," *The Arithmetic Teacher, 36,* 33–37.

Not only does this article have excellent ideas about introducing the basic ideas of probability and statistics to elementary school students, it has an excellent review of these ideas for teachers.

Classroom Tests

19. Flynn, Mary Kay, & Reese, Jean L. 1988. "Development and Evaluation of Classroom Tests: A Practical Application." *Journal of Nursing Education, 27,* 61–65.

Although the test described is for undergraduate nursing students, this is an ideal example of all of the steps, including validity, reliability, item analysis, and determining grades.

20. Fairbain, Donald M. 1993. "Creating Story Problems," *Arithmetic Teacher, 41,* 140–142.

There are some interesting suggestions here for creating questions that involve students in arithmetic classes.

21. Salend, Spencer J. 1995 "Modifying Tests for Diverse Learners," *Intervention in School and Clinic, 31,* 84–90.

This article extends the issues of modifying tests to meet the needs of special students.

22. Kleinheider, Janet K. 1996. "Assessment Matters." *Science and Children, 22,* 23–25, 41.

This article describes an assessment technique largely like a traditional test, but it incorporates some performance-based ideas. The description is primarily in the area of science, but it has potential in any subject area.

23. Kolstad, Rosemarie K., Briggs, L. D., & Kolstad, Robert A. 1985. "Multiple-choice Classroom Achievement Tests: Performance on Items with Five vs. Three Choices." *College Student Journal, 19,* 427–431.

A useful consideration of the forms of multiple-choice tests with older students.

Item Analysis

24. Nimmer, Donald N. 1984. "Measures of Validity, Reliability, and Item Analysis for Classroom Tests," *The Clearing House, 58,* 138–140.

A quick review of assuring classroom test quality.

25. Kolstad, Rosemarie K., Briggs, L. D., & Kolstad, Robert A. 1984. "The Application of Item Analysis to Classroom Achievement Tests." *Education, 105,* 70–72.

A quick review of item analysis techniques and a good example of why such analysis will strengthen tests.

Performance-Based Assessment

26. Brown, Janet H., & Shavelson, Richard J. September, 1994. "Does Your Testing Match Your Teaching Style?" *Instructor, 104 (2),* 86–89.

This article is an excellent beginning point for a teacher who wants to adopt performance assessments in the classroom. The authors want to use performance assessments as well as traditional tests. The examples given are mostly in the area of science, and some ideas about managing performance assessments are given. The second author, Richard J. Shavelson, is a leading authority in the field, and the references included will be useful for teachers wanting to go into more depth.

27. Palmquist, Bruce C. "Scoring Rubrics for Interview Assessment." *The Physics Teacher, 35,* 88–89.

Palmquist carefully describes a method of scoring a post-experiment interview with students to see if they understand procedures and findings, as well as the conceptual underpinnings. This procedure can be readily modified for other subject areas when the teacher believes that talking with a student may be a more authentic way of getting to what a student understands than through a written product.

28. Edwards, D. 1982. "Project Marking: Some Problems and Issues." *Teaching at a Distance, 21,* 28–34.

This is a provocative paper, dealing with projects done by adult learners, but it has applications for any projects done outside of the classroom.

29. Jones, Layman H. March, 1995. "Recipe for Assessment: How Arty Cooked his Goose while Grading Art." *Art Education,* 12–17.

A very interesting argument for not using special standards in grading students' art work. One may not agree with everything in this article, but it is a useful read before beginning to use art as a means of assessing students' knowledge.

30. Bergman, Abby Barry. February, 1993. "Performance Assessment for Early Childhood," *Science and Children, 30 (5)*, 20–22.

This article contains several practical suggestions for assessing science in kindergarten and first-grade programs, stressing the importance of teacher observation and well-planned products.

31. Grehaigne, Jean-Francis, & Godbout, Paul. "Performance Assessment in Team Sports." *Journal of Teaching in Physical Education, 16*, 500–516.

We are way outside of the cognitive domain, but elementary school teachers may be called on to assess aspects of their students' physical development, and this is a very careful analysis of physical ability and the ability to play sports.

Assessing Writing

32. Bereiter, Carl. 1980. "Development in Writing." In L. W. Gregg and E. R. Steinberg (eds). *Cognitive Processes in Writing* (pp. 73–93). Hillsdale, NJ: Lawrence Erlbaum.

This chapter may be a little hard to find, but there is no better description of the steps required for teaching children to write. This chapter is genuinely developmental, both in terms of age and stage.

33. Elbow, Peter. 1993. "Ranking, Evaluating, and Liking: Sorting Out Three Forms of Judgment." *College English, 55*, 187–206.

Although aimed at college English teachers, this article is well worth reading by teachers at all levels concerned about the process of grading writing. Elbow realizes the necessity for grading and the fact that grades must be reliable. He worries, however, that grades catch student interest more than the evaluative comments and suggestions for improvement teachers make. He argues strongly that grading/evaluating must be communicative. Elbow is a strong advocate of evaluating portfolios of student work and not grading individual papers. He suggests using minimal grades: for example, awarding only A's and F's, and leaving all papers in between ungraded. The title distinguishes between grading (ranking) and com-

ments that are designed to help students improve their writing ability (evaluating). He also says that teachers must find potential in writing (liking).

34. Faigley, Lester, Cherry, Roger D., Jolliffe, David A., & Skinner, Anna M. 1985. *Assessing Writers' Knowledge and Process of Composition.*

This book has excellent chapters (7–12) on evaluating student writing using performance assessment instruments. The book uses very specific examples of writing and rubrics. The examples are primarily useful with experienced writers.

35. McKendy, Thomas. (1992). "Locally Developed Tests and the Validity of Holistic Scoring." *Research in the Teaching of English, 26*, 149–166.

A useful critique of single grades on written material. Although teachers may be able to score written material reliably in this manner, the author gives a number of reasons why this may not be the best method.

36. Speck, Bruce W. 1998. "Directions in the Grading of Writing." In Zak, Frances & Weaver, Christopher C. (eds.). *The Theory and Practice of Grading Writing.* Albany, NY: SUNY.

This is perhaps the most helpful chapter in a book devoted to grading issues in writing. Particularly, this chapter deals with the idea of local versus national norms. This book would be of interest to secondary teachers.

37. Perera, Katherine. 1984. *Children's Writing and Reading.* London: Blackwell.

This book is not an easy read, but its compelling examples and its analysis of writing problems, particularly grammatical errors, makes it a worthwhile background text for any teacher of children really committed to improving student writing.

38. Czerniewska, Pam. 1992. *Learning about Writing.* Cambridge, MA: Blackwell.

This would be my recommendation for a text for teachers interested in developing an intensive writing experience in a classroom, particularly if children have had relatively little previous experience with writing. Particularly helpful are the chapters on cooperative writing and different kinds of writing.

Oral Presentations

39. Carlson, Robert E., & Smith-Howell, Deborah. 1995. "Classroom Public Speaking Assessment: Reliability and Validity of Selected Evaluation Instruments." *Communication Education, 44,* 87–97.

This article shows there are many ways of reliably and validly evaluating public speaking in the classroom. Of particular interest is the inclusion of three very different rating procedures developed by teachers. This article will be of interest to middle school and high school teachers who are trying to teach public speaking skills.

Journals

40. Matthews, Catherine E., & Cook, Helen. May, 1996. "Oh, Baby, What a Science Lesson!" *Science and Children, 33 (8),* 18–21.

This article describes some nuts and bolts about bringing an infant into an elementary school classroom on a monthly basis and the kinds of measurement and observational activities that might be useful for a science journal.

41. Prain, Vaughan, Hand, Brian, & Kay, Susan. 1997. "Writing for Learning in Physics." *The Physics Teacher, 35,* 40-41.

This article develops a few concrete ideas about journal writing activities in high school physics.

Group Work

42. Slavin, Robert E. 1982. *Cooperative Learning: Student Teams.* Washington, DC: NEA Professional Library.

This short pamphlet gives an excellent introduction to group learning. It has been revised, with a third edition in 1991. Each edition is worth reading, with the first considering intergroup competition.

43. Vermette, Paul J. 1988. *Making Cooperative Learning Work: Student Teams in K–12 Classrooms.* Upper Saddle River, NJ: Merrill.

A contemporary work that balances research and applications, this book has the single most useful chapter on assessing group work.

Portfolios

44. Bozzone, Meg A. May/June, 1994. "Professional Portfolio: Why You Should Start One Now." *Instructor, 103 (9),* 48–52.

This article has some specific ideas about the kinds of materials a new teacher may want to begin collecting for his or her professional portfolio and different ways of organizing it.

45. Hill, Bonnie C., Kamber, Patricia, & Norwick, Lisa. July/August, 1994. "6 Ways to Make Student Portfolios More Meaningful & Manageable." *Instructor, 104 (1),* 118–120.

This article describes one use of portfolios in which the primary purpose is to help students reflect on their work. The article has some ideas about portfolio management and using portfolios with children and parents.

46. Nidds, J. A., & McGerald, J. 1997. "How Functional Is Portfolio Assessment Anyway?" *Educational Digest, 65 (5),* 47–50.

This article provides a number of cautions about portfolio assessment, particularly in "high-stakes" assessment, based on the Vermont experience. A useful caution for teachers who want to introduce portfolios.

47. Karp, Karen S., & Huinker, DeAnn. January, 1977. "Portfolios as Agents of Change." *Teaching Children Mathematics, 3,* 224–228.

This is a practical article about using portfolios to help implement the National Council of Teachers of Mathematics Assessment Standards for School Mathematics.

Intelligence Tests

48. Glutting, Joseph J. 1989. "Introduction to the Structure and Application of the Stanford-Binet Intelligence Scale—Fourth Edition," *Journal of School Psychology, 27,* 69–80.

A comprehensive introduction to the current edition of the test. This would be helpful reading for any teacher before serving on a child study team.

49. Rothlisberg, Barbara A. 1990. "The Relation of the Stanford-Binet: Fourth Edition to Measures of Achievement: A Concurrent Validity Study." *Psychology in the Schools, 27,* 120–125.

A comparison of the Stanford-Binet to scores produced by the Woodcock-Johnson and Wide Range Achievement Tests.

50. Vig, Susan, & Jedrysek, Eleanora. 1996. "Stanford-Binet Fourth Edition: Useful for Young Children with Language Impairment?" *Psychology in the Schools, 33,* 124–131.

A research article that examines some of the limitations of the Stanford-Binet.

51. Klein, Perry. 1997. "Multiplying the Problems of Intelligence by Eight: A Critique of Gardner's Theory." *Canadian Journal of Education, 22,* 377–394.

A thoughtful critique of Gardner's theory compared to traditional ideas about intelligence.

Achievement Test Batteries

52. Hutchinson, Thomas A. "What to Look for in the Technical Manual: Twenty Question for Users." *Language, Speech, and Hearing Services in the Schools, 27,* 109–121.

An excellent preparation for attempting your first shot at reading a test manual.

53. Psychological Corporation. 1996. *Test Manual: Stanford Achievement Test, Ninth Edition. Primary 1.* San Antonio, TX: Author. [Republished in 1997 by Harcourt Brace Educational Measurement.]

54. Educational Testing Service. 1982. *NTE Core Battery: Test of Professional Knowledge.* Princeton, NJ: Author.

55. Hoover, H. D., Hieronymous, A. N., Frisbie, D. A., & Dunbar, S. B. 1997. *Iowa Tests of Basic Skills, Forms K, L, and M.* Chicago: Riverside.

56. Brookhart, Susan M. 1998. [Review of the Iowa Tests of Basic Skills.] *Mental Measurement Yearbook On Line, Vol. 13.*

57. Cross, Lawrence H. 1998. [Review of the Iowa Tests of Basic Skills.] *Mental Measurement Yearbook On Line, Vol. 13.*

58. Berk, Ronald A. 1998. [Review of the Stanford 9.] *Mental Measurement Yearbook On Line, Vol. 13.*

Individual Achievement Tests

59. Eaves, Ronald C., Vance, R. Hubert, & Mann, Lester. 1990. "Cognition and Academic Achievement: The Relationship of the Cognition Levels Test, the Key Math Revised, and the Woodcock Reading Mastery Tests-Revised," *Psychology in the Schools, 27,* 311–318.

A rather technical article that addresses the reliability and validity of several important classroom achievement tests, including the revised edition of the Key Math Test.

60. Nurss, Joanne R., & McGauvran, Mary E. 1986. *Metropolitan Readiness Tests, 5th Edition.* San Antonio, TX: Psychological Corporation.

61. Mabry, Linda. 1998. [Review of the Metropolitan Readiness Tests, 5th Edition]. *Mental Measurement Yearbook On Line, Vol. 13.*

62. Stoner, Gary. 1998. [Review of the Metropolitan Readiness Tests, 5th Edition]. *Mental Measurement Yearbook On Line, Vol. 13.*

63. Weller, L. David, Schnittjer, Carl J., & Tuten, Bertha A. 1992. "Predicting Achievement in Grades Three through Ten Using the Metropolitan Readiness Test." *Journal of Research in Childhood Education, 6,* 121–130.

This article discusses the strengths and limitations of the MRT as a long-term predictor of performance.

Dealing with Parents

64. Rich, Dorothy. May, 1998. "What Parents Want from Teachers," *Educational Leadership, 55 (8),* 37–39.

Some plain facts about parents' expectations of teachers, drawn from diverse school districts.

65. Rose, Mary C. December, 1998. "Handle with Care: The Difficult Parent Teacher Conference." *The Intermediate Instructor, 108 (3),* 92–93, 101.

This brief article has a series of things to consider before, during, and after a conference in which the teacher anticipates problems because she had to convey negative information or deal with information given to parents.

66. Burron, Arnold. October, 1995. "Heed Community Values If You Value Reform." *Educational Leadership, 53 (2),* 92–93.

A strong warning about community issues that may derail instructional and assessment reforms, particularly dealing with parents who hold strongly to traditional perspectives. The article makes several useful suggestions for bringing parents into the process.

■